TERRIFYING LOVE

TERRIFYING LOVE

Why Battered Women Kill and How Society Responds

LENORE E. WALKER

1817

HARPER & ROW, PUBLISHERS, New York

Grand Rapids, Philadelphia, St. Louis, San Francisco

London, Singapore, Sydney, Tokyo, Toronto

FIRST EDITION

Designed by Alma Orenstein

Library of Congress Cataloging-in-Publication Data

Walker, Lenore E.
    Terrifying love: why battered women kill and how society responds
    Lenore E. Walker.—1st ed.
        p.   cm.
    Includes index.
    ISBN 0-06-016160-4
        1. Abused women—United States—Psychology. 2. Justifiable
    homicide—United States. 3. Psychology, Forensic. I. Title.
    HV6626.W347   1989   89-11228
    364.1′523′082—dc20

89 90 91 92 93 CC/HC 10 9 8 7 6 5 4 3 2 1

To my son, Michael,
and my daughter, Karen,
with the hope that their generation
will be able to live together

CONTENTS

III

THE LAW

Terrifying Love is factually accurate, except that some names and identifying characteristics of the individuals discussed have been changed in order to protect their privacy.

I

CHEATING
THEIR DESTINIES

1

WHEN LOVE TURNS TO TERROR

W E LIVE IN A VIOLENT WORLD, and in a society riddled with violent images. Through the media, through advertising, and in many other ways, we've become perpetual observers—if not actual perpetrators—of violence. Such exposure does not necessarily make a person abusive. But it can, and does, enable her or him to grow more accepting of brutality in the environment, to perceive it as normal. Once that happens, emotional numbness begins to set in. That numbness is one of the reasons why people raised in an atmosphere of terror and brutality often fail to recognize the consequences of their own violent actions.

At home, in the workplace, on television, and in courts of law, images of the effects of both violence and sex-role stereotyping are rampant. So is promotion of machismo; so is the implicit infantilization of women; so is a tacit acceptance of pornography. These implications and statements of male superiority breed inequality in male/female relationships. They encourage men's control over women and the abuse of power. In the end, they lead to violence. And one of the most insidious forms of violence is domestic—violence that takes place in the home between man and woman, husband and wife. It turns love into terror.

In my earlier book *The Battered Woman* (1979), I explored the widespread phenomenon of physical, sexual, and psychological abuse of women by men in intimate relationships. Our society safeguards the sanctity of the home. Domestic violence has traditionally been considered a private matter—not the business of the police, the courts, or the state. Until recently, in fact, wife beating has often been something to joke about at cocktail parties. But the seriousness and savagery of battering relationships cannot be underestimated. Murder, suicide, permanent injury, kidnapping, incest, and child abuse are all inherent aspects of this syndrome. And if, as a feminist, I believe that our world will never be rid of violence until all societies treat men and women as equals, I also believe it is true that men and women will never be equals until women are physically safe in their own homes.

The Battered Woman is a book about people who live in domestic violence. Many battered women will die at the hands of their abusers. Some battered women, destined to die, refuse to be killed. They find the strength to survive by killing their abusive partners instead. In this sense, they indeed succeed in cheating their destinies. *Terrifying Love* is a book about those who live out the full consequences of domestic violence, riding its spiraling cycle to one irrevocable, inevitable end: battered women who kill in self-defense. It is also a book about what happens to some of these women after they kill—how our society deals with them in its mental health facilities, social service systems, and courts of law. Finally, it is the story of my own involvement in that process, my evolution from clinical psychologist to legal expert witness, which in its way has been my personal pledge to help battered women survive: to stand firmly as their psychologist-advocate, whether in the privacy of a psychologist's office or the public domain of a packed courtroom. While I have achieved success in this field, it is important for me to stress, above all else, my motivation. From childhood on, I've always had a genuine desire to make the world a better place. I believe that no single thing stands in the way of our positive evolution as cruelly and as insidiously as violence. And one of the cruelest, most insidious kinds of brutal abuse is the kind that takes place in our homes, in the intimacy of our interpersonal relationships. I believe, too, that no one, anywhere, is really free from the consequences of violence until all of us, everywhere, are absolutely free of it—in thought, in speech, in action. And as long as one woman is battered, none of us are truly safe. Neither is any child, and, as this book will show, neither is any man.

As you read the stories of these battered women I have known, you must remember that what happened to each of them could have happened to you or to someone you love. There is nothing special about these women's personalities, no great single event in any of their lives that made them choose to love an abusive partner. Their histories are similar to those of other women, except for the terrible secret of abuse they tried to hide as they did their best to cope with the men in their lives, men who sometimes loved them and sometimes beat them.

My own personal perspective has led me to believe that the need to abolish all violence lies at the very heart of the feminist cause. And I have written this book in the hope that it will further inform others concerning the terrible consequences of abuse of women, but also in the hope that some day, violence—whether physical, sexual, psychological, emotional, or spiritual—will never again be inflicted on any human being, anywhere.

Battered women who kill their abusers do so as a last resort. By refusing to die themselves, they gain a kind of personal empowerment—for many of them, for the first time in their lives. This book is about them. It is about who they are, why they do what they do, and how our society treats them after they kill. Issues of violence, terror, substance abuse, incest, pornography, of sanity and insanity, motherhood, social isolation, sexism, racism, anger, and healing are part of their collective story, and I will touch upon all these issues. I will also describe my own evolution from clinical psychologist to expert witness in cases of battered women's self-defense.

Growing up reading Perry Mason stories and detective

novels in New York City's now burned-out South Bronx, I never imagined the different turns my life and career would later take.

I come from a middle-class Jewish family where debate was encouraged and loud argument continual, but never violent. Maybe this is why, as a psychologist, I have an odd sort of tolerance for exploring violent situations. In a way, they seem personally unthreatening to me; I am aware that better behavior exists between people. As a woman, I have also been extremely fortunate in that my primary relationships with men—with my father and with my late husband Morton Flax—have been gentle, loving, nurturing ones. As a child I was taught to believe that people (men included) could be good and caring toward each other; this belief was confirmed in adulthood by some of my own experiences with intimacy.

I majored in psychology at Hunter College and taught elementary school in New York City. In graduate school at City College in the City University of New York system and then at Rutgers University, I studied school psychology, child psychology, and clinical psychology, completing my doctoral dissertation by studying preventive mental health issues. My career has involved a strong emphasis on teaching, education, and on health itself (rather than focusing only on the study of abnormality), on enabling people to use their own skills and to accentuate healthy behaviors. My studies in the psychology of systems and my experiential understanding of politics and the academic bureaucracy would later prove invaluable in enabling me to understand and to function in both the corporate world and the legal maze of our nation's courtrooms.

I began my clinical work as a child psychologist. Within a few years, I became a part of the women's movement, and by the early 1970s I began calling myself a feminist therapist. My clients were generally women, and a few men, who were probably very much like you or your loved ones. Through this work I became acutely aware of just how widespread abuse of women is in our society. It was an eye-opening, radicalizing experience.

It took me some time to formulate the Battered Woman Syndrome, a theory that will be discussed in depth in this book. Some time later, I also became familiar (from both a psychotherapeutic viewpoint and the viewpoint of a legal expert witness) with the phenomenon of battered women who kill. But, as I have stressed time and again, there is no real difference in psychological makeup between battered women who kill and those who do not. Most are average, "normal" women in many ways, women like you or your loved ones. The difference lies, perhaps, in the extremely life-threatening nature of the violence to which they are subjected, and from which some of them can escape alive only by ending their abusers' lives.

Despite my commitment to my work as a psychologist (or maybe because of it), I believe that battering relationships don't really benefit from couples therapy. They are better off dissolved; the cycle of violence, once begun, is nearly impossible to stop. And, contrary to myth, a battered woman, once out of the battering relationship, is unlikely to become involved with another batterer. If they become involved again at all, these women usually do so with gentle, nonviolent people. And, especially when their new relationships are supported by professional counseling, they are likely to succeed. This phenomenon has been truly satisfying for me to witness from a professional standpoint; it has also confirmed my belief that battered women, including battered women who kill their abusers, are by no means "addicted" to violent situations, and are neither masochistic nor sadistic. On the contrary: once free of abuse and terror, their lives can be very good indeed.

Since 1977, I have testified as an expert witness on behalf of battered women in more than 150 murder trials throughout the United States. All of these women killed their husbands or boyfriends after enduring incredible physical, sexual, psychological, and emotional abuse and torture. These women killed as a last resort; they killed in order to save their own lives and often the lives of their children.

Forensic psychology is a relatively new specialty area. In many ways, a psychologist working as an expert forensic witness needs to have the skills of both educator and clinical consultant.

The role of expert witness is, first of all, to tell the truth—to teach it in the courtroom, really—in such a way that both judge and jury can apply whatever specialized information they've been given in arriving at an appropriate administration of justice. In order to do this effectively, mental health professionals testifying as expert witnesses must be highly qualified in their fields. And they must be sure of their facts, because the adversarial process of courtroom law allows each side to challenge any facts or opinions put forth by the other side; the testimony of any expert witness is sure to be challenged.

My personal qualifications for the role of expert witness in battered women's homicide cases could never be seriously impugned. When I began testifying in court in 1977, I certainly knew more about the psychology of battered women than did most other psychologists in the country. I had completed a pilot research program in which I'd interviewed several hundred battered women. I had formulated specific psychological theories concerning the psychology of battered women, which I'd already begun to test out, in the major research program funded by the National Institutes of Mental Health (NIMH) and conducted at the Battered Woman Research Center in Denver, Colorado. I was about to publish a book on the subject, *The Battered Woman*, and several professional articles I'd written had already appeared.

In truth, though, few real facts were known about battered women back in 1977, at least far fewer facts than we know today. My work, while considered "exploratory research" by some scientists, employed methodologies deemed perfectly acceptable in standard social science research.* The problem of battered

---

*Since no one had actually studied large samples of battered women from a psychological perspective, I chose to concentrate on interviewing the women themselves, using both forced-choice and open-ended response questions in a systematic format that later became the model for the Battered Woman

women seemed so widespread, so urgent. I was entirely ready to put whatever knowledge I'd gain to work.

Back then, while stories of battered women who had been killed by their abusive husbands or boyfriends were commonplace, it was far less common to hear about battered women who struck back. But obviously some did, and then had no voice with which to speak of their reasons for harming or killing their batterers in self-defense.

Before I began working as an expert witness, I had been deeply involved in conducting extensive research into the psychology of battered women. My NIMH-funded project involved four hundred battered women; I was gearing up for a three-year involvement in it, which promised to be truly exciting. I knew that, as I learned more about the psychology of battered women from the data sure to be generated by our empirically based research, I would be able to develop better assessment techniques as a practitioner. Some of the best feminist researchers in Colorado were ready to begin working with me on this project; I was happily immersed in a myriad of details.

Then personal tragedy struck. In March 1978 (just three months after my father's unexpected death), my husband, Dr. Morton Flax, died suddenly. Mort, also a psychologist, had been executive director of a community mental health center in Colorado. He'd been my friend, colleague, lover, and partner. His encouragement had enabled me to dare to achieve some of my fondest dreams, and his sudden death left a very deep void in my life. In some way, I believe that my immersion in the drama, excitement, and tension of life as an expert forensic witness became a way for me to fill that void. The intensity of the work left little room for personal grief or anxiety.

Syndrome Questionnaire, used today for forensic evaluations. The sophisticated statistical methodologies employed in this study to control intervening variables made it unnecessary to use an experimental-control group research model. Results of this study have been published in my 1984 book, *The Battered Woman Syndrome.*

In the process of becoming a forensic witness, I brought my professional expertise to bear, attempting to educate lawyers, judges, and juries about the world of violence inhabited by battered women defendants. In turn, I gained a considerable education about the world of criminal justice and legal procedure—a world of formality and real-life drama, where human fate hangs in the balance, and a world largely ignorant of the battered woman's plight. My goal was, and still is, to give voice to these battered women who kill, because they are women too often silenced by vicious abuse. My goal is also to teach. I often think of myself now as an educator, trying to explain certain human behaviors to judges and juries.

There is a continuing debate within the feminist community about the proper role of an expert witness in trials of battered women who kill. Many people—such as Elizabeth Schneider, who writes for the *Women's Rights Law Reporter* and who is one of the nation's leading feminist jurisprudence scholars, on the faculty of Brooklyn Law School—believe that the social conditions that cause women to defend themselves by using violence are not clearly understood in the courtroom. Some of them argue that the Battered Woman Syndrome, as presented by an expert witness, may allow the court to view women who kill their abusive mates as mentally ill; in other words, the woman's own pathology, rather than the causative underlying social conditions, may be mistakenly blamed. Then, the reasoning goes, these and other women will never receive truly fair treatment as healthy human beings under the law. But badly needed court reform may never come, in that case, and women may therefore always need a spokesperson, such as an expert witness, to speak for them concerning the psychological dynamics of their life conditions.

This genuinely critical argument needs to be understood, as both sides are correct. Personally, I believe that expert witness testimony is extremely helpful so long as it educates a jury about issues they are not normally expected to understand. Although most of us are aware that sex role bias can have negative effects, the extent of the harm is debatable and not widely delineated. How it could cause a battered woman to strike back in self-defense, to the point of committing homicide, is knowledge not normally expected of a lay person; even many professionals don't understand it. From a purely practical point of view, at the present time in our system there is ample justification for expert witness testimony. I believe, too, that a good expert witness in these cases will always try to explain both general social conditioning and the individual's particular behavior, in order to properly and fully educate a jury.

A feminist psychologist or one very familiar with the current research on battered women, victimization, Post Traumatic Stress Disorder, and the concept of learned helplessness (all of which I explore in this book) can provide the most informative expert witness testimony when a battered woman is on trial. Shelter and task force workers with similar skills can also be good expert witnesses. It is a sad fact that, at present, some traditional mental health professionals frequently misinterpret test data, as well as misdiagnose, simply because they are unfamiliar with the pertinent research, its applications, and its implications vis-à-vis male and female sex-role socialization patterns. Such misguided "experts" play into the court's common misconceptions about pathology, too; so the truth is that there are dangers, as well as benefits, to using expert witnesses in some cases. The National Clearinghouse for the Defense of Battered Women in Philadelphia has been created to guide attorneys so that they avoid these pitfalls when preparing an abused client's defense.

Hopefully, those of us involved with reform will be able to educate experts and lawmakers alike so that eventually there will be sufficient judicial reform enacted to allow women to testify for themselves. Until then, each case must be decided on its own perceived merits; thus if there is any doubt as to the defendant's credibility—if critical information cannot otherwise be brought before the jurors, and if her ostensibly "abnormal" but self-protective behavior needs to be explained—then an expert witness should be called.

*   *   *

The first cases I was involved with in my hometown of Denver offered me a glimpse into the workings of our public defender system, and I was impressed with what I saw. Operating under financial constraints, overloaded with complicated cases, these attorneys genuinely try to assure that all defendants (most of whom are poor people of color, some of whom are women) receive justice. A good deal of their time is spent ensuring that their clients get a fair trial. Even when it seems that a defendant must be guilty of an alleged crime, these public defenders believe that their vigilance in ensuring the enforcement of the rules keeps the judicial system safe for the innocent, too. I believe that they are right.

Ideally, widespread reeducation will some day promote judicial reform, changing the rules to allow battered women to testify successfully on their own behalf. Until then, an expert witness must speak for them. Too often, our courts serve to complete the work of the batterer by continuing to arbitrarily control and then convict the battered woman. I would like to think of myself as one of the many people involved in changing this phenomenon. Most battered women who kill do so in self-defense. By the time they kill, they are already the most silenced, the most violated of women.

This book, then, is their story. None of these women are ruthless killers. All are victims. Their victimization, though, does not end when they kill a brutal spouse or lover. Battered women who kill in self-defense may go from being prisoners of interpersonal abuse to being prisoners of the state. They are not free until the jury returns a verdict of not guilty. My task as expert witness is, above all, to tell their truth.

There are many in the legal field who wonder if psychology belongs in the courtrooms at all. It is true that the discipline of psychology is rooted in the scientific tradition, rather than in the logical tradition of the legal system. These two traditions employ totally different ways of arriving at truth.* Perhaps, in the end, truth is most likely to be found at the intersection where all methodologies meet.

And that is precisely why a battered woman, subjected to the methodology of the law, deserves to be represented as well by an expert witness who is knowledgeable and practiced in the methodology of feminist psychology.

All people involved in violent situations may themselves be endangered at times. An expert witness is no different. I have testified in fear of my own life, in cases so filled with nearly unbelievable brutality that I felt shaken to the core. Judges have threatened to put me in jail for daring to defy their misogynistic orders. I have seen lawyers and helping professionals assaulted, nearly killed; for where murder, suicide, sexual abuse, and kidnapping are part of a situation, no one is really safe. I've been helped in confronting my own deadly terror, at times, by thinking of the suffering endured by battered women everywhere.

I have also been inspired by witnessing the courage and selflessness of others—women and men—who, day after day, in ways large and small, work ceaselessly to make this world a better, more just, and safer place for us all. So it is to them, too, as well

---

*In the scientific tradition, theoretical principles are used to formulate hypotheses (logical guesses) as to the truth in a given situation; experiments are then constructed, according to certain standard scientific methods, to test the hypothesis. Statistical analysis of the data collected is then done; if the result of final analysis shows a statistical probability of accuracy and if both experiment and results meet scientific standards, the hypothesis is considered acceptable; if not, it is rejected. The objective data determine what is to be accepted as scientific truth.

In the law, on the other hand, coming up with a hypothesis before all the evidence has been collected is considered nonobjective bias (in the field of psychology, not doing so would be considered subjective bias). In the adversarial system, both sides are allowed to put forth their very best arguments for their version of the truth. It is expected that objective truth will fall somewhere between the two positions.

as to those abused women dead or alive who cannot speak for themselves, that I dedicate this book.

Many things of a practical nature can, should, and must be done for battered women in our society. Resources already available, and proven effective, must be supported and expanded, including battered women's shelters and safe houses. Statistics show that approximately 50 percent of all women who stay longer than a week in a safe house or shelter never return to live with the batterer. And many more will eventually succeed in leaving the batterer if there is always a safe house or shelter open to them, even after they have returned home. The value of these places is that they immediately provide a built-in community and institutional support, chipping away at battered women's feelings of isolation, helplessness, and inferiority. Shelters save battered women's and batterers' lives. We need to create more long-term safe houses where women can begin new lives and stay, perhaps for a year or more, if they need the continued support.

We need to effect easy, effective, fair reforms in our system of law enforcement and of criminal justice. Ideally, battered women should be assured of adequate and effective police protection. They should have ready access to restraining orders. The system should promote a general facilitation of prosecutorial discretion and procedure when it comes to batterers. Battered women should be able to obtain temporary support, including child support—institutionally provided, if necessary—as well as speedy divorces. We must have genuinely effective, meaningful court regulation of child visitation rights. We must recognize the potential danger to women and children, and *listen* to them, so that we can provide adequate protection.

Eventually, special legal procedures for battered women defendants must be legitimized: procedures that recognize and validate the world view of women as well as of men, procedures that ultimately will allow battered women's voices to be heard. Once battered women are allowed to speak, they will be able to tell their own stories. And to know a battered woman's story is to understand, without a doubt, why she has killed. Until such time as special legal procedures are legitimized, however, it is imperative that qualified expert witness testimony be ruled admissible in our courts of law, in every case in which a battered woman is the defendant.

Women in general, and battered women in particular, need quicker, easier access to emergency medical facilities. They also need easier access to humane and responsive social service organizations, including access to career counseling, job training, decent job protection, safe child care, and the building of community support networks for women, for children, for people everywhere in America, as well as the rest of the world.

Truly humane societies are those, I believe, that have decided to begin the long march down the road toward the abolition of violence by promotion of equality between women and men. They are those societies that, every once in a while, stop along the way to take stock, and then decide to continue.

2

JOYCE HAWTHORNE'S STORY

IT WAS JANUARY 27, 1977, and things seemed more or less normal in the Florida town of Pensacola. But it wasn't even the end of the week yet, and Joyce Hawthorne was already exhausted. She'd just been to the doctor for the second time in several days, this time with her eight-year-old son. He'd developed a suspicious red line, resembling blood poisoning, at the site of an injury. Earlier that week, his older brother had been diagnosed with bronchitis. Now two of her five children needed to be awakened in the middle of the night for their necessary around-the-clock medicine.

Her fourteen-year-old daughter, America, had always been a big help in caring for the younger kids. But there was mounting tension at home that made this impossible; America had recently told Joyce that, three weeks earlier, her father had tried to sexually molest her. Now Joyce was afraid to leave the two of them alone together. And she worried about the implications of all this, too: could her husband, Aubrey, have been sexually abusing the two younger girls as well? She never thought of the possibility of him abusing the boys.

So often in the past, Joyce had watched helplessly as he brutalized them all. She'd protected the children as best she could

16

from his increasingly frequent, physically violent outbursts, but incest was something she'd never thought about before. America's admission only confirmed her growing conviction: Aubrey was not only a sick man but, no matter how hard she tried to please him, to be a good wife, he would never really change. Lately, Joyce had felt that she was "living with a time bomb," "walking on eggshells." Nothing she did seemed to please her husband; he always found fault with her. Sometimes she'd even cook two meals at night—one for the kids and another for him— because he was so particular. Every morning he'd leave for work only after reminding her that she'd "better not be unfaithful." (Joyce had never even considered the notion.) He'd check on her every movement when he returned after work. Things seemed to be getting worse every day; after seventeen years of marriage, Joyce's constant state of fear had become like torture to her. When she went to bed at night, she never knew if she'd be alive the next morning.

When Joyce had married Aubrey Hawthorne, she had been a seventeen-year-old bride who dreamed of being a good wife and mother. She'd believed strongly in the traditional values that assign women and men to different family roles: women stay home to take care of the house and kids, while men go out into the world to earn a living. Aubrey had believed in those values, too.

And both of them had fulfilled their roles. To the rest of the world they lived in, the Hawthornes appeared to be an average family.

In the summer of 1964, when they'd been married five years, Joyce invited Aubrey's cousins Dot and Charles over to make ice cream on a night when he was working late. When Aubrey came home, Joyce could tell he'd already had a lot to drink. She tried to give him some ice cream, but he refused; she noticed he was acting strangely. After his cousins left, he began to frighten her by turning the house lights off and on at random. They had an argument, which ended when he slapped her with his open hand several times. Joyce was scared. This wasn't the first time he'd been abusive toward her. Once, when she was pregnant, he had shoved her hard into a nearby chair, causing her to miscarry. Arguments frequently resulted in Aubrey accusing her of things she had not done and calling her terrible names.

This time, she took her two-year-old, America, and went to her parents' house. Once safely there, she called the sheriff's office to report the incident. The sheriff drove out to talk to Aubrey and called Joyce himself, telling her Aubrey was pleading for her to come home. The courts were likely to be hard on Aubrey, he warned her, if she persisted in filing charges.

But Joyce didn't go home right away. When a few days later Aubrey began threatening to kidnap the baby, Joyce went to speak to a judge. The judge told her the situation would only get worse, and advised her not only to file for divorce but to press assault charges. He also mentioned that Aubrey's employer would probably not tolerate keeping on an employee with a criminal record.

Joyce was horrified at the choice she faced: she could file for divorce, press assault charges, and cause Aubrey to lose his job, or return home to a violent situation. Those options seemed to her to be the only real ones.

Three days later, Joyce returned home. Aubrey was thrilled to see her. They got along wonderfully for a while. But the judge's prediction proved right; things got worse. When this second honeymoon was over, Aubrey began to abuse her again.

Sometimes his beatings caused injuries serious enough to require medical treatment. Still, Joyce rarely went to a doctor. She was too ashamed to reveal their secret, and she was frightened of what Aubrey might do to her if he ever found out she'd told another person. Even when she had no choice but to seek medical care, like the time she suffered the miscarriage, she never told anyone how the "accident" had happened.

Aubrey's abusive name calling worsened, as did his accusations of sexual infidelity. Joyce kept thinking that if she could only try harder to please him, to be a good wife, he'd stop hurting her and stop threatening to hurt the children.

He put a string on the outside gate lock so he could check on her comings and goings while he was gone. By this time, Joyce rarely left home except to run errands for the kids or shop for groceries. She was terribly embarrassed for Aubrey, and humiliated herself, when he accused her of sleeping with the mailman or with one of the children's teachers. But she knew she'd always been faithful to Aubrey. And she believed that some day he'd learn to trust her.

She knew that he drank too much, too. But she also believed that good wives never nagged their husbands. So she compromised, demanding that Aubrey drink only outside the house, in his workshed.

Sometimes, Joyce felt she'd be willing to do anything to make Aubrey feel happier, more secure, to make him stop drinking. Then he'd change, she told herself; he wouldn't be so cruel anymore. His bad side would disappear and the hard-working, kind, loving man she thought she'd married would remain. That was the real Aubrey, she told herself, the good Aubrey. But despite her hopes, his Dr. Jekyll/Mr. Hyde personality pattern became more acute. The violence and brutality increased; his kind, loving behavior became less frequent.

Not surprisingly, Joyce began to lose sexual desire for her husband. She went to a gynecologist, whose response was to give her vitamin shots to increase her arousal. He never asked, and Joyce never told him about the beatings, which had become more frequent by then.

One cold day in April 1969, shortly after the birth of their fourth child, Joyce and Aubrey went fishing in his boat. Joyce was still recovering from childbirth. But Aubrey nevertheless insisted on having sex among the sand dunes on the beach.

"No," said Joyce, "let's go home instead."

He became very angry then, breaking coke bottles and beer bottles, destroying their fishing poles. When she stepped into the car with him, he drove to the end of a bridge, got out to throw all their fishing gear into the water, then drove home.

At home, he smashed two of his favorite guns. His violent behavior worsened throughout the day, and he began to hit her frequently. At some point, Joyce's toe was hurt badly and she had to go to the hospital. While she was in the emergency room, Aubrey burned their boat, dumping his broken guns and a case of shells into the nearby river.

When she returned from the hospital and saw the damage caused by his rampage, Joyce realized that his violence could escalate into destruction of people as well as things, and that there was nothing she could do to control it. She decided that her only recourse was to try to keep him as calm as possible. From then on, she did her best.

By autumn of 1969 she was pregnant with their fifth child. Aubrey moved her and the children, without discussion, into an unfinished home he'd decided to buy. The place had no heat, no running water, no working toilets. Joyce and the kids were expected to endure these conditions until he got around to fixing things. They did. Life went on with Joyce struggling to protect them all as best she could.

In 1973, Joyce's family was traumatized by a terrible incident: her father was shot to death by someone trying to rob his small retail store. Although she and all her relatives were in a state of shock and grief over this, Aubrey took it even harder than the others. He drank more. His behavior began to spin more wildly out of control. One night he was driving them home from a dance, drunk and argumentative. Without warning he stepped on the accelerator, ran a red light, then slammed on the brakes. But not in time.

Later, Joyce would remember seeing them heading into a light pole. She was sure they'd both be killed. They weren't.

Later that year, Aubrey got angry with the family dog for straying outside their yard. He loaded one of his nine guns, then shot and killed it. The kids began to sob, devastated. He grabbed America's hair, tearing out a clump. He slapped another of the kids, then began crying himself. Joyce tried to comfort them all. But her feelings of anger were mixed with genuine terror: in a moment of rage, she knew, Aubrey could kill any one of them, and cry about it afterward.

Still, she felt incapable of leaving him now. She was suffering extreme emotional trauma as a result of her father's murder. So were her mother and brother, who could no longer sleep alone and were staying at Joyce and Aubrey's house every night. The presence of other adult family members seemed to calm Aubrey a little; he wasn't as physically abusive to her or to the children when her mother and brother were around.

Their doctor had given them all tranquilizers, which actually brought out the best in Aubrey. He cut down on his drinking for a while and became calmer, kinder, more considerate. But he was also having problems reaching orgasm during sex, probably because of the excessive amounts of alcohol he usually drank. When friends at work told him the tranquilizers were causing his sexual problems, he stopped taking them. The old abusive behavior quickly returned, worse than ever. He began to carry a gun at all times.

Aubrey's sexual abuse of Joyce increased. Exhausted by trying to meet his nightly demands, Joyce was tired and in pain much of the time. She knew that "good" wives were always supposed to be willing to satisfy their husbands. Still, she thought he was drunk and disgusting. But whenever she refused to have sex with him, Aubrey would reach for the gun he kept on the bedside night table and threaten her with it. He often required an hour or more to reach orgasm, never considering her needs or pleasure; while she nearly always gave in just to buy a little peace, most of the time she felt as if she wanted to scream. Her frequent vaginal infections made intercourse extremely painful and had her visiting the gynecologist frequently. That doctor's records later indicated that he suspected abuse at the time, but he never discussed his suspicions with Joyce.

A part of Joyce still kept hoping for a miracle, until that night in January 1977. She had spent the day at the doctor's office with a sick child, Aubrey's attempted sexual assault of America weighed heavily on her mind, and her own body and psyche were in a state of affliction and fear. When Aubrey came home drunk that night, she noticed something different in his demeanor, something even more violent than before, more uncontrolled, more terrifying. When he threw the hamburger she'd cooked for him across the kitchen table and threatened to kill them all, Joyce believed him. When he told her, within earshot of the children, that none of them should dare go to sleep because he intended to "make the rounds" that night, she believed him. When he told Joyce's mother and brother that they'd better leave unless they wanted to die, too, she believed him. Then he went to their bedroom and passed out in an alcoholic daze.

Joyce found as many of his guns as she could and hid them all.

She put the children to bed. She set the alarm so she'd wake up in time to give her two sons their medication. America helped her pull a mattress onto the hallway floor, outside the master bedroom. Then Joyce lay down and tried to get some sleep herself. But her nerves were entirely frayed; she couldn't sleep and became increasingly terrified.

Listening for any sound, any signal that another attack was about to begin, she wanted to jump out of her skin. But for a while, nothing happened. Minutes crawled by and became hours. The time came to wake her boys up and give them their medicine.

After that, for some reason she could not later explain, Joyce sensed that the time for crisis might be past. She decided to maintain as normal an appearance as possible—that would minimize the risk of angering Aubrey the next morning—and crept into bed next to him. He seemed to be asleep; maybe she too could get the sleep she so desperately needed.

Just as she was dozing off, he grabbed her. He was wide awake, demanding sex.

Joyce refused. She was in pain, she told him, and exhausted.

But there was no explaining to Aubrey. Angry, he reached for the night table where his loaded gun lay.

This is it, Joyce thought, this is the signal. Now he's going to keep his promise and kill us all. Then her mind went blank.

She would remember nothing until the moment, some time later the next morning, when she realized Aubrey was dead, stretched out on their bed with nine bullets in his body. Piled on the floor, in the middle of the room, were his five guns.

Forensic experts later theorized that Joyce must have reached for the loaded gun on her own night table at the same time Aubrey reached for his. Aubrey had insisted on keeping a loaded gun there too, after the intruder had killed her father. Then, the theory goes, she shot at his hand. She threw her gun to the floor, got out of bed, pulled another gun from the closet, and shot him in the buttocks as he rose up—on his hands and knees, perhaps—attempting to come at her. That second gun was tossed to the floor, too. She pulled another gun out, fired some shots at him, and threw it to the floor also, did the same then with another gun. By this time, Joyce's mother and America had run into the bedroom. Joyce's mother held a gun in her hand; both remembered Aubrey's earlier threats to kill the entire family. They later said that Joyce took the gun from her mother, firing again at Aubrey, then throwing it on top of the other guns heaped in the middle of the floor.

According to the pathologist who later performed the autopsy, any five of the nine shots that hit Aubrey could have killed him. When the police arrived, he was certainly dead: sprawled across the bed where he'd abused Joyce every night for years— nine bullets lodged inside him, five handguns and rifles piled on the floor, surrounded by his dazed wife and family.

January 1980

I first met Joyce Hawthorne three years after Aubrey's death.

An ordinary-looking woman of forty, about 5'3" tall, weighing about 150 lbs., she didn't attract much attention. Her smile was rare but sweet; her eyes sparkled when she laughed. She looked just like the church-going mother of five that she was. Judging by her appearance alone, no one would have known that she'd killed a man much larger than herself, firing five guns in the process, even if sometimes her facial expression, at rest, revealed her fear and unhappiness.

Accused of murdering her husband, she was about to go on trial for her life.

Joyce never denied that she'd fired the fatal shots; rather, although she had no memory of it, she claimed that she had been justified in firing them because she had wanted to protect herself and her family from assault, rape, and death.

Actually, this upcoming trial would be her second, ordered by Florida's First District Court of Appeals because of errors made during the investigation leading up to her first trial two years earlier, as well as several additional major legal errors made during that first trial; an appeal had been filed, and Joyce had been released on bond raised by using her home as collateral. Although she did not remember shooting her husband, she had initially confessed to doing it in order to get the police to release her five children, who were being held for questioning at the time.* Back then, a jury of twelve had found Joyce guilty of murder in the first degree, a verdict that would have carried a sentence of life in prison instead of the death penalty asked for by the prosecutor. But they hadn't been allowed to hear all of the existing evidence concerning Aubrey's brutality toward her and the children; this evidence had been disallowed by the first judge.

*Two years later, the appellate court ruled that the police should not have promised to release her children in order to force her to give a statement, especially after she and her attorney had already exercised her right not to talk to the detectives. It is never considered a "voluntary" statement when someone is forced to talk under duress; what is said is never considered to be legally reliable information. Furthermore, the higher court judges ruled that the trial court judge had been in error when he disallowed testimony concerning Joyce's long history as a battered wife.

This time, however, defense attorney Leo Thomas was ready to present the testimony of an expert witness.

He wanted to use my professional expertise on battered women and on Battered Woman Syndrome to help explain to a second jury why Joyce Hawthorne had been legally justified in shooting her husband.

In reversing the judge's previous decision, an appellate court had ruled that evidence about the extensive family abuse in this case could be introduced in the upcoming trial; but nothing had been specifically stated about the permissibility of allowing an expert witness to explain what Joyce's behavior had meant. Joyce, too, hoped that I would be able to give my professional opinion as to why it had been reasonable for her to believe she was about to die that fateful night in January 1977. But it was still the trial judge's decision as to whether such testimony would be allowed.

Battered Woman Syndrome had not previously been used in the state of Florida to support a self-defense argument (although several other states had, by that time, permitted such testimony in courts of law). Before, it would have been much more common for a woman like Joyce to plead insanity, arguing that her husband's terrible abuse had rendered her temporarily insane. (Francine Hughes, the battered woman portrayed by Farrah Fawcett in the 1984 television movie *The Burning Bed*, had actually been found not guilty by reason of insanity, in 1978, after killing her sleeping husband by setting him on fire.) Shortly after Aubrey's death, Joyce Hawthorne had been examined by a psychiatrist, who had found that she knew right from wrong, the legal standard for Florida's insanity plea. I, too, would find that Joyce Hawthorne was legally sane—but terrified that she and her family would be slaughtered, just as Aubrey had threatened. In my opinion, her belief that she and her children were in danger that night had been reasonable, and reasonable perception of imminent physical danger is the legal standard for acting in self-defense.

Based on my findings, I decided to prepare myself as an expert witness for her defense. I agreed with Leo Thomas that a second jury would have to be carefully educated as to how and why this soft-spoken, church-going mother of five had been able to kill the father of her children.

Fortunately for Joyce and her children, her plight had attracted Leo's attention from the first. Partner in the major Florida law firm of Levin, Middlebrooks, Mabie, Thomas, Mayes, and Mitchell (Joyce had gone to see another lawyer in that firm several years earlier, in a futile attempt to get a divorce), Leo Thomas was one of the best criminal defense attorneys in the state. .

He had arranged for her to be examined by mental health professionals, who found her to be legally sane. And Leo knew that, without understanding the long history of marital abuse Joyce had endured, the average person sitting on a jury could not be expected to comprehend why she had believed her husband would kill her when she refused his sexual advances. To begin with, in 1978 few people understood the concept of marital rape. Sex is usually thought to be part of the marriage contract. A jury would not necessarily understand how a woman could claim self-defense, especially if there was no corroborating evidence presented to document the fact that she was in imminent danger of being hurt or killed.

But Battered Woman Syndrome would provide the appropriate explanation; it would delineate the perception of imminency,* and show how that perception was affected by the woman's state of mind. It would make her state of mind comprehensible, because battered women are always afraid of being hurt; any crisis situation may be perceived as a matter of life or death. The struggle of the battered woman becomes, in the end, a struggle to stay alive.

I knew that the history of being a partner in a violent relationship was relevant to a defendant's state of mind; I knew it could change the understanding of reasonable perception of

---

*The term *imminent* as it is defined in self-defense statutes usually means "to be on the brink of," not "immediate," as is its more common interpretation.

imminent danger; I knew that the testimony of an expert witness could make the difference in allowing the jury to understand all this. And I also knew that Joyce Hawthorne might be convicted again—wrongfully—if the judge refused to allow such testimony. Joyce herself could not be expected to explain to a jury of her peers what it meant to be a battered woman; one of the effects of being repeatedly violated is the inability to break a code of silence, even when your life depends on it. Battered women, like other tyrannized people, lose the use of their own voices.

Leo Thomas realized that he would have to educate this second jury about battered women. He would have to make them understand why Joyce hadn't divorced Aubrey despite the daily horror of their marriage; he would have to corroborate Joyce's reports of domestic violence, even if no one else had seen Aubrey beat her; he would have to introduce convincing evidence to demonstrate that Joyce's fear had been reasonable on the night she finally killed him. All this would mean persuading the jury that Aubrey Hawthorne's repeated abuse of his wife had so affected her state of mind that she'd believed she needed to shoot him, to stop him from hurting her—as she perceived him coming toward her, even before he'd actually touched her—on that night in January 1977. Leo would have to help Joyce persuade the jury that her acute state of terror had induced her to use no less than five guns that night, firing at least nine bullets into her husband's body; that, in fact, her behavior had been a demonstration not of anger but of fear.

Until I met Joyce Hawthorne in January 1980, I was one of the few psychologists in the United States who provided therapy services for and conducted government-funded research with battered women. *The Battered Woman* had been published the previous year. Several earlier articles on the subject had appeared in professional journals. I'd been invited to testify before congressional committees preparing policy-making legislation on domestic violence. I'd been asked to consult with several government agencies seeking answers to the battered woman's plight. I had testified as an expert witness in several court trials, on behalf of battered women who'd killed their abusers. As a long-time social activist, I found the new opportunities for systemic change exciting. After reading about my testimony in another case, Leo Thomas had requested my involvement in Joyce's upcoming murder trial. As an expert witness for the defense, explaining the pertinent data on battered women would be my job.

I began to research the facts of her case, starting with police records predating that first trial.

When the police arrived at the scene of the homicide, they had arrested Joyce on charges of first-degree murder. Prosecutor Ron Johnson, the same prosecutor I was to face in her second trial, had asked for the death penalty, claiming that Joyce committed a truly heinous act by killing Aubrey Hawthorne in cold blood while he slept peacefully in bed. That first jury of twelve had believed Johnson, especially in light of the fact that Joyce's defense attorney had been unable to introduce evidence concerning her long history of abuse. However, they had sentenced her to life imprisonment rather than to the requested death penalty. Perhaps they also believed the testimony of the forensic pathologist, who stated that, as evidenced by the path of the bullets embedded in his body, Aubrey could not have been sleeping. Perhaps they knew, somehow, that there was more to her story than the "bare bones" evidence the judge had let them hear. If the judge were to disallow expert witness testimony again at her second trial, a similar situation might occur. Expert witness testimony would be crucial in helping a jury understand why Joyce Hawthorne's actions were legally justifiable.

I set about gaining more important collaborative information by reading various other related documents Leo had sent to my office: police reports, doctors' records, witness statements, transcripts of the first trial. After interviewing and evaluating Joyce, I decided that a consultation with Leo would also be necessary before I'd feel ready to testify.

Members of Joyce's church chipped in to raise money for her and America's airfares. The two traveled to our Denver offices for the special psychological evaluation developed at our Battered Woman Research Center. At that time, I was the only psychologist in the country capable of providing such a detailed assessment for forensic purposes. My assistant Roberta Thyfault and I had obtained permission for Joyce and America to stay in the guest dorms at Colorado Women's College, site of the Battered Woman Research Center.

This was their first trip so far from home. We wanted them to see some of our beautiful state, especially in light of the fact that Joyce might eventually wind up spending a good deal of time in prison; she was still charged with first-degree murder. After completion of the interview and evaluation procedure, we encouraged them to take a bus trip into the Rocky Mountains. Both women say those lovely memories are still with them today, happily separated from the many other painful, ugly memories of their life with Aubrey Hawthorne.

"What's it like to interview a woman who's killed someone?" Roberta had asked nervously, while we prepared for Joyce Hawthorne's arrival. One of the research program's interviewers, thoroughly familiar with the formal assessment procedure we'd developed at our Center, Roberta had handled the eight-hour procedure at least thirty times by then, and knew how to use it to gather information we'd need to know. I'd chosen Roberta for her special competence. As evaluators, our goal would be to reconstruct Joyce Hawthorne's state of mind at the time she'd killed Aubrey, even though she herself could not remember.

"It's not much different from interviewing other battered women," I'd replied. "But it's important to remember that even though she's charged with committing a serious crime, she is considered legally innocent until she's declared guilty by a jury of her peers, after a fair trial. We've got to protect her rights even more carefully than we usually do, especially while her case is pending. Remember that if she's convicted she could spend the rest of her life in jail."

"That's not really what I mean. I guess I want to know what

it feels like to spend the whole day with a murderer. You've done it before. Were you scared that you might be hurt? Did you ask some questions in a different way, or avoid certain topics, maybe, so as not to upset her?"

I'd never really considered things in that light. Although I'd been interviewing battered women for six years—and, for the past three years, battered women who'd killed their abusers—my training as a psychologist had taught me to adopt a nonjudgmental attitude. Maybe that was why I had never viewed these women as murderers. None of them had seemed dangerous to me; their homicidal acts had appeared to be the inevitable outcome of another horrifying, brutal fight, one that they had survived however they could.

I thought this through then, sharing some of my thoughts with Roberta: the violence these battered women endured was not the stereotypical stuff of movie scripts and teleplays, not a series of bouts between two trained contestants equal in physical strength. Most women are at a serious disadvantage when facing an attack from a man who is not only physically stronger but more ready and willing to fight. And battered women who kill are really like battered women who don't kill—they endure the same harassment, the same psychological torture; they experience the same terror—except that they have partners who are ready, able, and willing to kill them. When a battered woman kills her abuser, she has reached the end of the line. She is absolutely desperate, in real despair. She believes, with good reason, that if she does not kill, she will be killed.

Later Roberta would meet Joyce and conduct the standard, lengthy interview. Afterward she would admit that she hadn't felt any difference in Joyce's presence than she had in dealing with the other battered women she'd interviewed. Except for Joyce's fear that her husband really would kill the entire family that night in January 1977, she had been very similar to others. We were both convinced she'd shot Aubrey to protect herself and the people she loved from the terrible fate she believed lay ahead.

March 1980

Pensacola, Florida, is better known for its white sandy beaches and nearby naval base than its courtrooms. The particular courtroom where Joyce Hawthorne would be tried for first-degree murder was unusually crowded. Television cameras rested outside the courtroom doors after the busy morning. Inside, the seats were filled. I sensed reporters scurrying for the little standing room remaining when I first walked in, escorted by the bailiff.

My reputation as a "tough" expert witness had preceded me. I supposed it was an accurate one, although I thought of myself primarily as a psychologist whose task was to explain human behavior accurately to judge and jury. My goal as a feminist was to speak truthfully for battered women. Like Joyce Hawthorne's, these women's voices have often been silenced by abusive blows; we hear them, momentarily, only when they are forced to strike back and kill.

After being sworn in, I sat in the witness box with my files open before me, pen in hand, yellow legal pad nearby. I waited for the jury to return. Because I felt entirely ready to respond to direct examination, I was surprised to hear prosecutor Ron Johnson stand and begin a long speech to Judge William Anderson, explaining his objections to my testimony.

The judge delayed calling in the jury. They would have to wait, out of earshot of the courtroom, so as not to hear any part of the debate concerning the admissibility of my testimony. I heard Leo Thomas respond for the defense and found myself the silent center of a swirling legal argument. Hearing these men discuss, represent, and misrepresent me, I found myself wondering why there was such a big fuss about it all—such a big fuss, just to get a woman's voice heard.

"Dr. Walker is not being presented to testify as to Joyce Hawthorne's mental status," I heard Leo say. "We are not trying to test Florida's insanity standards under the law."

But I'm a psychologist, I thought to myself. *Of course I evaluated her mental status.*

"She will only speak," he continued, "to Joyce Hawthorne's state of mind at the time of the incident."

What is the legal difference, I wondered, *between mental status and state of mind?*

Apparently, this was the prosecutor's reasoning, too.

"If Dr. Walker tells the jury what effect the Battered Woman Syndrome had on Joyce Hawthorne's state of mind at the time she killed Aubrey Hawthorne, then she will be testifying as to a mental condition," Ron Johnson countered. "No notice of an insanity plea has been received, and therefore she shouldn't be permitted to testify. The state has the right to examine the defendant if an insanity plea is filed; therefore, we would have been denied that right."

Pretty pompous, I thought silently, *as well as mistaken, to argue that the state has rights generally belonging to defendants. What the state really has is a burden: to prove beyond reasonable doubt, according to the standards of American justice, that this crime was committed by the defendant.*

"The prosecutor has had sufficient notice as to Dr. Walker's examination and conclusions," said Leo. "In fact, he took her deposition himself. If he wanted his own expert to evaluate the defendant, why didn't he just ask?"

I stifled a small laugh. I knew Leo would have fought like a tiger to keep his client from being examined by any state-appointed psychologist. An excellent defense attorney, fully aware of all the potentially unnecessary risks that might jeopardize his clients' rights, he knew just how to play by the rules as well as fight by them.

"Judge, this is justifiable homicide we are arguing, not excusable homicide, which would have been a mental health defense. Dr. Walker can testify as to the reasonableness of Joyce Hawthorne's perception that she was in imminent danger when she shot her husband. We say she acted in self-defense, not out of a disturbed mental condition."

Yes, I thought, *all people have perceptions that govern their behavior, and only a few of these perceptions can be considered*

*a product of mental disease or defect, as the insanity law re-
quires.*

Ron Johnson assumed a threatening stance. "If you let her
testify, Judge, then she takes away the role of the jury to decide
if Joyce Hawthorne's perceptions of danger were reasonable.
You'll open the door to allow any woman to kill a man she doesn't
like, and get away with it!"

Where does that come from? I wondered. *Maybe this man's
passion is interfering with his ability to reason?*

"She is a noted feminist," Johnson continued, "she admits
to it right here on page 15 of the introduction to her book *The
Battered Woman,* so we all know she's biased against men. This
woman would have decent people justify the actions of any
woman who kills a man, just because he tells her to obey him. It
will be open season on killing men, your honor, and you mustn't
allow it!"

*Open season on killing men because I'm a feminist? How
ridiculous can he be?*

I knew of no feminists who'd advocated killing men as a
way to equalize power. Personally, I was there simply to speak
about Joyce Hawthorne, a woman who had shot and killed her
husband because her long history of being battered by him had
given her reasonable cause to believe, on the night of January 27,
1977, that he would keep his promise to kill her. Under the law,
this reasonable perception of imminent bodily harm or death
would justify her shooting him.

I heard Leo Thomas echo some of my thoughts to the
judge.

"Dr. Walker will not be invading the jury's province. The
appellate court judges in the case of *Ibn-Tamas vs. the United
States* ruled that they needed a psychologist to explain the defendant's state of mind. This is not a feminist issue, your honor.
It is about what happens to a woman when she lives with a man
whom she loves and who beats her."

I leaned back in my seat in the witness box, realizing that
this debate would be long and perhaps futile; I might never be

allowed to testify for Joyce Hawthorne, after all. Still, it was an argument I'd heard countless times: in classrooms, at professional meetings, in every arena where the phenomenon of battered women who kill had come up as an issue, whenever the rest of the system had already failed—after police, lawyers, and judges had refused to arrest, prosecute, or sentence a man for the criminal act of beating his wife or girlfriend. The tragic fruits of violence were a result of its unchecked nature. Our system repeatedly failed the battered woman, leaving her alone to defend herself and her children from further harm.

Now I wondered: would the system fail another woman? Would these heated, oft-repeated legal arguments hinder, obscure, and ultimately prevent the telling of her story?

I left my thoughts abruptly. Judge Anderson was telling both attorneys that he'd heard enough legal arguments. Also, he said, he had read the briefs prepared by each side citing case precedents. He was inclined to agree with the prosecutor, he said; but he would allow the defense to make a "proffer," an offer of proof, to try to persuade him otherwise (and to go on record, of course, in case his decision were to be appealed again).

An offer of proof is done without the presence of the jury. If the testimony is then ruled admissible, it must be repeated in the jury's presence. (That is why it is so terribly important to get the right information on record during a proffer; it is what appellate court judges base their opinions on. If Judge Anderson decided not to allow my testimony, and if Joyce was convicted again, that same testimony would provide the basis for another appeal.)

I steeled myself to the probable task of having to repeat myself, nearly word for word, more than once. But I was entirely willing to do that; I had made up my mind long ago that I'd repeat myself as many times as necessary if it meant the difference between life and death for a battered woman.

Leo Thomas stood and began to ask me the questions we'd prepared. Here we go, I thought.

"Please state your name, occupation, and business address to the court reporter for the record."

"My name is Dr. Lenore Walker, I am a clinical and forensic psychologist, and I practice in Denver, Colorado," I responded, my voice a little shaky with stress and with waiting.

"Are you licensed to practice psychology in any state?"

"Yes. I am licensed to practice psychology in New Jersey and Colorado, as those are the states in which I've lived and worked."

"Do you hold any board certificate?"

"Yes. I have been awarded the Diplomate in Clinical Psychology from the American Board of Professional Psychology."

"What does that mean?"

"Most states recognized the diplomate as proof of excellence in the practice of clinical psychology, and so offer the license to practice in that state without having to sit for the regular state examination. It is similar to Board Certification for physicians."

Leo's questions went on for a while, asking me to describe my education, training, teaching appointments, clinical psychology jobs, my expertise on the subject of battered women, and my professional relationships with colleagues. I was asked to list books, articles, and chapters I'd written, to talk about research projects I'd been involved in, to recap my testimony before Congress, all with the intention of establishing that I was recognized among peers, as well as among national policy makers, for my knowledge about battered women.

Leo turned to ask Ron Johnson if he wished to conduct his *voir dire,* the examination of an expert witness' qualifications. Sitting—smugly, I thought—at the prosecution table, Johnson refused, saying it would prove a waste of time if my testimony were later disallowed. So Leo continued with his next line of questioning.

"Now, would you define a battered woman to the Court?"

"Yes. The definition that I have used of a battered woman is a woman who has been physically, sexually, or seriously psychologically abused by a man in an intimate relationship, without his regard for her rights, in order to coerce her into doing what he wants her to do at least two times, often in a specific cycle."

"Are there specific psychological theories which your research has uncovered in this area?"

"Yes. Until I began doing some of the research in the psychology of battered women, battered women were believed to have something psychologically wrong with them—some kind of a mental disease. Most often psychiatrists and psychologists thought that women who remained in a battering situation were masochistic or had other personality disorders, and that somehow they did something to deserve it, to provoke it. My research has contradicted those old ideas and has offered theories in the field of psychology, which are now being widely accepted and disseminated."

"What are some of the new ideas, Doctor?"

"The two major theoretical constructs are the construct of learned helplessness, which is the application of a psychological process that was discovered by a psychologist named Martin Seligman in his laboratory work with animals about twenty years ago, and that ten years ago was applied to human beings in experiments with college students, and more specifically to women and battered women—which is the contribution my work has made: I applied learned helplessness to battered women. And the second is the cycle theory of violence."

"What is the learned helplessness theory?"

"The theory of learned helplessness explains how people lose the ability to predict whether their natural responses will protect them after they experience inescapable pain in what appear to be random and variable situations.

"The process of learned helplessness results in a state with deficits in three specific areas: in the area where battered women think, in how they feel, and in the way they behave. People who suffer from learned helplessness restrict the number of responses that they make to those with the highest probability of success. When a battered woman perceives she is in danger, if she has developed learned helplessness, she is likely to respond using the most predictable method of protecting herself. Sometimes that means using deadly force."

"And how about the cycle of violence?"

"One of the most important things that we discovered from the early interviews was that battered women and violent relationships are not consistent; that violence does not occur all the time in these relationships, nor does it occur in a random way. Rather, there seems to be a pattern that starts out slowly with some tension that builds up, explodes in some kind of an acute explosion, and then there is a third phase where the man is either kind, loving, or contrite, or he simply stops abusing for a short period of time; so there is a period of quiet, of less tension or none, and then the cycle of violence starts all over again. Each couple has their own unique pattern to the cycle, which can be measured by a trauma psychologist."

"Do some people have a predisposition to developing learned helplessness based on certain sex roles and sex role education?"

"Yes. Many of the battered women that we have been studying seem to have a vulnerability to falling into a learned helplessness pattern. Much of that comes from early socialization in sex roles that keep them very rigid in the way that they would respond to things; or sometimes it happens as a result of childhood abuse, sometimes during adolescence; and sometimes it happens only after they've lived with a batterer for a short period of time. What we have found is that the earlier this occurs, the more likely it is for the woman to have less capability of making an effective response to terminate the violent relationship."

"What would happen to a woman with such vulnerability if she married a man who began to hit her?"

"She would be more likely to develop adequate strategies for coping with the violence early on, but be less able to get out of the situation. By the time she might be able to develop effective strategies or even utilize some of the services—much like with the earlier research with animals and with other people—it would be more difficult for her to do that; and that's where the learned helplessness theory comes through."

"Mr. Thomas," Judge Anderson interrupted suddenly,

"since this is a proffer, can we get to the point? What is the opinion you want this witness to express that has a bearing on issues in this case? If you can lead me into that, maybe I can get a better idea of it."

"I think we need to lead up to it," Leo responded, "but if the Court will allow me to append it to the record, fine."

"Well, really," said the judge, "if I know the issues we are dealing with and the opinions being expressed, I think we can determine then whether we need to get all this background into it."

"All right," said Leo, and switched the sequence when he returned to questioning me. "As a result of your training, expertise, and research, Dr. Walker, have you had the opportunity to examine and diagnose Joyce Hawthorne and form an opinion as to whether or not she is a battered woman?"

"Yes, I have."

"What sort of examinations and so forth did you conduct with Joyce Hawthorne?"

"Doing a standard clinical psychological interview, I interviewed Joyce Hawthorne for approximately three hours. I read through many of the materials that you had provided for me, and Joyce Hawthorne came through our research center and spent approximately eight hours with one of our trained interviewers completing the entire assessment package, consisting of the structured Battered Woman Syndrome Questionnaire and other psychological scales that we have administered to the four hundred battered women who have come through our research center. We prepared a detailed summary of her childhood, relationship, and abuse history."

"Have you personally interviewed Joyce and reviewed those tests?"

"Yes, I have."

"Now, first of all, do you have an opinion as to whether or not Joyce Hawthorne is a battered woman?"

"Yes. In my professional opinion, Joyce Hawthorne has indeed been a battered woman."

"As a result of your background, training, education and expertise, do you or do you not feel that you can characterize, identify, and explain certain behaviors of Joyce Hawthorne?"

"Yes, I believe that with my background, I certainly can."

"And do you feel that this identification is necessary for a full and complete understanding of her behavior?"

"Yes, I certainly do. Most people do not understand the psychology of battered women, although battered women have been around for ages. It's only recently that we understand what they think, what they do, and why they do what they do."

"Have you testified in any other court as an expert witness?"

"Yes, I have."

"And do you recall on how many occasions?"

"Somewhere between eight and twelve times."

"Are there specific characteristics of batterers and battered wives?"

"Yes, there are."

"Have you identified those characteristics in the case of Joyce Hawthorne?"

"Yes, I have."

Leo turned to the judge, cutting short his questions after sensing the judge's impatience. "That is my testimony, your honor."

"Mr. Johnson," asked Judge Anderson, "do you have any questions now?"

"Not unless the Court thinks her testimony may be admissible," said the prosecutor, "and then I would question her, your honor. I would object to it on the grounds of her sample, and also on the grounds of relevance."

It seemed that Judge Anderson agreed. "I'm having a lot of trouble connecting it up with what issue in the case this is to relate to," he said.

"Your honor," Leo responded, "this relates to an explanation of the emotional responses of Joyce Hawthorne, responses that could very well be different in a different situation. But because of her conditioning—which, of course, could be explained by Dr. Walker—Joyce would respond in certain ways to certain things."

"Isn't it true that just about everybody . . . that their conditioning accounts for the way they respond . . . ?"

"Pardon?"

"Isn't it true of just about everybody," said the judge, "that their conditioning and things that happen to them during life, condition them to respond in certain ways?"

"But this is a particular group, Judge, that responds; and that's what we're dealing with."

"Is it aiming toward any issue that is a defense issue in the case?"

"Absolutely, your honor."

"What is the issue?"

"Whether or not she acted in self-defense; whether or not she believed that she was in fear; and that's absolutely what we're aiming at. That is the whole purpose of this testimony."

"That is what you want to do? Show that she believed she was in fear? That is opinion testimony."

"Let me elicit a little bit more along those lines."

"Okay."

Leo turned to me again. "Dr. Walker, did you review with Joyce and the other materials the events of the night of January 27, 1977?"

"Yes, I did."

"And as a result of reviewing the transcripts and interviews and her past history in childhood and all those details, do you have an opinion as to her emotional state on that night and early morning hours of January 27, 1977?"

"Yes, I do."

"And in your opinion what was her emotional state?"

"It is my professional opinion that Joyce Hawthorne believed that she was in imminent danger of being killed that night."

*   *   *

Looking back on that afternoon in court, I can remember the nearly optimistic feeling I had then. I was reasonably certain that Judge Anderson would listen to Joyce's story. That the conviction in my voice would somehow persuade him to allow my testimony, to ensure that the jurors would not base their final verdict on stereotype or myth.

It was a shock to hear him finally rule that my testimony would be disallowed.

It occurred to me then that in a way I, too, was being battered into silence by the court. A myriad of legal technicalities would be manipulated to stand in the way of an expert witness speaking to a jury, explaining to them why she believed Joyce Hawthorne, a woman who had never committed another violent crime in her life, had been driven to kill her cruel and abusive husband.

Doesn't anyone want to hear what women know? I wondered silently, catching Leo's eye in dismay.

Doesn't anyone care?

3

LEARNED HELPLESSNESS
AND
THE CYCLE OF VIOLENCE

A S I STATED IN MY TESTIMONY before Judge Anderson, and
as I've stated, as expert witness, during dozens of trials
since, my research with battered women has led me to
theorize the existence of a certain pattern that evolves in battering relationships, a pattern I call the Cycle of Violence. (This
theory bears a complementary relationship to Seligman's theory
of learned helplessness, which will be explored in further detail
later in this chapter.) Even though it does not occur in all battering relationships, it was reported to occur in two-thirds of the
sixteen hundred incidents in our studies on battered women. The
Cycle of Violence must be understood if we are to develop a
genuine understanding of the dynamics of domestic violence in
our society and of the psychology of battered women.

I break the Cycle of Violence into three phases: the tension-building phase; the acute battering incident; and the tranquil, loving (or at least nonviolent) phase that follows.

During the tension-building phase, minor battering incidents occur; slaps, pinches, controlled verbal abuse, and psychological warfare may all be part of this phase. The woman's attempts to calm the batterer can range from a show of kind,
nurturing behavior to simply staying out of his way. What really

42

happens in this phase is that she allows herself to be abused in ways that, to her, are comparatively minor. More than anything, she wants to prevent the batterer's violence from growing. This desire, however, proves to be a sort of double-edged sword, because her placatory, docile behavior legitimizes his belief that he has the right to abuse her in the first place. Any unexpected circumstance that arises may catalyze a sudden escalation of violence, an explosion; in the initial part of the tension-building phase, battered women will do almost anything to avoid that.

They go to great lengths to manipulate and control as many factors in their environment, and as many people, as they possibly can. They may also "cover" for the batterer in an attempt to win his favor, making excuses for his bad behavior, and in general isolating themselves from others who might help them. This increasing isolation is common to all battered women; the effect it has on exacerbating her already-established psychological terror cannot be stressed enough. As the Cycle progresses, the battered woman's placatory techniques become less effective. Violence and verbal abuse worsen. Each partner senses the impending loss of control and becomes more desperate, this mutual desperation fueling the tension even more. Many battered women say that the psychological anguish of this phase is its worst aspect. (Some will even provoke an acute incident, just to "get it over with" and, at the cost of grave physical injury, save themselves from real insanity or death.) But, sooner or later, exhausted from the unrelenting stress, the battered woman withdraws emotionally. Angry at her emotional unavailability and, because of that anger, less likely to be placated, the batterer becomes more oppressive and abusive. At some point and often not predictably, the violence spirals out of control, and an acute battering incident occurs.

During the acute phase—set apart from minor battering incidents by its savagery, destructiveness, and uncontrolled nature—the violence has escalated to a point of rampage, injury, brutality, and sometimes death. Although the battered woman sees it as unpredictable, she also feels that the acute battering incident is somehow inevitable. In this phase, she has no control;

only the batterer may put an end to the violence. The nature of his violence can be as unpredictable as the time of its explosion, and so are his reasons for stopping it. Usually, the battered woman realizes that she cannot reason with him, that resistance will only make things worse. She has a sense of being distant from the attack and from the terrible pain, although she may later remember each detail with great precision. What she is likely to feel most strongly at the time is a sense of being psychologically trapped.

Many battered women don't seek help during an acute battering incident. They often wait for several days afterward before seeking medical attention, if they do so at all. And, like other survivors of trauma and disaster, they may not experience severe depression or emotional collapse until days or even months later.

There is plenty of strong, sane rationale behind the battered woman's apparent passivity in the face of acute violence. Her batterer is in nearly all cases much stronger than her physically, and she knows from painful past experience that it is futile to fight him. Acute battering incidents are often so vicious, so out of control, that innocent bystanders may be injured just because they're in the wrong place at the wrong time. And anyone attempting to intervene, even another strong man, is likely to get hurt. Even if she managed to call the proper authorities, they might not respond effectively. Police in law enforcement departments across the country attest to the difficulty of breaking up an acute battering incident; even they view this kind of call as being extremely dangerous.

When the acute battering incident ends, the final phase in the Cycle of Violence begins. In this phase, usually all tension and violence are gone, which both members of the couple experience as a profound relief. This is a tranquil period, during which the batterer may exhibit warm, nurturing, loving behavior toward his spouse. He knows he's been "bad," and tries to atone; he promises never to do it again; he begs her forgiveness. (There are some similarities here to the behavior of a binge alcoholic—in fact, many batterers are active alcoholics. He is the one who begins and ends the battering incident; he is the one in power.)

During the third phase, the battered woman may join with the batterer in sustaining this illusion of bliss. She convinces herself, too, that it will never happen again; her lover can change, she tells herself. This "good" man, who is gentle and sensitive and nurturing toward her now, is the "real" man, the man she married, the man she loves. Many battered women believe that they are the sole support of the batterer's emotional stability and sanity, the one link their men have to the normal world. Sensing the batterer's isolation and despair, they feel responsible for his well-being. The truth is, though, that the chances of the batterer changing, actually seeking or receiving professional help, are very small, especially if the woman remains with him. Usually he seeks help only after she leaves, as a way of getting her back. In fact, almost 10 percent of the batterers in one of our research samples committed suicide after their women left them, lending credence to the battered woman's intuitive perception of her importance to the man's well-being and of the psychological dynamics in the relationship and debunking the myth that in a battering relationship it is the woman who is crazy.

It is in this phase of loving contrition that the battered woman is most thoroughly victimized psychologically. Now the illusion of absolute interdependency is firmly solidified in the woman's psyche, for in this phase battered women and their batterers really are emotionally dependent on one another—she for his caring behavior, he for her forgiveness. Underneath the grim cycle of tension, violence, and forgiveness that make their love truly terrifying, each partner may believe that death is preferable to separation. Neither one may truly feel that she or he is an independent individual, capable of functioning without the other.

In fact, many battered women who kill their abusers start out intending to commit suicide themselves. Suicide seems the only way to break the batterer's control over them and avoid further abuse. Somehow, though, these women experience a flash of insight: perhaps it is that they are truly unloved by the man who has beaten them, that they are truly separate from him, or that they can only stop his violence by killing him. This insight may give the battered woman ultimate control over what happens to her.

When professional intervention does not occur, battering relationships may escalate in violence to the point of suicide or homicide. It is a fact that many, many more women die each year at the hands of their abusive husbands then kill their abusers.

After years of research and of practicing psychotherapy, both with battered women and with batterers, and as part of a psychotherapy team working with battering couples (which I did with my late husband, psychologist Morton Flax, and with other psychologists over the years), it is my professional opinion that battering relationships rarely change for the better. Even with the desire of both partners, the inequality inherent in the relationship, the brutalizing division of power, is resistant to change. The violence in such relationships seems almost ingrained, although it may sometimes abate in frequency and severity. Physical abuse may stop for a time, but almost invariably the psychological abuse increases, and eventually the physical abuse will begin again. The best hope for the battered woman to stop the violence is to end the relationship altogether. This resolution is at psychotherapeutic cross-purposes when both partners are taken into consideration, since the batterer will almost always function better with the woman than without her, whereas the woman will almost always function better when she is out of the relationship for good.

There is usually no way the battered woman can permanently alter the man's battering behavior by changing her own. Batterers are violent for their own personal reasons, not because of anything their women do or don't do. And I believe it is entirely comprehensible that a woman—helpless in the face of a superior physical might directed against her, psychologically brutalized by continued entrenchment in the Cycle of Violence, emotionally devastated by unalleviated stress, entrapment, and terrible isolation—would try, in a moment of crisis, to stop the flow of unendurable events by taking one of her abuser's weapons into her own hands and using it in self-defense.

The question most often asked about battered women is, "Why don't they leave?" The underlying assumption is that then the battering would stop. Years of research have proved that assumption to be untrue; the abuse often escalates at the point of separation and battered women are in greater danger of dying then. The apparent passivity and immobility of battered women is difficult for most people to understand. But some important research in the field of human behavior, and several important theories that have evolved out of that research, are helpful in making the battered woman's behavior understandable.

Intermittent Reinforcement

One such theory is the social-learning theory of intermittent reinforcement. Behavioral psychologists have found that behavior that has been intermittently reinforced is the most difficult behavior to stop. In a battering relationship, the batterer's chief power is his seemingly random and variable unpredictability. The battered woman may not know, from one minute to the next, whether she'll be faced with her "good" husband or her "bad" husband. Sometimes he indulges her, reminding her of their courtship period when he proved he was capable of long periods of loving behavior. At other times he displays physical and psychological cruelty. Likewise, she may not know if sex will be pleasurable and loving, or if it will take the form of violent rape. In situations where the nature of the couple's sexual experience differs according to the whims and personality changes of the batterer, loving sex often has the effect of a positive reinforcement for the battered woman. Because it is sometimes pleasurable, at the times when it is abusive she may still hope that "the next time will be better." For many of the women we've evaluated over the years, this has been the case.

Post Traumatic Stress Disorder

Another important concept worth understanding is the recognized diagnosis of Post Traumatic Stress Disorder (PTSD), which battered women, like many Vietnam war veterans, may develop. Those who study PTSD have found that, after experiencing severe and unexpected trauma, or being repeatedly and unpredictably exposed to abuse, most people tend to develop certain psychological symptoms that continue to affect their ability to function long after the original trauma. They may believe that they are essentially helpless, lacking power to change their situation. Continuing and unpredictable disasters, such as earthquakes, randomly administered electric shocks, or acute battering incidents, can have the effect of stimulating the development of coping responses to the trauma at the expense of the victim's ability to muster an active response to try to escape further trauma. Furthermore, and whether this is true or not, the victim ceases to believe that anything she can do will have a predictable positive effect. Repeated trauma, such as battering, also causes the victim to develop certain coping or adaptation responses. She can no longer predict the outcome of responses she might make and therefore chooses only responses that have a high probability of protecting her.

The proven pattern of response theorized by the concept of PTSD, of which the Battered Woman Syndrome* is a subcate-

---

*Battered Woman Syndrome has been officially recognized as a subcategory of PTSD by experts in the field. Like Rape Trauma Syndrome, Battered Child Syndrome, and Child Sexual Abuse Accommodation Syndrome, there are significant behavioral, cognitive, and affective symptoms that are recognizable to appropriately trained mental health professionals.

In 1986, feminist psychiatrists, psychologists, social workers, and nurses battled with the American Psychiatric Association over their newly proposed diagnostic criteria, scheduled to be placed in the revised third edition of the *Diagnostic and Statistical Manual of Mental Disorders* (DSM-III-R), the official publication of the American Psychiatric Association and the nosology (classification) system used to diagnose most clients who seek psychotherapy in this country. One of the new categories proposed was called Masochistic Personality

gory, ties in dramatically with Seligman's theory of learned help-lessness. Indeed, if we can understand and apply both theories, we have a clearer understanding of the battered woman's di-lemma.

Learned Helplessness

Martin Seligman, a psychologist at the University of Pennsyl-vania, originally placed dogs in cages from which they could not escape and administered electric shocks to them at random and variable times. He found that the dogs quickly learned there was nothing they could do to predictably control the shocks. Even-tually, dogs in the experiment appeared to completely cease

---

Disorder, and its criteria could have easily been confused with Battered Woman Syndrome, which is a subcategory of Post Traumatic Stress Disorder. Later, the title was changed to Self-Defeating Personality Disorder, and another category, Sadistic Personality Disorder, was added. Neither category was properly devel-oped, and neither met scientific standards.

Meetings were held with Robert Spitzer, then chair of the task force charged with the DSM-III revision, his self-selected task force members, and other members of the American Psychiatric Association governance, who re-tained ultimate control over what was published in the diagnostic book. In the end, there was agreement that the newly proposed categories (including one that classified menstruating women with premenstrual syndrome as mentally ill) were based on clinical consensus of a small number of like-minded physicians and that more research would be needed prior to including the categories in the diagnos-tic system.

Unfortunately, however, the psychiatrists in charge of the research have different standards than psychologists and other researchers. From the looks of things today, the feminists' protests have not been taken seriously, and these new categories may yet be permitted in the fourth edition of the DSM due out in 1992. If this happens, it will be a setback for battered women and other victims of violence. Nevertheless, it is also important to remember that the dispute was fought out in public, and every major women's magazine, and most newspapers and local media ran stories exposing the politics behind the creation of psychiat-ric classifications. Therefore, there is hope that no one will take them too seriously.

all voluntary escape activity. Furthermore, when researchers changed procedure and tried to teach the dogs to escape, they appeared to instead remain entirely passive, sometimes lying in their own excrement, refusing both to leave and to try to avoid the administered electric shocks. However, a closer look revealed that these dogs were not really passive. They had developed coping skills that minimized the pain, lying in their own fecal matter (a good insulator from the electrical impulses) in a part of the electrical grid that received the least amount of electrical stimulation. Seligman found that eventually the dogs would learn to escape after being repeatedly dragged to the cage exits. Once they had learned to escape in this manner, their "learned helplessness response," which was to trade the unpredictability of escape for the more predictable coping strategies, disappeared.

With people, Seligman found that it was the cognitive aspect of this syndrome, that is, the individual's thoughts, that proved all-important. In other words: even if a person has control over a situation, but believes that she does not, she will be more likely to respond to that situation with coping responses rather than by trying to escape, similarly to the way Seligman's dogs responded once they had "learned" helplessness. Thus, when people are involved, the truth or facts of a situation turn out to be less important than the individual's set of beliefs or perceptions concerning the situation. Battered women don't attempt to leave the battering situation, even when it may seem to outsiders that escape is possible, because they cannot predict their own safety; they believe that nothing they or anyone else does will alter their terrible circumstances.

What this theory means, when applied to battered women, is not that a woman can learn how to be helpless; rather, it means that a woman can learn she is unable to predict the effect her behavior will have. This lack of ability to predict the efficacy of one's own behavior changes the nature of an individual's response to situations. People suffering from learned helplessness are more likely to choose behavioral responses that will have the highest predictability of an effect within the known, or familiar, situation;

they avoid responses—like escape, for instance—that launch them into the unknown. It is a reasonable measure of the battered woman's human fear to state that she believes the demons she knows well are probably preferable to the demons she does not know at all.*

Based on my research (in which I refined the scaling techniques used to signify or infer the presence of learned helplessness), I have come up with five factors in childhood and seven factors culled from adulthood experiences that I have successfully used to identify the presence of learned helplessness in an individual. Time and again, this list of factors has proven to have remarkable predictive and confirming value. Joyce Hawthorne, for instance, experienced four out of the five significant factors as a child (factors 1, 3, 4, and 5, below), and all seven of the significant factors in adulthood (see below) during her marriage to Aubrey.

The five childhood factors are:

1. Witnessing or experiencing battering in the home.
2. Sexual abuse or molestation as a child or teenager.
3. Critical periods during which the child experienced noncontingent control.†

*Some research indicates that many battered women may be "externalizers," that is, people who believe that things happening to them are caused by powers outside of themselves, over which they have no personal control. ("Internalizers," on the other hand, are people who tend to believe that they have great influence over the events of their lives.) It has also been found that externalizers seem to succumb to learned helplessness more easily than internalizers. My own research, reported in *The Battered Woman Syndrome*, indicates that battered women are both internalizers and externalizers, believing in their own ability to cope with the situation, which is nevertheless created by powerful others (their batterers).

†The term *noncontingent* reflects the fact that, even if children in this situation experience some control, they often do not connect what they do with the outcome. During such periods, children might experience such factors as early parent loss; alcoholism of a parent; frequent moves; or shameful or stigmatizing situations, such as poverty, that might result in the child dressing differently from others.

    4. Stereotyped sex-role socialization supporting rigid tradi-
tionality.
    5. Health problems or chronic illness.

The seven factors that occur in adulthood during the battering relationship itself, and which I found to be associated
strongly with the current accepted measurements of development
of learned helplessness, are:

    1. A pattern of violence, particularly the occurrence of the
Cycle of Violence, with its three phases of tension building, acute battering incident, and loving contrition or
absence of tension. An observable escalation in frequency and severity of the abuse is another pattern, even
when the Cycle of Violence is not prominent.
    2. Sexual abuse of the woman.
    3. Jealousy, overpossessiveness, intrusiveness of the bat-
terer, and isolation of the woman.
    4. Threats to hurt or kill the woman.
    5. Psychological torture (Amnesty International defini-
tion*).
    6. Violence correlates (including the woman knowing
about the man's violence against others, including children, animals, pets, or inanimate objects).
    7. Alcohol or drug abuse by the man or woman.

Taken as factors contributing to the makeup of a life and
a mode of behavior, these factors can contribute greatly to our
understanding of the battered woman's psyche, of the motiva-
tions behind her actions or lack thereof. Because of the comprehensive clarity and educational value of these factors, I often like

*The Amnesty International definition of psychological torture includes
the following elements: verbal degradation; denial of powers; isolation; monopo-
lizing perceptions; occasional indulgences; hypnosis; threats to kill; induced
debility; drugs or alcohol.

to use them in the form of a chart when I testify before a jury. Unless a jury is allowed to understand the bearing that learned behavior patterns have in determining the actions of battered women (and especially of battered women who kill), they may find themselves at a loss in attempting to deliver a reasonable and just verdict. And the battered woman, victimized by her man, runs the risk of being victimized yet again by an uncomprehending legal system.

Lack of Police Intervention

If battered women often meet with outright enmity in the sexist arena of the courtroom, they often meet with outright indifference or inaction when they turn to the law enforcement agency of first resort: the local police.

Until recently, police rarely provided battered women with effective or adequate protection. Most police officers seem to feel that what goes on between husband and wife is outside the realm of public law and order. Many men join the paramilitary police force to meet their own macho needs for power and control; these men may side with the batterer, certain that the battered woman must have done something to deserve the abuse.

In one of our samples, 90 percent of the battered women who reported assault to the police actually did sign complaints, but fewer than 1 percent of the cases were ever prosecuted. And the rate of conviction of batterers until recently was dishearteningly low.

There are simple solutions to this. For one thing, the police, not the battered woman, should be legally obliged to sign any complaint issued against a batterer, forcing the state to enforce its own law. In addition, police should be able to immediately issue and enforce temporary restraining orders forbidding the batterer to do any further harm. It is a notable fact that most batterers seem to comply with restraining orders, even though they are "only pieces of paper," commonly thought by the police to be difficult to enforce. For some women, just obtaining a restraining order, or order of protection, as it is sometimes called, makes her feel more powerful, more in control. And police tend to respond more supportively toward women who get them; perhaps because it signifies to them that these women "mean business." Although spouse abuse is either a misdemeanor or a felony crime in all states, judges tend to issue greater sanctions when a batterer violates a restraining order than they do for the assaultive act itself. Furthermore, battered women who have previously obtained a restraining order and later kill their batterers in self-defense are more likely to be believed than those women who had never taken any self-protective legal actions.

Until such time as the police can really protect women from abusers, more women are likely to die at the hands of battering husbands or boyfriends. And the socially ingrained attitude of neglect on the part of the police (another result of institutionalized sexism, which leaves the business of "disciplining" women to the men who believe they "own" them) is likely to continue.

The following story is an all-too-typical example of such neglect and inaction on the part of police, lack of intervention that in Darlene's case had tragic consequences.

DARLENE'S STORY

A young Black woman in her mid-twenties, Darlene had lived with Richard for two years. He was charming and handsome, new to town when they'd first met, and Darlene had quickly fallen in love.

"He treated her nicely at first," members of her family would later recall. "But as soon as she let him move in, he became mean to her and to all of us. He didn't let her see us much, and we'd always been a close family."

Blaming Darlene, though, for letting Richard separate them (the woman is almost always blamed in these cases for not employing adequate social skills or for failing to keep everyone happy), the family stopped persisting in their demands to see her. But they kept up contact by telephone.

"We guessed maybe he was hurting her," they recalled, "but we didn't know what to do about it. Darlene kept telling us she had everything under control. She made excuses for his bad behavior, so what could we do?"

Finally, though, Darlene decided she couldn't take any more. She made up her mind to leave Richard, who by now was beating her frequently.

To escape another beating, though, she had to leave her home—a home filled with the furniture she'd saved all her money to buy, a home that was her pride and joy—and hide. On the pretext of taking his clothes to the laundromat, she did leave, staying first at her cousin's place, later at her aunt's. When Richard tracked her down, she called the police, begging for protection. Police records would later show that she had told them Richard was threatening to set her home on fire.

"We can't do anything about a threat," the police told her.

"Can't you stop him?" she pleaded. "He really will do it."

Like other battered women, Darlene knew all too well that Richard could easily destroy her personal property to punish her for walking out on him. He knew how proud she'd been of her home. His need to control her outweighed any love or compassion he might have felt.

Later that same day, Darlene called the police again.

"He's threatening to kill me," she reported tearfully. "I need some protection, or he'll do it."

"Sorry," she was told. "We can't do anything until he actually tries to hurt you. Besides, you're safe there where you are."

But Darlene didn't feel safe. She knew how violent Richard could be. Every strange sound made her jump with fear; neither family nor friends could calm her down.

Richard began stalking her by phone, alternately begging her to come home and threatening to hurt her or destroy her possessions. After a number of phone calls like this, he told her he was planning to leave town the next morning.

Daring to hope that he really would move away and leave her alone, Darlene fell asleep that night. But she slept beside the loaded gun her family had given her for protection.

Morning came. Darlene began to do some chores around her aunt's home.

The next thing she knew, Richard was banging on the door, demanding to be let in. Afraid that he'd try to kill them all, Darlene and other family members hid. But Richard left, bumping into Darlene's brother on his way out.

"Leave her alone," Darlene's brother demanded. "She wants you to go away."

"Okay," Richard promised, speaking "man to man" with the brother. "Tell her to give me back my clothes, and I'll give her back the key to her house. I won't stay where I'm not wanted. I'll come by again in an hour."

After listening to Richard's message as relayed by her brother, and daring to hope that he really meant to let her go this time, Darlene packed his clean clothes into a bag and prepared to give them to him when he returned.

Watching nervously, she saw Richard drive up in his van. She went outside to get the exchange over with quickly. He stayed inside the van as she handed him the clothes. Then, making her realize that her dream of escape had been too good to be true, he began arguing with her.

Witnesses saw Richard start to get out of the van. Certain that he was going to make good his threat to kill her now, Darlene brandished the gun her family had given her and started shooting wildly. Richard jumped back into the van, drove it onto the sidewalk and over the lawn, chasing her as she tried to run, backward, into the safety of the house. She'd almost gotten there when she tripped and fell. One of her wooden shoes, too clumsy to run in, had fallen off.

Richard hit her straight-on with the van. He smashed her flat against the house. The brick wall tumbled around her lifeless body as her family watched helplessly.

Then he sped off, to be arrested and charged with second-degree murder a few hours later.

"Why didn't you charge him with first-degree?" I asked Joe Cotter, the assistant D.A. assigned to this case.

The calls to the police, recorded the day before, proved that Richard had been planning to kill her, I thought. And had it been the other way around—had Darlene killed Richard—certainly she would have been charged with first-degree murder.

"No," Joe replied. "He didn't admit to it, so it isn't a fact, and therefore it can't be called premeditated."

"So what? That man terrified her. His behavior was typical: a batterer stalking a woman, unable to let her go. And his threats to kill her are also corroborated by members of her family. Besides, he went right to where she was staying!"

"It's her word against his, Lenore, and we can't use hearsay statements she made to her family because she's not available to corroborate them. So if the suspect keeps quiet and denies even the obvious, he has a better chance of getting off."

"Sure, she's not here to corroborate her statements! Because she's dead, because he finally killed her, just like he tried to do every time he beat her! No one believed her, even though she kept getting more and more frantic. So now she's dead, what more proof do you need?"

Joe sighed. "The problem is that I can't get Darlene's family to cooperate, Lenore. Maybe you can help? If they don't testify, Richard might even go free. He's pleading self-defense, because she had a gun and she was shooting at him."

"Wait a minute, Joe. How can he claim self-defense when he tracked her down, argued with her, drove his van up across the sidewalk and onto the grass, and smashed her to death with it? If he was so scared, why didn't he just drive away?"

"His lawyers will claim that he loved her, that he couldn't think straight with a gun pointed at him."

"Do they really think a jury will buy that?"

"What's a guy to do when the lady he loves runs away,

hides out from him, and then starts shooting at him—when all he did was come to kiss her goodbye?"

"Oh my God, Joe. What about all the harassing phone calls, all the threats, all the prior abuse?"

"I know about all that, but it's not going to be enough. We have to put it out in front of the jury. And the people who can testify to the truth of it won't talk to me. I'm white. I represent the system they think failed to protect Darlene on purpose."

I calmed down, beginning to see his point. "Okay. What can I do?"

"First of all, I don't even know if I can get your testimony admitted. The rules of evidence are different for the prosecution than they are for the defense. But will you at least see the family, interview them if you can, and come up with a professional opinion? I want to know for sure: was Darlene a battered woman, was she repeatedly beaten and terrorized by the man who killed her? And, if you think so, will you help me prepare her family to testify at trial?"

Early the next morning I entered my office to find my waiting room filled with nine angry Black people: Darlene's family.

It took very little time for us all to begin talking together honestly. They were pleased that, for once, the D.A.'s office seemed to be spending some money to hire me to help them, money they thought was usually reserved for cases involving rich white people.

"No one cares that a decent young Black woman was killed," someone said. They were incensed at the lack of action taken by the police in the days preceding Darlene's death; they mistrusted the justice system the police represented. And rightly so, I thought. Like women, Blacks are kept on the fringes of this society's power structure, and some think Black women are the most oppressed group of all.

"Do you need to know who gave her the gun, Dr. Walker?"

"Why does that worry you?"

"Because Black people get in trouble for having guns. We

won't get a brother in trouble. So if we have to say it, we just won't testify. It wouldn't matter, anyway."

"Well, I understand why you feel so discouraged. The police and the whole system failed to protect Darlene. And maybe it won't work, trying to put Richard behind bars. But Joe tells me he can't get a conviction at all without you telling the jury what you know. So if you don't testify, he might really get away with murder. Isn't it worth a chance?"

The tension broke then, and everyone began talking at once. I immediately knew that, upon hearing what these people had to say, any jury would convict Richard.

With the information her family provided and the police records, I had enough to support testimony concerning Darlene's status as an abused woman, a battered woman, a woman who had shot that gun at her abuser in a desperate attempt to stay alive.

Unfortunately, she had failed in her attempt. Like so many other battered women, her cries for help had gone unanswered, and she died because no one, certainly not the police, had protected her.

In the end, Darlene's family made wonderful witnesses. Each one of them testified, clearly and eloquently, as to what they had seen. During their testimony, there wasn't a dry eye in the courtroom.

Joe never could get my testimony admitted. The judge ruled it irrelevant, since I had never interviewed either Richard or Darlene. But Joe did manage to tell the jury what I would have said, in his closing argument. It was odd to hear my words coming out of his mouth. Still, the jury heard it all, and that was the important thing.

Richard was convicted of second-degree murder and sentenced to sixteen years in prison; the judge found aggravated circumstances, so he got double the eight-year sentence he might otherwise have received. In a way, Darlene's death was avenged. Yet that doesn't really make me feel better. It could have been prevented altogether.

Why do institutions designed to protect us fail women in instances of domestic violence?

The following is another story of overt neglect on the part of the police and criminal justice system—another system where that neglect had fatal consequences.

PAM'S STORY

Pam Gunther did everything the system allowed her to do to escape from her abusive husband, Dave: she filed for divorce, obtained a restraining order, then took her two young children and fled to a nearby safe house when Dave's threats became too frightening.

When she returned home one evening to get some additional clothes for the children, Dave held her at gunpoint for six hours. Neighbors called the police, who finally arrived, and managed to talk him into letting her go. They arrested him, charged him with burglary—not assault or kidnapping, holding her hostage, or attempted murder—and allowed him out on bond within two hours, less than a third of the time he'd kept Pam hostage with a gun to her head.

Terrified, Pam returned to a battered women's shelter. She knew she'd narrowly escaped death this time but was unsure she'd be as lucky again.

She was right.

One week later, Dave shot and killed Pam as she and her two children were leaving a restaurant. They'd dined there with her former boss and friend, who was also shot and critically injured.

Finally, Dave was charged with first-degree murder—too late to protect Pam.

When Dave had been charged with burglary, the community's pleas to the police and the D.A.'s office to charge him with a higher-level crime and revoke his bond had been ignored. Shelter advocates and others had been labeled as "overreacting," "hysterical" women. The subtext, of course, is that they were seen as meddling in police business, which is not considered to be the business of women.

Meanwhile, the police had failed to do their job. And another woman had died at the hands of her batterer.

As I write this, four women in New York who received orders of protection have been killed by batterers. Four more women were murdered in Colorado, also with restraining orders in hand. Candlelight vigils have been held by battered women resource workers nationwide to honor the dead women: women who all along had feared they would be killed, women our society failed to protect. We must ask ourselves: as a society, why do we permit this slaughter of women to continue?

A United States Commission on Civil Rights investigation* has shown that police records on battered women are consistently inaccurate, a situation that is attributable, I believe, to inadequate reporting techniques.

The tragedy is, too, that when police do intervene they are ineffective. They seem reluctant to arrest or in any way restrain the batterer. What is the cause for this? Institutional, socially

*The investigation was completed in 1978 and published as *Battered Women: Issues of Public Policy.* In 1982, the Commission published *Under the Rule of Thumb: Battered Women and the Administration of Justice.*

Another study, funded by the Police Foundation in Minneapolis in 1981 and 1982, showed that arrest is the most effective police response for reducing further battering. (Sociologist Richard Berk and criminologist Larry Sherman gave the police three options from which to choose: arrest; order a walk around the block to "cool off"; do nothing. Arrest turned out to be overwhelmingly the best response.) After a night or even a few hours in jail, many batterers seem to learn that there are serious consequences for beating their wives or girlfriends. Although they may not stop the psychological abuse, in cases where they have been incarcerated the physical abuse often ceases or diminishes. This study has prompted a change in police procedure there toward arrest and incarceration of the batterer until arraignment in court.

ingrained sexism again? Policemen identifying with batterers—as men, as members of a social club that does not admit women?

Sociologist Murray Straus* has estimated that, in any society, between 25 percent and 67 percent of all homicides occur within the family, inside the home. (Although his lack of a feminist perspective causes him, I believe, to misinterpret some of his data on incidence and prevalence of violence between men and women, his work has given us the best picture available of the enormous levels of violence that exist behind closed doors in America.) Social psychologist Angela Browne and sociologist Kirk Williams have found that more than 50 percent of all women homicide victims are murdered by former abusive male partners.† And a study of domestic violence in Kansas City showed that fully 80 percent of all homicides resulting from domestic violence had a history of previous police intervention (on the average, one to five such interventions). This statistic speaks eloquently of the true consequences of nonintervention in the Cycle of Violence, for these homicides are the result of battering that, though publicly acknowledged, has gone unchecked and uncontrolled.

Psychologist Angela Browne's research data indicates that the number of women killing men has decreased by 25 percent in the last few years. This decrease is mostly accounted for in those communities that provide the most comprehensive services for battered women and their children. These services are essential, for the wealthy as well as for the middle-class, working-class, and poor battered woman.

Among the women in our early samples, only 10 percent ever bothered to call the police for help, apparently with good

*Straus is Professor of Sociology and a Director of the Family Research Laboratory at the University of New Hampshire, in Durham, N.H. With R. A. Gelles and S. C. Steinmetz, he coauthored *Behind Closed Doors: Violence in America* (Doubleday, 1980).

†The study results will be published in 1989 in *Law and Society Review.* Angela Browne is the author of *When Battered Women Kill* (Free Press–Macmillan, 1987). Kirk Williams is associated with the Family Research Laboratory at the University of New Hampshire.

reason: almost all of the women who had called stated later that the police had provided absolutely no help at all. In fact, they often made things worse; once they were gone, after some feeble and ineffective attempts to placate the batterer and after the batterer saw that nothing had been done to stop him, he often continued his abuse with renewed violence. Today, with a larger number of communities adopting proarrest policies, the percentage of battered women receiving effective police intervention is higher.

It is clear that we need to find or create sensitive, effective legal intervention for battered women, beginning with police protection.

4

THE EXPERIENCE
OF TERROR

Terror of her abuser is a seed that is planted in the psyche of the battered woman by repeated subjection to psychologically sadistic manipulation and physical bullying; it grows and grows until she is incapable of believing in the effectiveness of taking positive action on her own behalf, until she has become a true victim of learned helplessness. It is common for a severely battered woman to believe that the batterer is omnipotent, capable of coming after her no matter where she is. Even capable of transcending death itself to inflict pain and terror on her again. This supposedly irrational fear finds its logical basis within the context of the battering situation, for it is the situation itself that invokes it.

But is terror a legally definable emotion? If so, how does one measure it? Battered women experience a bloodcurdling kind that leaves a hole in the pit of the stomach, that makes a person shake from the inside out. What must it be like, coming home day after day without ever knowing if you will be physically safe there or not? Or going to sleep at night, not knowing if you'll wake up the next morning?

And how does one measure psychological degradation, the feelings of humiliation and shame experienced by the battered woman when she senses she will never be able to please the man she loves? To be sure, continual, unpredictable insecurity in the presence of ever-building violence must dramatically influence the way a human being views the world. And while many other emotions play a part in the tragic stories of battered women who kill, nearly all of them kill not out of anger, jealousy, or other emotions, but out of terror. They are in terrible fear for their lives. They kill in self-defense; their ultimate fear is that they will be murdered themselves if they do not kill.

Unfortunately, this fear is definitely not irrational. Although I am concerned here with addressing the issues of women who kill to save their own lives, it is statistically far more likely that battered women will die at the hands of their abusive partners.*

The increased terror experienced by the battered woman during separation, divorce, and child custody proceedings is based undeniably in reality. Separation creates a period of unprecedented danger in battering situations, a danger not often recognized by others. The batterer would often rather kill, or die himself, than separate from the battered woman; he is always more terrified of abandonment than of violence. Studies show that batterers fare poorly on their own; on the other hand, battered women and children, once free of the batterer, tend to do rather well. The batterer's fear of abandonment is based on self-

---

*In the first two months of 1987 alone, seven women were murdered by abusive mates in the metropolitan Denver area. By the end of that year, the number of known dead battered women rose to nineteen. There were four murder-suicides in a two-month period in late 1988. This is not an isolated regional phenomenon. The battered women's shelter staff in Norfolk, Virginia, counted sixty-nine dead battered women within the first nine months of 1987, and in Suffolk County, New York, within one month in early 1989, four batterers killed their women and children. In the study cited in the previous footnote, psychologist Angela Browne together with sociologist Kirk Williams analyzed recent American homicide statistics compiled by the Centers for Disease Control in Atlanta, Georgia; they found an increase in the number of women being killed by abusive partners in thirty-five states; in twenty-five states, most of these women were killed after they separated from or divorced their partners.

knowledge; he senses he will do badly on his own, and, in fact, if abandoned the chances of his dying by his own hand are fairly high. The battered woman perceives that he will do anything to keep her from leaving him. Her fear for her life, and for the lives of her children and other family members and friends, is likewise based on undeniable truth that, if she does not know consciously, she will certainly intuit. Life hangs in the balance: hers, his, everyone's.

PATRICIA'S STORY

Patricia Burns was terrified that her husband, Clarence, would make good his threats to find and kill her if she ever tried to leave him. But, after years of abuse, Patricia, an elementary school teacher in Denver, Colorado, decided that she could endure no more. She was afraid for her life if she stayed with him, too.

Patricia did everything the system tells women to do. Her attorney prepared the necessary papers, filed them on her behalf, and asked for and received a restraining order from the courts. Still terrified of Clarence, Patricia did just what her counselor told her to do: she kept up normal appearances until she and her fourteen-year-old son had safely left home. In fact, she cooked Clarence breakfast that morning the way she'd done every day for the past fifteen years. When he'd left for work, she wrote him a note telling him that they wouldn't be coming home any more.

Patricia was very happy with her job and didn't want to give it up. Nor did she want her son uprooted from friends and school; she felt that he'd suffered enough. So she tried to suppress her terror and her desire to flee the state. She and her son went to stay with family.

As his first week alone wore on, Clarence became increasingly frantic. He managed to track down Patricia's movements and, one afternoon, to locate her parked car. He climbed into the trunk and locked himself in.

Later Clarence would claim that he'd just wanted to talk

with Patricia. He would claim he'd taken along a gun because he planned to kill himself. But Patricia got into the car without knowing that he was there. When she parked it again, Clarence unlocked the trunk from the inside and stepped out to follow her.

Within a short period of time, Patricia Burns lay dead on the Denver sidewalk outside her family's home. Clarence had shot her five times in the face.

Clarence Burns was arrested and charged with first-degree murder. Two public defenders were assigned to prepare his defense. (This was the same public defender's office that I'd worked for as expert witness for five years. They had a complete file on the psychological dynamics of battering relationships, much of which they would choose to ignore in this case.)

Clarence was sent for psychological testing, the psychologist determining that the stress and pain of his separation had caused him to become "temporarily insane." His previous threats to kill Patricia were ignored completely in the report, as was his well-known history of violent behavior. During his trial, the jealous accusations he'd made of his wife—so common in battering situations, yet almost always unfounded—were presented. Without their accuracy being checked at all, Patricia Burns was accused, postmortem, of having had a lover. Clarence's attorneys prepared to claim a "heat of passion" mental health defense.

"No way!" the assistant D.A. responded. "We'll offer a second-degree murder plea arrangement, and nothing lower." Secretly he didn't believe that the state had enough evidence to win a conviction of first-degree murder, even though Clarence's previous threats to kill Patricia had been sworn to in the initial restraining order process and clearly stated to her own divorce attorney, who had persuaded her that it was safe both to stay and to fight legally. (It is my feeling that racism may have influenced many of the pivotal decisions in this case. Patricia was white; Clarence was Black. In prejudiced minds, does the life of a white woman married to a Black man have the same value as other lives?) So the decision was made to plead Clarence's case to second-degree murder. The prosecutor fully expected the judge to hand down a ten-year sentence.

Instead, Denver District Court Judge Alvin Lichtenstein found mitigating circumstances, based on the inaccurate psychological evaluation presented, and sentenced Clarence to four years in the penitentiary. He then suspended the sentence with provisions for Clarence to attend a community corrections program for two more years. Clarence could go to work, as he normally did, during the day, but had to report to the halfway house facility at night. Judge Lichtenstein later justified his actions by claiming that he didn't want Clarence's son to be deprived of financial support.

This judge's unjust and inappropriate sentence might not have attracted nationwide attention had he not added a lecture from the bench that demonstrated his sexism as well as his ignorance concerning domestic abuse.

"Patricia Burns provoked her own murder," he decreed. "She fooled her husband by cooking him breakfast, being nice to him, and then, without warning, leaving him. This behavior would understandably drive any normal man to lose control and kill."

Judge Lichtenstein never mentioned this marriage's long history of battery and abuse. Those who knew the details of the case were aghast. Within a few minutes after he'd addressed the court, a newspaper reporter phoned my office. She repeated what the judge had said, still in shock herself. I was outraged.

"Women can no longer tolerate the injustice handed down by ignorant, old, white, male judges," I said, for the first time, but not the last.

I allowed her to print my comments. The local media picked them up quickly; within two days they had made headlines across the nation. Women's rights groups immediately began to plan protests. The D.A. vowed to file an appeal. Misuse of judicial process would be claimed.

Battered women were featured on nightly news reports in the metropolitan Denver area. Several days later, a large rally sponsored by several organizations was held in Denver. Dottie Lamm, wife of Colorado's governor and a newspaper columnist and social worker in her own right; Nancy Dick, the lieutenant governor; Pat Schroeder, our local congresswoman; and many others were among the politicians, people of influence, and ordinary, outraged citizens who attended. Speeches were given decrying this unjust decision, along with other sexist judicial decisions that had victimized women. Reform was in the air.

Judge Lichtenstein bowed to political pressure and asked to be removed from his criminal court docket. He was reassigned to a civil docket by Chief Judge Clifton Flowers. Before he left, he reversed his original sentence without a hearing, reinstating Clarence Burns's sentence to four years at the state prison in Canon City. The defense filed an appeal; women's groups filed a brief supporting the D.A.'s position, and their strategy paid off. Eventually, Judge Lichtenstein's decision was reversed; the chief judge accepted responsibility for holding a new sentencing hearing.

Without much media attention this time, Clarence Burns was sentenced to ten years in prison. In Colorado, with half-time off for good behavior being standard procedure, he will soon be eligible for parole.

Not much of a deterrent for killing a woman, is it?

During the time of Clarence Burns' prosecution, an interesting side issue had developed within the Colorado Women's Bar Association. Usually a staunch advocate for women's rights and especially for the rights of battered women, a small group split in its support of Judge Lichtenstein. These women claimed that, while others may have had trouble with Lichtenstein, they "personally" did not. "He gets along really well with me," was the comment most frequently voiced by those women who supported him.

Such a comment is a demonstration of the internalization of oppression that can occur among women who are trying to work in a world run by men. In some ways, the women supporting Judge Lichtenstein were themselves merely mimicking the placatory behavior of battered women.

The truth is that strong women who speak out against the entitlement values of men (the perks that men expect) are often punished, some by sexual and physical abuse, some by opposition to their careers, some even by death. Yet all are forced to live with the threat and the fear of harm.

The most common question asked of battered women is: why do they stay with the men who beat and rape them? Why don't they leave? Why do they remain in an abusive situation as the violence escalates out of control?

To understand this, we must understand something of the socialization process of little girls in our society, the process that teaches girls to grow into women who accept the temper tantrums of men without allowing it to diminish their love for them, until it is too late. This process does not affect only those women who are abused physically but impacts on all women who endure the psychological abuse of men, too. In our culture, women are usually trained to believe that men are invariably "imperfect," that they must put up with any and every imperfection in the men they love, in order to get any love in return.

Battered women are not blind; most of them understand that there is something seriously wrong with the men who alternately hurt and nurture them. Like most women socialized in our culture, as well as in other cultures, the battered woman is trained to make excuses for a man's imperfections, even at the risk of her own physical well-being. And, equally crippling to her, she is trained to blame herself for some of his worst behavior. If she were a good enough wife, goes her internal line of reasoning, she could make him stop beating her; he would not have to hurt her. The truth is different, of course. Men who batter in one relationship tend to batter in their next relationship, too; this behavior is compulsive on the batterer's part, essentially unmotivated by any action the woman takes or does not take. Batterers abuse women and children for their own reasons; they alone are responsible for continuing or for changing their behavior. (I try to suggest to my therapy clients that they check out a man's behavior with his former wife or lover, in order to help her see that she is not to blame. If he is a batterer, his reaction to any infraction of his self-imposed "rules" will remain the same in all his relationships with women; his need to control a woman by creating his own behavioral standards and then attempting to enslave her to them will not change.)

Only about 20 percent of batterers are also violent to individuals outside the home. Many batterers have successful careers and are highly respected in their communities. Many, too, would not be as productive or successful were it not for the quiet aid and silent career participation of their battered wives. In this sense, they seem indistinguishable as a group from other men. But batterers do seem to have dual personalities: a "good" side and a "bad" side. Their behavior inside the home is extreme, seeming to swing quickly back and forth between personalities. Unlike true psychopaths, they do experience guilt and shame at their "bad," violent actions, but seem unwilling to control their behavior.

In general, the "typical" batterer has a poor self-image and low self-esteem (traits he shares with the "typical" battered woman). He may excuse his violent behavior by blaming the battered woman for some imagined infraction of his personally set rules. He cherishes traditional values regarding family, and believes in the validity of stereotypical sex roles and in the supremacy of the male. He is likely to externalize responsibility for many of his actions. He experiences chronic, almost pathological jealousy; he may also experience (perhaps chemically abnormal) reactions to stress, compulsively drinking at times in an attempt to alleviate the feelings of unhappiness or stress, "blowing off steam" by turning violently on his wife or girlfriend and children. He may often use sex as an act of power, aggression, and violence, or to enhance his shaky self-esteem; he may engage in increasingly "kinky" and violent sexual behavior in order to become aroused or to maintain arousal. He may be bisexual. In his heart, he believes that his acts of violence are excusable and should go unpunished; furthermore, he does not expect that his violence will go as far out of his conscious control as it often does.

In one study, Dr. Daniel Sonkin, a San Francisco psychologist, found that 95 percent of men who sought treatment for their battering behavior admitted to abusing more than one woman.* Likewise, Dr. Anne Ganley has found that the batterers she treats often go on to batter another woman in their next relationship; each partner of the batterer is different enough in behavior and character for Dr. Ganley to have drawn the conclusion that the abusive behavior stems from the male batterer himself, not from the relationship.†

It is true that battering relationships defy some of our most treasured concepts about family, marriage, and love. We've all been raised to believe that it "takes two" people to make a fight. But that truism does not hold in battering relationships, where only the man needs to be violent. He can and does pick fights on his own, sometimes waking a woman up from sound sleep to initiate an acute battering incident.

In our society, too, a woman's behavior in times of interpersonal conflict is usually defensive rather than aggressive. Women are taught to keep themselves as safe as possible. While a few women do adapt to living in constant terror by learning violence themselves, and while it is true that some mutually violent relationships may develop over time, it is also almost always the case that the man has the terror-producing advantage. And women learn to recognize the cues that will precede an acute battering incident: a certain look in his eyes, a change of facial expression, a particular behavioral routine, or some other warning ritual. Often no one else believes them if they seek help, or else they are so silenced by their own psychological paralysis that they cannot

*See *The Male Batterer* (1985), written with Del Martin and Lenore Walker. Sonkin has also written, with Michael Durphy, *Learning to Live without Violence* (Volcano Press, 2nd ed., 1989). He is working on another book, *The Wounded Man.*

†Anne L. Ganley, a psychologist at the Veterans Administration Hospital in Seattle, Washington, is the author of "Perpetrators of Domestic Violence: An Overview of Counseling the Court-Mandated Client," in Daniel Sonkin's book *Domestic Violence on Trial: Psychological and Legal Dimensions of Family Violence* (Springer, 1987).

seek help at all. So they do the best they can to keep their rising terror at a manageable level. If they don't, they are much more likely to be killed. Much has been made of the seemingly "odd" behavioral patterns some battered women may employ as survival techniques. Not enough, though, has been made of the striking courage and stoicism of these women who still manage to function day to day, keeping homes and tending children, under conditions of excruciating physical and psychological duress.

But living in constant terror exacts its price. One of the results would appear to be an emotional immunity of sorts, an imperviousness to the reality and consequences of violence, and also to the reality of death. Battered women who kill their batterers almost never understand that they have actually killed them, until they are informed by the police. In fact, both the battered woman and her batterer seem to have trouble believing that genuine harm and damage will actually result from a battering incident; in this type of relationship, denial runs rampant. And rampant denial, wedded to terror and violence spiraling out of control, can predictably lead to fatal consequences. Even after a homicide, denial and the battered woman's belief in the omniscience of her batterer serve to deaden death's effect. The battering situation breeds its own logic of thought and action.

After killing or seriously injuring her batterer, it might "normally" be expected that the battered woman would notify the police, or at least call on someone else for help. But by the time she kills, the abused woman is often so damaged herself, physically and emotionally, that she may be in a dissociative state.

Beverly Ibn-Tamas, whose story follows, couldn't believe her abusive husband was dead, even though she'd fatally shot him twice.* Dragged down to the Washington, D.C., homicide divi-

---

*Joyce Hawthorne, whose story begins this book, often stated to me that one of the most important beliefs she'd cherished during her many long years of legal battle after she shot and killed Aubrey—a belief that kept her spirits up—was the feeling that, if she got too depressed, Aubrey would rise from his grave and come after her again. And, she said, she felt that he'd already beaten her long enough and hard enough.

sion in a state of hysteria, she said she "just knew" that her husband could not be dead. He hadn't wanted to die; therefore, he would not. To her he was still alive: terrible, threatening, omniscient.

BEVERLY'S STORY

A licensed practical nurse, Beverly had suffered a history of violent and brutal abuse during her marriage to Yuses Ibn-Tamas, a highly successful and respected neurosurgeon. He had pushed, shoved, and punched her, choked her to the point of unconsciousness, thrown her across the room, tossed her from a moving car and threatened her at gunpoint; he had wrongfully accused her of sexual infidelity with other men, as well as with several of her women friends. Beverly had become more and more isolated from other people.

Her husband had grown increasingly involved with Black Muslim activists over the years; she disliked his involvement with the group and disliked his friends but was prohibited by him from having friends of her own. When she became pregnant, Yuses's abuse worsened. He began to beat her more frequently, sometimes seeming to aim his blows intentionally at her abdominal region.

Beverly had left him several times before, when the abuse became particularly intense. She'd even enlisted the help of her in-laws (who, after her death, denied ever witnessing or knowing about Yuses's violent behavior, a common denial among surviving relatives of the batterer, as we will see in other women's stories).

But on the day in January 1977 when he began to beat her pregnant belly fiercely with a hair brush, then threatened to kill her with a handgun, something inside Beverly reacted to her terror. She struggled with Yuses for the gun, got it, and shot him through the chest at point blank range.

Yuses stumbled down the stairs of their lavish home in Washington's "Gold Coast."

So absolute had this man's power been over her, though, for

so long, that Beverly wasn't even sure she'd hurt him at all. She thought maybe he was just heading into another room to get a gun she knew he kept hidden in a cabinet there. So she followed him, terrified that he was finally going to kill her.

When she entered the room and saw that he'd stopped running and had turned to face her, she was sure he'd already gotten the other gun. He would kill her now, she thought.

She aimed the handgun and shot him again.

This second bullet hit Yuses right between the eyes. He immediately crumpled to the floor.

As a neurosurgical nurse, Beverly seemingly should have known that this second wound was fatal. But, as was typical in battering situations, logic did not prevail. In her tortured heart, she truly believed that her husband was omnipotent and could heal himself. That was the reason for her hysterical resistance when arresting officers arrived.

He isn't dead! she repeated to herself, over and over again: he isn't dead!

When I interviewed Beverly, she had already endured several lengthy legal procedures and spent five months in jail.

She still loved the man she'd killed; she was still mourning his death. Tragically enough, in the courtroom, at her own trial, she couldn't bear to speak of his violent behavior and terrifying abuse of her. To the end, she acted as though such talk would constitute betrayal of the love they had at one time shared.

This case was the second on which I was called as an expert witness. Unfortunately for Beverly, my testimony was disallowed. And thus began a six-year legal battle over admissibility (the D.C. appellate court ruling eventually set the rule under which future cases would be argued). Beverly Ibn-Tamas was convicted of second-degree murder, but the compassionate judge who heard the proffer of my testimony sentenced her to only two years in prison. Despite the moderate punishment, here was another woman suffering at the hands of an abusive husband, and at the hands of a slow-moving, uninformed legal bureaucracy.

It is in the nature of repeated exposure to violence that denial sets in. This denial, even up to and beyond the moment of homicide, can act as a sort of human survival mechanism. But the reality of acute battering incidents is that they are genuinely life-and-death situations, replete with all the inherent terror that violence wreaks upon its victims. Rage, fear and pain are unlimited and uncontrolled during an acute battering incident. So intense is the fear evoked, in fact, that death—of victim, perpetrator, or both—is often viewed as a relief. The battered woman who kills knows, instinctively, that at some point there will be no cessation of brutality and no way out. The batterer will stop at nothing unless he is stopped himself.

The coercive, sadistic behavior of the batterer often includes threatening to damage or destroy loved people or favorite objects of the battered woman. As a way to terrorize and control their women, batterers have even been known to hold pets hostage. And the psychologically manipulative techniques employed by batterers often involve public humiliation; as a result, battered women almost invariably experience social restriction and increasing isolation, which has the effect of accentuating and exacerbating their daily experience of terror.

Usually, the battered woman is not "permitted" to do anything that isn't first approved by the batterer. This type of control and forced isolation can produce many of the same kind of coping skills, passivity, and learned helplessness behavior that are produced by exposure to physical violence. Social isolation also induces depression; many battered women suffer severely from depression and despair.

Women are easily demeaned in social situations. Traditionally, they are expected to be always "proper" and "polite" in public. Furthermore, women are traditionally expected to remain unassertive, to accept all male behavior without comment. At some point in her relationship, the battered woman will be abased socially by the batterer, via ridicule, criticism, or other forms of verbal and psychological abuse. In addition, her own fear of the batterer's pathological jealousy serves to cut her off from others.

And once she is totally cut off from people outside the battering relationship, she is paralyzed with loneliness; her victimization really is complete.*

Women who seek psychotherapeutic help while still in the battering relationship are all too likely to be misled by uninformed professionals. Psychotherapists without specialized training in abusive relationships tend to focus on the emotions and behaviors of the individual client. Women, desperate to believe that if they change their own behavior they will change the battering situation for the better, and thus free themselves of their unrelenting terror, comply with the sometimes-misinformed prescriptions of these professionals. They are only ground down into further despair when they realize that nothing they do themselves makes any difference; the batterer has absolute control. And he is willing to break all bounds of human decency: he will lie, cheat, brutalize, violate—and kill.

The following story illustrates this truth. It shows, too, that the battering situation knows no cultural or economic boundaries; neither does its peculiarly isolating nature, and neither does its terror.

It is the story of Gertrude Kapiolani Toledo, called Kappy by her friends, heiress, beauty queen, descendant of royalty, and a battered woman.

KAPPY'S STORY

She was born Gertrude Kapiolani Miller in Honolulu, Hawaii, part of the Alii, or Hawaiian royalty, and granddaughter of

*However, most women who have left a battering relationship, especially those fortunate enough to seek and receive professional intervention, will say that the fear of loneliness they'd initially experienced proved to be exaggerated. These women quickly relearn that they are fully capable of acting positively on their own behalf. They cease to live in terrible isolation and, even in moments of loneliness, are likely to admit that the intense loneliness they experienced while living in the battering relationship was far worse than that which they occasionally experience living by, and caring for, themselves.

Hawaii's first delegate to the United States Congress. A real-life beautiful princess, Kappy was named Miss Hawaii in 1954.

Later she traveled the world for a number of few years as the companion of Abe Saperstein, owner of the Harlem Globetrotters. Sometimes she'd take center court to perform hula dancing at halftime. She and Saperstein had a daughter, Celine, in 1959, and Kappy returned to live in Hawaii shortly before Saperstein's death.

In 1962, she married Robert Toledo, the son of a Waianae Coast dairy farmer. Bob Toledo was of Portuguese Hawaiian descent. He was a man of considerable bulk, weighing probably more than 300 pounds. A superb businessman, he wasted no time in turning the family dairy into the finest on the island. He became a multimillionaire.

To the people of Oahu, they seemed an extraordinary couple—the Hawaiian princess, descendant of King Kamehameha, and the towering Waianae Coast Dairy King. They were successful in building a financial empire together.

But Kappy's marriage was not as successful as it seemed. Bob Toledo was beating her.

At first, she didn't really keep it a secret. Kappy was strong and self-confident; she'd had a successful career herself, was used to adoration, had lived independently in the past. Her first instinct was to fight back legally. She threatened to leave Bob and, after a particularly brutal beating that put her in the hospital, filed for divorce.

Predictably, though, Bob apologized. He sent her to vacation on another island. Promising he'd never do it again, he begged her to drop the divorce proceedings. Although Kappy told the truth of his brutality in detail for both legal and hospital records (which were preserved), she gave in to Bob's plea. She'd given birth to a son, Stevie; after all, she reasoned, he was the father of her child.

For a while, things were reasonably calm between them. But Bob's behavior soon became violent again. He continued his abuse of her and the children, even to the point of threatening to kill her with knives. Sometimes, Kappy got angry and struck back at him in whatever way she could: one night while he was sleeping she cut the hairs on his chest into the shape of a cross; one afternoon she crashed her own car into his empty one. She wasn't really a "typically" submissive battered woman, and she got beaten badly for that.

After a while, though, like other battered women, she stopped telling outsiders the truth. And she began to lie, to cover up for her husband.

Their money bought nice things for the children and a good education for Celine. (Stevie wasn't much of a student, never graduating from high school.) Kappy and her daughter owned and rode horses. Riding around the island was Kappy's escape from her life at home. Although her royal money had long since been spent, she still had the title of royalty; riding allowed her to mingle with the island's other socialites. She used her social influence to lobby for favorable dairy legislation, which gave Hawaiian dairy farmers exclusive rights to sell milk in the state. During a particularly bitter milk strike, Bob Toledo became the leader of the island's dairy farmers, gaining rights to fully 20 percent of the island's milk production. Their joint fortunes increased.

Kappy had been diagnosed years earlier as having mitral valve heart disease, a congenital syndrome. The medication prescribed for her was a blood thinner, Coumadin; but she refused to take it, because she knew she'd bleed worse when Bob hit her. She knew, too, that if she took the medication she would have to give up her beloved riding, her only real escape from Bob's cruelty because it too could cause internal bleeding.

Her own father had been a wife beater. When she was thirteen, she'd seen her mother suffer an incapacitating stroke after a particularly severe beating. Nevertheless, she gambled with her fate.

In 1979, Kappy suffered a stroke that left her paralyzed on her right side, and unable to speak.

Her tough spirit helped her rehabilitation. She managed to

recover a good deal of speech; with the help of physical therapy, she became able to walk short distances with a cane. For longer outings, though, she was confined to a wheelchair.

She still looked much like a regal beauty queen when sitting still: her long hair was meticulously braided daily, with the help of her maids. Kappy could think clearly when not under stress, and she could make good decisions about things requiring routine, uncomplicated judgment. But she had suffered sufficient frontal lobe damage to change her whole life.

Prior to her stroke, Bob had demanded sex from her daily. Afterward, he never touched her sexually. Later, Kappy would say that she didn't know which she'd hated more, his incessant demands or his complete rejection.

Now that she was an invalid, he needed less overt violence to control her. He still threatened to cut her with his knives the way he'd always done; now, though, instead of actually brandishing a knife at her he would only describe it, telling her she'd bleed to death from even a tiny cut, since she no longer had any choice about taking the Coumadin.

Bob had always been a heavy drinker. Now, he seemed to be drinking even more. His cruelty increased, as did his irrationality.

He built a beautiful home with a lovely view on their dairy property in Waianae, and moved Kappy out there from their city home in Kahala. She liked the house, but when he threatened to kill her and bury her "where the cows were," she became terrified, feeling vulnerable and isolated there. She asked her cousin, Sammy Amalu, to send some of the young men who served as his bodyguards to stay with her sometimes, whenever she became especially afraid of Bob. (Sammy was also confined to a wheelchair and needed constant care.) Her contact with Sammy and the bodyguards was often the only contact she had with any adults other than her household maids and dairy employees.

Meanwhile, Bob Toledo had become romantically involved with a secretary, Martha, who worked at the Hoauli Credit Union, which held the loans on their dairy enterprise. Although Martha later denied any intimate relationship between them, it seems unlikely that Bob, with his seemingly insatiable sexual appetite and chauvinistic attitude toward women, would have permitted a merely platonic relationship. He bought Martha a new Lincoln Continental, a $250,000 apartment in town, and shared with her a joint bank account that at one time had more than $80,000 in it.

When Bob moved out of the Waianae house permanently, in the summer of 1983, he rented an apartment close to the dairy in Makaha, in a luxury building on the beach. His apartment overlooked the big waves that made the island a surfer's paradise. People who knew him noticed that his behavior had changed dramatically. His drinking had increased. He seemed extremely depressed. And his outbursts of violence were more frequent, observed now by people other than just Kappy. He also seemed to have lost a good deal of interest in the dairy business. The past few years had seen a real shake-up in the Hawaiian dairy industry, following a scandal involving heptachlor, a cancer-causing chemical that was suspected of tainting Hawaiian-produced milk. This scandal seemed to further depress Bob, who took it almost personally.

Bob's friends explained away his behavior by saying that he was a man with "family problems": an invalid wife, an alienated daughter, a son who had academic and social problems. Who could blame him, they said, for taking a mistress, for wanting a little fun out of life?

His relatives and immediate family (who had never liked Kappy) urged him to divorce her, and to keep as much of their joint estate as possible for himself.

"Divorce her, buy her a small place in town, and give her $2,500 a month for expenses, to have the maids take care of her," his sister suggested.

"Cut her out of your will," urged his nephew-in-law, a Hawaiian law school graduate practicing in California.

Both were obviously ignorant of Hawaii's "tenants-in-entireties" law, which effectively barred Bob from ever disinheriting his wife. But the value of their joint property was approximately $15 million. Much was at stake.

"Don't live with your mistress before the divorce," advised Gil Ayers, manager of the Hoauli Credit Union, obviously more concerned about the appearance of social impropriety surrounding one of the union's greatest borrowers than about the wreckage of human life Bob Toledo had left in his wake.

Bob moved Martha out of the new apartment, renting another one in the same luxury building for her and her brother. He moved out of the Makaha condominium he owned, and into the new apartment in town himself. He was paying all the rent for both places. Clearly, he was desperately motivated, both emotionally and financially, to want a divorce from Kappy.

Meanwhile, though, his behavior was deteriorating even further. He began to scheme—with overtones of sadism in every imagined plot—to scare Kappy to death.

An invalid isolated at home with her maids, Kappy experienced a variety of reactions at Bob's request for a divorce. She was hurt, and jealous of the woman she knew to be Bob's mistress. She felt inadequate because of her chronic invalidism; she knew that her girlish beauty had faded long ago; she felt betrayed and shamed. On the other hand, she certainly didn't love Bob anymore; she despised him, in a way. And she was also frightened of him, of the violence she knew he was capable of. If they were to divorce, she decided, she wanted to be able to live comfortably. Furthermore, she wanted to pass a share of her wealth on to her children, especially to Celine, who had never gotten along with Bob and stood a good chance, despite his adoption of her, of being cut from his will.

Kappy hired Walter Chuck, one of the most respected older attorneys in Hawaii, to represent her in the divorce proceedings.

When Bob visited Kappy those days, he still beat her. He no longer needed to use enough force to leave visible bruises; she was too frail for that. Instead, he was more likely to come up behind her and begin choking her. Or to slip into her bedroom unannounced, in the middle of the night, and wake her while holding a knife to her throat.

"Die!" he yelled at her, more than once. "Die or I'll kill you! You're no good for anything any more. Why doesn't your heart just stop?"

At other times, he'd force her to walk unassisted, back and forth, back and forth, until she'd literally drop to the floor in exhaustion. After one particularly brutal session of forced walking, he disappeared into the bathroom and returned with feces smeared all over his penis. He demanded that Kappy "suck it off." She gave him a look full of contempt—her disgust momentarily overcoming her terror—and refused, calling him a dirty old man. After that, he left the house for several days.

One night in October 1983, Bob stormed drunkenly into the home he no longer lived in and smashed some heavy antique dining room chairs. Another night, soon after that, he came to the house, drunk again, and challenged one of Sammy Amalu's bodyguards to a fight.

Exhausted from the continual stress, Kappy went to the Honolulu Victim Kokua Services to ask for a restraining order. Knowing how common it was for women to change their minds after the domestic crisis had passed, the district attorney's victim/ witness advocate there took down the information she provided but told her it would take a full week for the restraining order to be issued. This practice was used to cut down on the paper work involved in those cases in which women changed their minds after registering a complaint. The following day Kappy saw Walter Chuck, who advised her to drop it. Chuck had had another client in the past who'd filed for a restraining order against a violent husband; the husband in that case had violated the restraining order anyway, and murdered her. Since then, Chuck had always clung to the belief that it had been the restraining order that had enraged the man, contrary to most of the available statistical evidence.

Bob's rages and aberrant behavior worsened. So did

Kappy's terror. As the weeks passed, it almost seemed as if Bob would get what he wanted after all; Kappy was hospitalized with heart problems. In the hospital, he continued to harass her. One of Kappy's nurses noted on a medical chart that Bob Toledo had been asked to leave because of the disturbance he'd created there; an earlier note on some of the pertinent nursing documents expressed Kappy's wish that he not be permitted to visit her at all. But he was still her husband, so her wishes were disregarded.

Still, Kappy's health improved. Once discharged, though, she was seized with terror at the thought of going home where Bob could harm her at will. She decided to equalize their power somewhat, and sent one of her maids out to buy a gun.

Kappy hid the gun in a corner of the pool table in the downstairs game room. Whenever she left the house, she put the gun in her handbag. Having it made her feel safe somehow, although she never expected to use it.

For his part, Bob had stopped dropping in as frequently. It seemed that he was beginning to make a new life for himself; he'd lost a great deal of weight, had bought new clothes, and went out often, now that he was living in town. He still visited the dairy daily, but left most of the business details to his manager and foreman.

In the meantime, he'd had his attorney offer Kappy a woefully inadequate divorce settlement, which she refused. He must have known his offer of $2,500 per month in living expenses was absurd.

He and his nephew-in-law continued to discuss ways to deprive Kappy of her share of the joint property. One plan was to challenge the legality of their marriage; there were rumors that one of Kappy's previous marriages had never been legally terminated. Bob's nephew-in-law told him that, if he could get his hands on Kappy's birth certificate, he'd initiate a search.

Walter Chuck, meanwhile, suggested to Kappy that she try and talk with Bob. That way, he said, they could realistically begin to untangle their assets and proceed with a legitimate and fair divorce. Kappy, beginning to be worried about having enough money to live on, agreed. Economically desperate, she pushed aside her fears of being beaten or killed. Armed with knowledge of her fair share of their assets, she called Bob and invited him to come visit her at home.

It was November 1983 when he received her call. Bob was searching through papers in his office with his business manager Albert Wong, trying to find the documents his nephew-in-law wanted. The documents weren't there; he welcomed the invitation from Kappy as an opportunity to continue his search at the house.

Kappy had prepared a list of the items she wanted included in their divorce settlement. On the November morning Bob came to visit, she felt a little more secure than she ever had before; she'd kept her new gun on hand, just in case.

Once there, Bob continued his frantic search for her birth certificate. While he ransacked drawers, she tried to discuss their assets with him, pleading for new tires for her car and a larger cash allowance, asking for her half of the dairy income. She talked in her halting voice, a constant reminder of the stroke she'd suffered. Listening to her in the background, while he rummaged desperately through drawers, failing again in his search, Bob became more and more furious. Finally, he turned to her in a rage.

"I wish you'd die!" he yelled.

Kappy could see the edge of a knife peeking from the file folder he held in his hands. That's when she stood, unsteadily, and reached for the gun. She pointed it at him.

"This is a real gun," she said.

"I'm not afraid of your pea-shooter," said Bob. He took out the knife and pointed it at her. "I can stick this knife in you, and you'll bleed to death. Then I'll just put your hands around the knife and everyone will think you killed yourself."

This was too much for Kappy's damaged brain to sort out clearly. She saw that he was furious, in a rage the way he'd been all those other times he'd hurt her. She lacked the ability to comprehend whether or not anything he'd said made sense. As he approached her, she believed that he was finally going to do what he'd said he would do all these years: he was going to kill her.

Kappy shot the gun five times.

Four of the bullets went wild, hitting different parts of the room. Bob must not have believed that she'd be capable of hitting him, even though she was shooting with her undamaged but nondominant left hand, because he continued to approach her, she'd remember later, with a smirk on his face. Then he crouched down in a martial arts attack position (this fact was later supported by the pathologist's report).

A moment later, Bob Toledo lay dead on the floor, killed by the fifth bullet, which freakishly had bounced off a top rib near his clavicle, entering his heart.

Detective Yamashita, the first police detective to interview Kappy after the homicide, apparently was put off by her wealth and status. Later, he would testify at her trial that he'd never believed her version of the story (even though it never changed and was entirely consistent with the physical evidence and the witness statements presented). He must have believed that, because Kappy was wealthy, she could buy a good defense, and that Bob Toledo's death had been prearranged—from the request for a restraining order several weeks prior to the homicide, to Kappy's purchase of a gun, to her calling Bob up to come to the house in order, Yamashita thought, for her to kill him. Her story, he said (fortunately, recorded on audiotape), was "as phony as she was."

At her trial, witnesses for the prosecution lied, minimizing Kappy's physical disability, testifying that she could do "almost anything." What a cruel joke for her—the former beauty queen, the fallen princess, a once-prodigious equestrian.

The prosecution would attempt to make the jury believe that Kappy had planted the knife in Bob Toledo's hand after shooting him. There was conflicting testimony surrounding this point; she had been overheard telling her maid to "put the knife in his hand," whereas she could later recall telling her maid to "put the knife back in his hand." It is likely that, as is common with brain-damaged people in times of great stress, Kappy was extremely confused. Apparently she did try to put the knife he'd dropped back in his dead hand, but slipped and fell while bending over to do it; when she saw her maid enter the room, she yelled for her to do it. Instead, the maid threw the knife across the room.

Kappy's money helped her hire a good defense attorney. John Edmunds, one of Hawaii's finest attorneys, proved to be very protective of his client. It was he who contacted me initially, sending along pertinent reading materials, flying into Denver himself for a meeting before allowing me to interview Kappy.

I was impressed immediately with John's methodical attention to details and his insistence on excellence from all those who worked for him. He found the best experts to work on this case, urging everyone to "showcase" and improve their particular skills. When he approved of an individual's work, he offered sincere and loyal friendship. The same qualities that made him a superb friend made him an especially tough adversary; I would not have wanted to testify in a case with him on the other side.

Kappy's trial lasted five weeks (running from June into late July 1984). By the time it was over, I had been to Hawaii three times, interviewing and evaluating Kappy, as well as other witnesses, accompanied by a bodyguard John Edmunds had assigned for my safety. Kappy herself was constantly accompanied by bodyguards and a private nurse. I believe that the presence of these people and the great confidence she rightly placed in her attorney helped allay some of her fears; at her trial, she could take the necessary chances and display real emotion, to her advantage, during direct examination. During her cross-examination by the state's attorney, Reynette Cooper, she responded fearfully to Ms. Cooper's harsh questioning, sometimes inappropiately giggling, and probably helped her case, enabling the jury to see the impact of having lived helplessly for so many years in terror and violence.

Kappy's money worked as a double-edged sword, though. Had she been a person of ordinary means, she might not have been charged or tried in the first place; because of her physical and mental handicaps and the lack of evidence of a crime, the prosecutor could have chosen not to charge her. She also faced a trial in probate court, after the criminal trial was over; her twenty-year-old son Stevie was challenging her rightful inheritance. To win control of her money, in the end, she needed to be found not guilty, but also competent to manage her large estate. Edmunds fashioned a meticulous defense, aided by his superb staff and by her civil attorney, Walter Chuck.

The prosecution was vigorously supported by Bob Toledo's relatives. They had never liked Kappy, thinking her a snob because of her royal background and probably hoping to inherit a large part of her considerable estate if she was judged guilty. Class prejudice had much to do with the handling of this case. Reynette Cooper, the chief prosecutor, had grown up as a poor child of Portuguese Hawaiian extraction in Waianae. She'd known Bob Toledo as a generous man whose ethnic roots matched her own; he was a philanthropist in the Portuguese Hawaiian community, giving away his money to help poor kids like herself get a college education. She seemed to have had trouble, personally, believing that a man like Bob would ever have beaten his wife.

Kappy Toledo's trial received an enormous amount of coverage in the Hawaiian press. It was a dramatic story. Testimony on both sides was bitter, haunting, heart-breaking.

Dr. Charles Golden, a nationally known neuropsychologist, testified on Kappy's behalf. She'd suffered so much frontal lobe brain damage during her stroke, he stated, that she could not have premeditated murder, an act she had never carried out before.

Reynette Cooper tried to prove that Kappy's motivation for killing Bob had been to get him out of the way in order to retain her royal social contacts. She introduced, as evidence, the fact that Kappy and Sammy Amalu had joined the prestigious Polo Club a few months before Bob's death and had also thrown a fabulous party at the Waianae home shortly after joining the Club. Anyone who knew the island's socialite standards knew how foolish Cooper's accusations were; the island royalty would have considered it far better for Kappy and Bob to live apart, in civilized fashion, without disgrace, scandal, or murder. But Reynette

Cooper, herself a "poor kid" from the wrong side of the social tracks, played to those members of the jury who could not be expected to know these unwritten social codes.

The prosecution ran into trouble when it put Bob Toledo's mistress, Martha, on the witness stand. Martha had neglected to tell Cooper about the Lincoln Continental Bob had given her and about their joint bank account; when the bank officer in charge of the account testified for the defense, it proved an embarrassment to the prosecution and hurt their case. (It was probably a mistake, too, from the jury's point of view, to put youthful, able-bodied Martha on the stand, providing such a marked contrast to Kappy's fragile, aging, infirm elegance.)

The prosecution posed the following question: Why should either one of the Toledos have died after both had finally agreed to divorce? Reynette Cooper claimed that the facts showed Kappy was greedy, and angry because Bob had left her for another woman.

But the facts gathered by the defense showed otherwise. Bob Toledo, John Edmunds insisted, had been the greedy one—newly reconciled with a family that had always been hostile to Kappy and wanted a piece of her estate for themselves, spreading his cash thin with expensive new purchases, with a new girlfriend on his considerably slimmer arm, he had wanted the entire Toledo estate for himself. And he'd been willing to kill Kappy, or at least to make her believe he'd kill her, to get it.

While prosecution and defense were bandying accusations back and forth, other interesting facts based on the autopsy of Bob Toledo were coming to light, facts that would have incontrovertible bearing on the outcome of the trial.

Although no one could have known it on the day of Bob's death, he had been suffering from brain damage equally as debilitating as Kappy's, although in a different way. That November morning, two brain-damaged people had faced each other in the Waianae house with lethal weapons; neither one truly had had the capacity to reason under stress.

The autopsy of Bob Toledo's brain revealed that he had long

been suffering from a rare disease called tuberous sclerosis, which causes deterioration of the brain resulting from tuberous lesions. Little is known about it, as the diagnosis almost always comes after death; most who suffer from it are retarded. In rare cases, like Bob Toledo's, people with the disease remain intellectually intact. Evidence suggests that the condition is inherited genetically; reading up on it, I found myself wondering if this could have been the cause of Stevie Toledo's inability to learn in school. Not that it would matter; the diagnosis cannot be made until a postmortem autopsy, and the condition is unfortunately incurable. In Bob Toledo's case, the main tuberous lesion was located in the part of the brain that is believed to regulate rage/aggression reactions.

Unexpectedly, this new fact provided a whole new twist to the analysis of Battered Woman Syndrome I'd usually done. It was not always necessary, of course, to present a physical rationale for the batterer's abusive and violent behavior. But in Kappy's case, we had it. Whatever else the prosecution might attempt to make of the facts, here was absolute, incontrovertible evidence of Bob Toledo's capacity for violence, and the evidence had been provided by the state's own pathologist.

It confirmed, beyond a shadow of a doubt, that Kappy's fear of Bob's rage and violence had been entirely reasonable. Not only did he have a long history of wife beating; now there was physical evidence of brain damage that would have caused him to be explosively violent. This fact was the one hurdle the prosecution could never surmount.

Toward the end of the trial, the defense put on a spectacular courtroom demonstration that, with Kappy's willing assistance, revealed once and for all to the jury the full extent of her physical disability. Once she had ridden like the wind, John Edmunds stated in his closing argument; but, despite all her money and social influence, she would never be whole again. She had been an invalid, incapable of premeditating murder at all, living in a state of isolation, terror, and physical vulnerability at the moment when, in reasonable fear of her life, she killed her violent husband.

The jury was convinced. Instead of convicting Kappy Toledo of first-degree murder, they returned a verdict of not guilty.

The ending of Kappy's story is bittersweet. In a way, and as if to support my own beliefs about the difficulty of breaking the Cycle of Violence, her behavior after the trial was consistent with what a battered woman might be expected to do before she is fully recovered from the trauma of being terrorized. In a way, too, it is consistent with the emotional truth of Kappy's life, that of an aging invalid, isolated and lonely, unable to genuinely reason in times of crisis.

Kappy quickly forgave her son, Stevie, for testifying against her at the trial. She forgave him, too, for attempting to wrest her fortune from her in probate court. After those proceedings were over, she invited him and his wife, Michele, to move into the beautiful, isolated Waianae home with her. They agreed.

Today Kappy, Stevie, Michele, and Stevie's young son, also named Bobby Toledo, are living there together.

Rich or poor, the women described in this book are a small minority: a minority that did not sit and wait to die. Instead, in a moment of self-defense (or, in some cases, self-realization), they finally took matters into their own hands and killed their abusers.

Even when damaged physically and emotionally like Kappy, these women are the lucky ones. Despite any subsequent abuse they may experience at the hands of the legal system, despite the wrenching mourning process they endure, almost all of the women in our studies who killed in self-defense breathed a sigh of relief when they learned that the batterer was really dead. Finally, they were released from terror.

Unlike many battered women—and notably unlike most battering men—the women who kill their abusers are ultimately capable of individuation, of separation. At a moment of acute crisis, and even when she is horribly damaged, as Kappy was, the battered woman who kills realizes that she would rather live, and that, in the truest sense, the choice is hers to make.

Facing My Own Terror

Until January 14, 1986, I thought myself pretty well insulated from real terror, even as an expert witness testifying in cases that involved unbelievable violence. After all, the batterer was dead in most instances; he could not harm his woman ever again, much less me. Sometimes, I found myself becoming somewhat afraid in instances when the dead batterer's friends or family acted with hostility toward me, or when an unfriendly judge became angry.

But, until that day, I had never experienced the bone-chilling shadow of true terror in my own life. I had never known the fear of feeling utterly vulnerable to violence, of feeling that there really was no safe place to hide.

On that day I was vacationing in Ocho Rios, Jamaica. I'd just returned to my hotel room after a lovely afternoon spent climbing Dunn River Falls, snorkeling in the magnificent blue Caribbean, relaxing on the beach with my twenty-two-year-old son Mike and eighteen-year-old daughter Karen. The phone rang. It was Jessie, the secretary back in my Denver office.

"Lenore, sit down because I have some bad news to tell you. I want you to hear it from me, instead of learning about it some other way."

I could feel my heart beating loudly. Please, I thought, hurry and tell me, whatever it is.

"Jeanne Elliott was shot in the courtroom this morning," Jessie said slowly. "It was the husband of one of her clients. Apparently he intended to kill her. She's in surgery right now, and we don't know if she'll live."

I heard myself gasp, cry out. I remember being afraid to ask any questions, terrified of what I would hear. I do know that I went into a state of shock.

Jeanne was one of my closest friends. We'd worked together, as attorney and expert witness, on some of our toughest cases. Our clients had all been brutalized by abusive men; most of them lived in a state of daily terror. Jeanne and I had often pretended fearlessness ourselves in an attempt to provide these women with the strength they needed to endure bad times. I'd always admired Jeanne's strong advocacy stance. She'd been the source of my own courage on many occasions. Now she was lying on an operating table, her life hanging in the balance.

I managed to regain enough composure to ask Jessie for a few more details. At the time, she could give me only a sketchy account.

"The man who shot her is named Gerry Utesch," Jessie said. "He's an Aurora policeman." Jeanne, she told me, had been arguing in front of a judge that Utesch should give her client (his wife, from whom he had been separated and whom he had psychologically battered for years) the money he'd been ordered to pay months ago, so the bank wouldn't foreclose on their house. She was also asking him to make current his support payments for a teenaged child with special needs. As Jessie continued, it didn't sound to me at first like anything but the familiar domestic legal motions an attorney would go through in a routine divorce case.

But in battering cases, nothing is ever really routine.

"We don't know why he shot her," Jessie continued, "or how many times." She gave me the telephone number of the hospital intensive care unit. Jeanne had been rushed there, from the Aurora courtroom.

After Jessie hung up, I stood cradling the phone receiver, in silent shock, for a long time. When I finally replaced it, I still felt numb. I simply could not imagine the courageous, feisty Jeanne, one of my finest friends, cut down so easily by a murderer's bullets.

Then I suddenly experienced a rush of intense emotion that I could not control. I was first aware of unbearable anger; then a deep, gut-wrenching sorrow; then, overwhelming all other sensations, terror. This wasn't an ordinary experience of fear. It was profound, something that shook me from the inside out.

I cried for a long time, until I had no tears left. Mingled with my grief for Jeanne was real fear for my own safety, and for the safety of those I loved. I'd always thought of myself as an empathetic individual; my work as a psychotherapist had required me to be. But for the first time, I realized that I was experiencing what my clients experienced every day—terror.

Several months earlier, Jeanne and I had discussed the seemingly increasing violence of batterers toward the women we'd been working with. She and I shared observations often. We talked a great deal on the long drives we had to take, back and forth into the small mountain towns surrounding Denver while working on one particular case together. We'd both had personal experience in being around violent people. As a therapist, even when personally, overtly threatened by violence in a therapeutic encounter with a batterer, I was less inclined to react fearfully than to employ well-learned crisis intervention techniques: "talking the batterer down," aligning myself with him psychologically to let him know that he was not being judged. These techniques allowed the batterer to give up the idea of violence, which, in therapeutic terms, I saw as an attempt to ward off his own feelings of abandonment and disintegration stemming from a fear of loss of control. Also, when interviewing or evaluating in a professional context, I had always truly felt that I was there to help; in some way, this had given me the sense that I would not be hurt myself. Intellectually, I believe, both Jeanne and I had accepted the possibility of being hurt ourselves by any of the more out-of-control batterers we might come across in our work. But it's one thing to talk about such danger, to intellectualize it. In our hearts, neither of us really expected it to happen.

Even when Jeanne had called me earlier the previous fall to say that a police psychologist had warned her client that Gerry Utesch was threatening to "put a bullet in her spine and watch her die slowly," neither of us really perceived the threat with genuine terror. (The police psychologist had never returned

Jeanne's calls to him, so Jeanne had simply assumed he had the situation under control.)

Gerry Utesch had been on the Aurora police force for years. I'd even known him briefly when he was a juvenile officer sitting on the Aurora Community Mental Health Center board of directors, an organization of which my late husband had been the executive director. But everything I now knew about him had been irrevocably colored by his horrendous act.

At the trial, his own supervisor had described Utesch's self-proclaimed "solution" to his own divorce. His rage at women in general, and at his wife and her lawyer in particular, had begun to spill over. He needed desperately to be through with the divorce; at the same time, his fear of abandonment kept him tied emotionally to a wife who no longer wanted anything to do with him. In this sense, Gerry Utesch was a typical batterer. More dangerous than many, however, because he was legally allowed to carry a gun.

Utesch shot Jeanne four times as she stood in the courtroom, just as the judge ordered him to leave with her, to ensure that his wages would be garnished so he'd meet his financial obligations to his former wife and children.

"I'm not going with her," he defied the judge, "because Ms. Elliott is not going anywhere." Then he took out the police weapon concealed inside his jacket. He fired four police-issued hollow-point bullets.

Jeanne, a former army sergeant, later told me how she'd held her hands up to her face, successfully deflecting the first bullet. She had probably saved her life with that single reflexive motion; the bullet grazed her nose and hand and not her head, as had been intended. But a second bullet tore into her abdomen, ripping her internal organs apart. Jeanne hit the floor and, by instinct, began to roll.

A sheriff's deputy tried to grab the gun away from Utesch. But Utesch managed to fire two more shots before he was wrestled to the ground.

The third bullet was the one he had promised to fire. It hit Jeanne in the spine, paralyzing her permanently from the mid-chest down.

My son and daughter reacted differently to this tragedy. Karen was empathetic and in grief. She seemed able to express the pain of the whole experience: Jeanne's, her own, mine. She and I cried together. But my son became angry with me. His feelings of grief and terror became channeled into rage, an expression of feeling more acceptable to males in our society.

"How dare you put yourself in this kind of danger?" he asked accusingly. "It's not fair to the people who love you. It could have been you standing in that courtroom along with Jeanne, or along with any of the other attorneys you work with!"

When I heard him, I knew he'd spoken the unspeakable. He'd hit on the danger potentially lurking, always, in wait for those who intervene with domestic violence. Here I was, advocating for battered women without regard for the inherent danger, deceptively thinking myself somehow removed from the violence of battering situations. But was I ready to give up my life for the work?

Jeanne managed to live through her terrible ordeal, but just barely.

She was in intensive care for three months, and endured surgery several times. She then spent many more months in rehabilitation. I and many other friends made sure that she was never alone. The nurses and doctors were wonderful, allowing at least one of us to be with her twenty-four hours a day. Jeanne's family, friends, and former clients—battered women for whom she'd advocated—came from all over the country to be with her; the cards, flowers, and offers of help never stopped. I believe that these continual expressions of genuine love helped Jeanne survive her many medical complications. And they helped her overcome her despair. She never had to worry when awake or asleep; someone she loved and trusted was always there to protect her. Interestingly, my son, Mike, spent many nights sitting with Jeanne in her hospital room. It was an important healing experience for him, allowing him to feel his sorrow and guilt without getting stuck or channeling it into anger.

Seeing Jeanne fight, day after day, reduced some of my own terror. Her courage gave me back some of mine; and when she naturally developed Post Traumatic Stress Reaction I was able to use some of my professional skills to help her. In doing so, I realized that I was helping myself, too, intervening with the fear that had overwhelmed me and cutting it down to a manageable size. Eventually, I was able to function normally again. I was able to enjoy life thoroughly again. But, though my fear had become manageable, I found that it never completely went away.

Gerry Utesch was sentenced to thirty-two years in the state penitentiary in Colorado. Some fathers' rights groups attempted to make him a kind of hero; they honored him for refusing to pay child support (even though the money he'd been ordered to pay was minimal in relation to his salary). At his trial, he tried to minimize his behavior by alleging that the unbearable stress of divorce had made him more likely to kill or hurt someone. But no expert witness testified on his behalf.

During the time of the trial, several of my friends decided to share office space so that none of us would be alone during working hours. Why invite trouble? we reasoned, forgetting that Jeanne Elliott had been shot in an open courtroom, with more than thirty people watching helplessly. Thus a simple truth fuels women's terror: if a batterer wants to kill or maim you, he can do it.

Unless there is a miracle, Jeanne Elliott will never walk again. She continues to advocate for battered women; recently appointed a county court referee in Denver, she is often called on to mete out justice to batterers. Yet, while her courage has been an example for me and for others, I know that the undeniable terror remains, deep down inside. And this confirms my belief: as long as there is even one batterer left, none of us are truly safe.

II

WHY BATTERED WOMEN KILL

5

JUST LIKE YOU AND ME: A PROFILE OF BATTERED WOMEN WHO KILL

BATTERED WOMEN WHO KILL can perhaps be set apart from those who do not kill in terms of the perceived danger of their situations, and the severity and brutality of the violent physical, sexual, and psychological abuse they have endured. Sexual abuse plays a big part, as does alcohol and/or drug abuse on the part of the batterer. And so does incest; in many of the cases we have on record in which battered women killed their abusers, the batterers had made sexual advances to, or had actively sexually abused, one or more of their children.

There are far more intrinsic similarities than differences between battered women who kill and those who do not. There are also many more similarities than differences in our society between battered women and women in general. And it is my contention that death and murder always lurk as potentials in violent relationships.

Battered women come from all types of economic, cultural, religious, and racial backgrounds. They are millionaires, and they are women on welfare; they are uneducated women, and they are practicing professionals with J.D.s and Ph.D.s; they are mothers, and they are childless; they are religious, and they are atheists; they live in rural areas, and in cities, and in small towns all over this country and all over the world. They are women like you. Like me. Like those whom you know and love.

Whether we like it or not, and whether we are aware of it or not, we all live in violent societies. Some kind of physical assault occurs in nearly one-half of all American families.* For our purposes in drawing a generalized picture of the "typical" battered woman (and later of the "typical" battered woman who kills), we consider a woman to be battered if she is subjected repeatedly to coercive behavior (physical, sexual, and/or psychological) by a man attempting to force her to do what he wants her to do, regardless of her own desires, rights, or best interests; if she is intimately involved with this man not but necessarily married, although she often is; and if, as a couple, they have experienced at least two acute battering incidents, often going through the Cycle of Violence at least twice.

The typical battered woman has poor self-image and low self-esteem, basing her feelings of self-worth on her perceived capacity to be a good wife and homemaker, whether or not she also has a successful career outside of the home. Although she is more liberal than her mate in her sex role attitudes, she behaves in stereotyped, traditional ways in order to please the batterer, who generally holds extremely rigid and traditional values regarding home and family life. She may believe that she is the one at fault for not stopping her batterer's violent behavior; consequently, she suffers great guilt. Caught between the pillars of guilt and violence, she lives with a great deal of denial of her own fear and rage; this denial enables her to function day to day. She may appear to be passive, but the truth is that she can be strong, often

---

*A 1976 epidemiological study by Murray Straus, Richard Gelles, and Suzanne Steinmetz gives a figure of 28 percent in that one year, but they believe the actual number to be twice that. Gelles and Straus replicated these statistics in their 1986 study, published in their book *Intimate Violence* (Simon & Schuster, 1988).

Gelles and Straus have also published *Physical Abuse in American Families: Risk Factors and Adaptations to Violence in 8,145 Families* (Transaction Books, 1989).

manipulating the people and objects in her environment extensively, at least enough to avoid being killed.

As a result of all these factors, she suffers from continual stress and is particularly subject to psychosomatic ailments and depression. An extremely isolated individual—because she often avoids exposing the terrible secret of her husband's unpredictably violent behavior to others, and because his domineering and jealous nature often prevents her from seeking the friendship of others—she believes that she alone is the only person capable of changing her predicament; if she can't, she thinks, no one will. And she believes that, if she can only find the right formula, her batterer's "bad" side will disappear, and she will be left with the wonderful, kind, sensitive man she remembers from the past.

In trying to differentiate those battered women who kill from those who do not, we can look for special characteristics common to this particular group.

Dr. Angela Browne, who in 1979 began working on our research project that involved four hundred battered women, compared the forty homicide cases we had completed by 1983 with a subsample of one hundred battered women who had been living out of the battering relationship for less than a year.* The only real differences she found were in the women's perceptions of violence. Women who killed, she found, perceived their men as using greater violence, more frequently, resulting in more and in graver injuries to them, than did those battered women who did not kill. The ones who killed described themselves as growing increasingly more desperate in their attempts to stay as physically safe as possible.

They described their men as making more death threats. Their men were also more likely to use weapons to terrorize them. They tended to abuse alcohol more frequently and seemed to be growing continually more dangerous toward the women, toward their children, and toward others.

*See her book *When Battered Women Kill* (Free Press–Macmillan, 1987)

Battered women who do and do not kill are essentially a heterogeneous group. Like Browne, in a 1986 study of my first one hundred battered women self-defense cases (as I came to call them), I found that, while these women used a variety of methods to kill their tormentors, guns were used by 75 percent of the women. (Actually, in many of these cases, the woman did not choose to use a gun but shot the abuser after he threw a gun at her, in some cases ordering her to shoot him before he shot her.) Another 13 percent used knives as the lethal weapon, usually in the middle of panicked physical combat (it is extremely difficult for the average woman to strike fatal blows with a knife unless she is assisted by an adrenal flow of terror). Five percent of the women in this study killed their batterer with a car. One used a sledge-hammer; one poisoned her husband; one set him on fire, probably after his death. The remaining women (four of them) hired another person to kill their abusers, and each of these four women received much longer sentences than those who had killed the batterers themselves. More recently, the battered woman self-defense has been adapted and admitted in court to assist battered women accused of such contract killings.*

Batterers most likely to be killed were the ones who continued to verbally degrade and humiliate a woman while she had the weapon in her hands. So were those men who had sexually abused her or her children. So were those men who ordered the woman to kill them—using her, perhaps, to commit their own suicides. And many of these women initially intended to kill themselves but, at the last minute, killed their abusers instead.

Each and every woman in our study had endured extraordinarily brutal and terrifying abuse before killing in self-defense. To know their stories is to understand why they did it.

Like other battered women, those who killed could never

_____

*My Battered Woman Syndrome testimony was introduced by Boston attorney Nancy Gertner in 1989 at the trial of Lisa Becker Grimshaw in Springfield, Massachusetts, and Denver attorney Stanley Marks in 1988 at the trial of Donna Yacklich in Pueblo, Colorado. Donna's case is described in Chapter 13.

predict exactly when an acute incident would occur or how bad the violence would be. All mentioned the fact that their batterers were extremely jealous of every other person in their lives, including family, friends, people at work, and especially children. Their men were all unusually suspicious and possessive, and often threatened to hurt or kill the woman's relatives and friends.

All of the battered women who killed were subjected to verbal abuse and criticism that often amounted to acute psychological torture.

While they often later remarked on the unusual sensitivity and sensuality of the batterer when he was on "good" behavior, many also noted his unusual sexual behavior: tendencies toward actively violent perversity, and, in some of the cases in which battered women killed, father/daughter incest and child abuse.

Nearly all of them noted that their men had difficulty controlling intake of alcohol. Every one of them had been threatened with guns, knives, or other weapons. And every one of them was aware that the batterer truly was capable of killing either her or himself.

When a battered woman kills, she most likely senses an increased loss of control in the batterer and in the level of violence. She senses, too, that she is somehow less essential to him than she has been before; that this time he may well go all the way and commit murder. Sometimes she knows this, sometimes merely intuits it; in all cases, a sense of absolute horror is present. As the violence escalates out of control, the woman's perceptions of it change.*

At a certain point in a battering situation, the violence has

*Minnesota Multiphasic Personality Inventory (MMPI) profiles of women who live in violence demonstrate notably changing patterns as the violent incidents in their lives escalate in intensity. A specific Battered Woman Syndrome pattern on the MMPI has been found by psychologists Lynne Rosewater, Mary Ann Dutton-Douglas, and Lois Veronen in separate studies. (The MMPI consists of 550 true-or-false statements that, when scored, give objective personality information. It is one of the most used personality tests, particularly for forensic cases.)

accelerated to such a level that it will not diminish again as it has done in the past, in line with the previously established pattern of the Cycle of Violence; consciously or not, the battered woman who kills senses this. Once this point is reached, the physical brutality appears to spin wildly out of control. Battered women who kill have almost invariably done so after having experienced such an uncontrollably savage acute incident, or after the recurrent onset of tension-building phase behavior, in order to prevent such an acute incident from happening again. Each woman seems to feel that she just cannot cope with the impending brutality or the psychological tension any longer. Few state later that they ever intended to kill; all say that they simply wanted to stop him from hurting them like that again. Almost every battered woman tells of wishing, at some point, that the batterer were dead, maybe even of fantasizing how he might die. These wishes and fantasies are normal, considering the extraordinary injustice these women suffer at their men's hands. But it is equally true that the small number of women who kill their batterers do not necessarily want them dead at the time; rather, they are seeking only to put an end to their pain and terror.

Are They Rich or Poor?

The myth of the battered woman as an uneducated woman living in poverty, while true in some cases, is not supported by the statistics. Woman battery is a universal phenomenon, occurring on all levels of society (an estimated 50 percent of all women are battered at some time in their lives) and in all cultures. Many of the still silent-battered women in America, and all over the world, are from middle-class and upper-income backgrounds, with the family wealth controlled by their husbands. Many of these women are successful professionals themselves: lawyers, doctors, corporate executives, college professors, and, yes, psychologists. And they are far less likely to leave the battering relationship than their working-class or lower-income counterparts.

There are reasons for this phenomenon. In our society, the poor are more likely than middle-class or upper-income women to have extensive contact with community and social service agencies; in effect, they are more likely to be aware that help, though burdened with bureaucratic red tape and an insidious victimizing process of its own, exists for them outside of their homes and immediate families. Thus, the women most likely to leave a battering relationship are often those who are eligible for such services, that is, lower-income women.

Working-class, middle-class, and upper-income women are often much better off financially when married. Their spending power is increased, as is their accumulation of property. Middle-class and upper-income women may also fear social ostracization as a result of making their battering public. They may fear hurting their husbands' careers. They may believe that the social esteem and respect accorded their husbands will automatically cast doubt on their own version of things, in the eyes of their community. Along these same lines, middle-class and upper-income women realize (truthfully, in many instances) that others in the community will not come to their aid because those others may have financial, political, and social ties to the batterer; should he suffer disgrace or exposure, they stand to lose as well. Thus, powerful members of the woman's community, rather than helping her, may collude in covering up the batterer's criminal behavior. This response supports the commonly held view of battered women, explored earlier in the chapter on terror, that their husbands are nearly omniscient and certainly much more powerful than anyone who might expose them.

Kay Sandiford has written of the long history of abuse she suffered from her husband, Frank, in the book *Shattered Night* (Warner Books, 1984). Her story, like Kappy's, shows beyond the shadow of a doubt that the economically privileged battered woman can have just as much, if not more, trouble separating from the batterer as the battered woman who lives in poverty. For it is *the escalation of violence itself that dictates the outcome in these cases,* not the economics of the situation.

KAY'S STORY

Italian by birth, Frank Sandiford had come to America to study medicine. A charming and handsome man, he easily won the heart of the sophisticated Baltimore socialite, Kay, a recent divorcée with a young son. Early in their relationship, Kay became pregnant, and Frank persuaded her to let him perform an abortion himself. He kept the surgical instruments he used, and would later use them to shame and terrorize her frequently throughout their marriage.

Although the attractive young doctor made Kay happy at first with his devoted attentions, Kay sometimes found herself wondering about his motives. Did he love her, she asked herself, or her money? Other nagging doubts were raised when, after taking some medication Frank had prescribed for her, Kay's mother suddenly died.

But Kay suppressed her burgeoning fears. Frank was an ideal husband in so many ways: good-looking, sensitive, bright, attentive, with a brilliant professional future. When he suggested that they move to Houston so he could train with the great cardiologists Michael DeBakey and Denton Cooley, then at Baylor University, she eagerly agreed. Although it was her money that purchased their lovely old mansion in River Oaks and her social connections that accounted for their upper-class contacts, Frank soon became such a well-known surgeon that his earnings could eventually have supported their elaborate lifestyle. To everyone who knew them, they seemed an ideal couple: attractive, wealthy, successful, demonstrably in love.

But all was not well with them. Bit by bit, Frank developed a tendency to abuse Kay verbally and—in seemingly minor ways, at first—physically.

The first acute outburst of physical violence shocked and horrified Kay. As his beatings grew more frequent, she soon became a woman living in constant fear. Eventually, her fear of Frank, and of others discovering the secret truth beneath the veneer of love, wealth, and success that seemed to surround them, crept into all areas of her life. Her actions and thoughts became distorted. So did her behavior.

Kay wore long sleeves and pants when playing tennis, so that her partners would never see the bruises riddling her arms and legs. As Frank's outbursts became more and more violent, she grew terrified that others would find out. She sent her son to a boarding school in the East so he would not witness the abuse. She worried about her maid spreading word of her husband's tirades.

Frank's behavior had changed, too. Things were going badly for him professionally; his hot temper was making it increasingly difficult for others to work with him. All Kay heard about this, though, were his complaints about his colleagues. As time went on, he became paranoid about the other professionals he worked with and began to plot grisly scenarios of revenge against them in retaliation for real or imagined slights. It was rumored, at the time, that he left DeBakey's research team after a dispute over his uncontrollable temper. But Cooley, who had split with DeBakey by that time, took him on immediately.

No one suspected Frank of foul play when other doctors' patients mysteriously died, while his alone survived, assuring him of senior status at the University of Texas Medical Center, right under Cooley himself. But at home, Frank would terrify Kay with gruesome tales of arranging to have his colleagues' patients killed. Although she never checked out any of these tales, the mere fact that he would think in that way was frightening to her.*

On one of their many trips to Italy (where Frank was revered as a hero for his surgical skills), Kay learned of a plan he had to smuggle a gun back into the U.S. and murder Cooley, his mentor. Then, Frank reasoned, he would become the nation's top cardiac surgeon. Kay was even more frightened than she'd been before. She knew from personal experience that Frank was capable of

---

*Later, operating room nurses would testify that Frank had often fallen apart under stress, especially when surgery was not going smoothly. He sometimes threw sharp instruments across the operating room, bullying and frightening them all with his unpredictable temper. They described him as a "Dr. Jekyll/Mr. Hyde type of man."

great violence. She no longer believed that he was capable of real kindness or of genuinely loving anyone.

Sometimes, when she had been driven to a point of helpless desperation and despair and talked of killing herself, he'd actually encouraged her, urging her to imagine a romantic scenario for her own tragic death. By now, she believed that she would be free of Frank only if she died herself. It seemed he was angry with her much of the time. He was furiously jealous and possessive, too. Kay didn't know of the affair he was having at this time with a younger woman, but she probably would not have done anything about it had she known. Even though he still treated her like a beloved Dresden doll in the presence of others, she knew the shadow underneath that charm. Kay's self-esteem was at an all-time low. She wanted very much to die.

Working up her courage one night, she took all the pills she could find in her medicine cabinet and lay down in bed to die. Frank came home; she told him what she'd done. His response was to cover her with a blanket, kiss her goodbye, and leave the house, without notifying medical authorities or anyone else.

Kay lost consciousness.

To her surprise, though, she woke the next morning alive, and feeling awful. Frank was nowhere around. Kay called a close friend, then drove out to a cottage she kept on a lake about an hour outside of Houston, to think seriously about herself, her life with Frank, and her future plans. They had discussed divorce in the past. Now Kay decided she would no longer think of killing herself; she would simply divorce Frank.

She hadn't counted, though, on his anger at her for staying alive.

Throughout the next several days, they had an increasing number of arguments, during which Frank seemed to be getting more and more out of control, both verbally and physically. Desperate, Kay called her family lawyer back East and confided her troubles to him. He suggested she see a Houston lawyer, who in turn suggested that she consult attorney Marion Rosen. Kay might be better off with a woman attorney, he told her, in what now looked like it was about to become a bitter high-society divorce.

Marion Rosen gave Kay the advice she usually gave clients in terms of protecting their assets. "Start changing all your joint accounts back into your own name," she suggested, "and put all your jewelry into a safe deposit box." When she learned of Frank's temper, his violence, and Kay's most recent suicide attempt, Marion further advised her to hide Frank's guns and never stay alone with him at home. Marion Rosen had had ample experience with other cases involving domestic abuse. She believed what Kay told her, and her advice was excellent.

Kay followed this advice to the letter. She began the chore of visiting banks and making necessary financial changes. And she remembered to hide Frank's .357 Magnum under the bedroom love seat.

She'd bought the gun as a birthday present for him several years earlier. Like many other batterers, Frank was fascinated, almost obsessed, with firearms. Somehow, he'd managed to persuade Kay, scared as she was of him, to buy one for him. Since then, Frank had been seen shooting the gun in their backyard. He'd said he was shooting at some squirrels. Others maintained he was actually shooting at some young children who'd trespassed to play in their backyard. But no one had done anything about it at the time. The incident would probably have passed completely unmentioned again, if not for the events that were to transpire.

The evening of January 29, 1980, Frank came home in a terrible mood. Later, the maid would remember him screaming abusively at Kay in the dining room. He'd demanded that she go over some of their financial records to account for the past year's tax debt; the fact that Kay hadn't yet completed the task became his excuse for abusing her. Kay noticed, with terror, that his facial features were beginning to distort: a sure sign that he would soon begin to hit her. She left the dining room table to go upstairs for their tax files, hoping it would calm him down. When she reached the top of the stairs, she realized that he was following her. When she entered her bedroom, she could hear him stomping angrily behind, yelling that he was going to kill her.

Almost instinctively, Kay reached under the love seat cushion for the .357 Magnum and ran out onto the landing. Frank was heading straight toward her, brandishing a tennis racquet. He hit her on the head with it.

That was when Kay shot him, twice.

The force of the bullets spun him around, and he fell backward down the stairs. Kay screamed. The maid ran in from the kitchen, saw Kay standing on the second-floor landing with a gun in her hand, and ran back out. She was afraid Kay had finally gone crazy and would kill her, too. Kay didn't, of course.

Called soon after the shooting occurred, Marion Rosen gave her client more good advice: she told Kay not to sign away her right to remain silent and not to say a thing. She then set to work getting Kay released from jail into a private psychiatric facility.

Once there, Kay realized what she'd done and became thoroughly despondent. She wanted to neither live nor die. She proved useless in helping her attorney prepare a defense.

Kay's psychiatrist, Jim Claghorn, was baffled. Although her depression certainly was severe, she didn't at all fit the legal definition for insanity. She hadn't been seeking revenge; she didn't seem angry; she'd known nothing of Frank's extramarital affair, and therefore wasn't jealous. Her most pronounced emotion, in fact, was fear. The psychiatrist wondered: what had her motivation been to kill her husband? And why did she want to kill herself now, too? Most importantly, how could he keep her alive if he discharged her?

Jim Claghorn called me about this perplexing case. Knowing, through colleagues, of my work with battered women, he asked my associate and me to come to Houston on a consulting basis and examine Kay. I agreed.

I found that, without a doubt, Kay was suffering from Battered Woman Syndrome. This and other pertinent information would later be used to good effect in her trial, held during the first two months of 1981.

Marion Rosen put together a superb defense for Kay. Among other articles introduced as evidence were the surgical instruments Frank had used to perform an abortion on her, which he later used to terrorize and humiliate her. So strong was the evidence that, while Kay was found guilty of manslaughter, she was placed on probation for ten years. She never had to serve a minute in prison—a most unusual sentence, by Texas standards.

This judgment turned out to be a good one. Kay did so well that, after a few years, the probation department found it no longer necessary to supervise her behavior. She eventually made another marriage, this time with a kind, gentle man. Kay is finally living the decent life she deserves.

Fear of poverty will cease to be a viable threat for any woman only when she accepts her right to economic parity and freedom, then demands it, then receives it. Kay Sandiford's first real act of separation from Frank was the legal separation of their financial assets. Ideally, less privileged homemakers should likewise have access to all the medical and other benefits given to those who work outside the home. Our system has kept women in or out of the job market according to the needs of men. Male superiority in the economic realm can contribute to male feelings of superiority, to damaging macho posturing and sex-role stereotyping in the intimate environment of the family home. Our society reinforces inequity in intimate relationships between men and women by reinforcing economic inequities in the world outside.

As long as one group of individuals, anywhere, is socialized to consider itself superior to another group, or to have more rights than another group, or more real power, there will be violence. As long as men consider women to be their property, and as long as that view is supported by the law, some of them will feel free to abuse, damage, and destroy their women as they see fit.

6

THE ROLE OF ALCOHOL

STATISTICS SHOW an undeniable association between alcohol abuse and battering.* In nearly all the cases in our sample where battered women killed their abusers, the batterer's inability to control his alcohol intake had increased progressively over time, as had his violence, his unpredictability, and the bizarre nature of his behavior. (Research may some day find that there are chemical changes induced in batterers by their reactions to stress, similar to those changes induced in some alcoholics, that indicate concurrent neurological differences or abnormalities present in the batterers' brain patterns.) Alcohol does not *cause* the man's battering behavior in these cases, but, as is true in most crime, its presence as a factor increases the risk of severe injury or death.

The following story is a good example.

*Sociologist Pat Eberle analyzed alcohol data from our research project and found that more than 60 percent of the battered women interviewed said that their abusive partners had serious drinking problems and frequently abused alcohol. However, when analyzing the data on 1600 battering incidents (four per woman), Eberle found that only 20 percent of the men always were drunk when they battered their women. See my book *The Battered Woman Syndrome* (1984) for more details.

OPAL'S STORY

Bob had been a hard drinker most of his life. It got so that he couldn't start the day without a can of beer.

Opal, his sixty-four-year-old wife, didn't really like him drinking so much. But she didn't nag him about it, either. She'd stuck by Bob through thick and thin, marrying him before he went into prison to serve a ten-year sentence for killing his former wife. When he got out, she'd helped him build up a contracting business. They'd had their ups and downs, but there'd never been any physical violence between them at all until, during their last three years together, Bob's drinking began to increase.

His behavior had also become rather strange. He had insisted that Opal move with him to the country north of Dallas, into a house they'd built together. This move took her far from her children, who lived in eastern Texas.

Soon after the move, he began to complain that he couldn't remember things any more. He also said he was having a lot of difficulty concentrating. Opal thought she noticed him shaking if he didn't get a drink when he wanted it. She even thought he sometimes acted a little like he had the DTs. Because he was getting arrested for driving while under the influence, he became less inclined to want to drive.

Bob began pressuring Opal to sign over all her social security checks to him. He claimed this was one more way for her to assure him that she really did love him. Things between them were getting very tense. His behavior grew more unpredictable by the day, and increasingly tyrannical. He started threatening her with his guns.

Opal became terribly afraid. She felt that she was always waiting for some horrible thing to happen—never quite knowing when it would but knowing somehow that, when it did, Bob would be the instigator, and that she had no power to stop him.

One afternoon, without any warning, Bob grabbed one of his guns and began shooting at Opal inside their home. Two bullets pierced the ceiling. Another lodged above the front doorway—

that was the shot that came closest to hitting Opal as she tried to escape the house. Afterward, she cowered in a corner of the living room, afraid to move at all.

Bob sat in his armchair, gun in hand, a large pump rifle next to him on the floor. After a while, he seemed to quiet down. He seemed to nod, then appeared to be napping.

As quietly as she could, Opal tiptoed into his bedroom and got the .357 Magnum she knew he kept in his dresser drawer. Then she reentered the living room, planning to sneak out to safety through another door. Just as she'd nearly reached her goal, she saw him raise his hands. His body moved forward. She knew it! He'd only pretended to be sleeping. He'd really been watching her all the time. Thinking that he would surely shoot her now, Opal turned and fired the Magnum straight at him.

Bob died from a single wound to the top of his head.

The state prosecutor tried to portray Bob as a defenseless man who'd been fast asleep when, for no reason, his "angry" wife had blown him away.

Opal was defended vigorously by Eldred Smith and his son Stephen, two excellent attorneys, who took care to demonstrate the dead man's many guns to an all-woman jury. The pump shotgun alone, they pointed out, could have killed everyone on a neighborhood block. I testified as an expert witness for Opal, detailing the years of increasing abuse she had experienced in her marriage to Bob. Through this and other means, the defense wanted to persuade that jury that it had been entirely reasonable for Opal to believe that Bob hadn't really been asleep, that he'd been lying in wait to shoot at her again. She had therefore killed him first, they claimed, in self-defense. Opal's family also testified for her, successfully documenting the terror and abuse she had endured in her last years with Bob.

In this case, justice was truly served. After deliberating for less than two hours, the all-woman jury voted unanimously to acquit her.

It does indeed seem to be a classic fear on the part of many men that a woman will wait until he is asleep, then kill him. In fact, at our Battered Woman's Research Center we have come across several cases in which that did happen, but far fewer than might have been expected according to the folklore. There have also been several cases in which it appeared to the battered woman that the man was asleep because he was lying down in bed or sitting in a chair. However, given the high alcohol content found in each man's blood during autopsy, the woman's common story that her batterer would typically beat her, sit down to rest a while, then return to beat her again, must be believed. Many of these men were so used to imbibing enormous quantities of alcohol that they could still be actively beating a woman with blood alcohol levels measuring .30 and higher (that is, three times the level at which a normal person becomes intoxicated). While pathologists may sputter about death being caused by alcohol poisoning at such dangerously high levels, it is probable that certain men can be so addicted to alcohol that they can tolerate it in extraordinarily high doses, sometimes without even displaying typical signs of drunken behavior.

In the next story, excessive drinking also contributed to the violence of the battering relationship.

SALLY'S STORY

Sally had lately become ill with a variety of medical problems that finally forced her to quit her job as an X-ray technician for a northern California health maintenance organization. Her husband Bill had been steadily employed throughout their marriage, but during the past three years he'd taken to drinking heavily and had also begun to complain bitterly about his job and his current boss. Sally was used to hearing his constant complaints, usually in the form of disjointed, drunken ramblings.

Bill had begun to hit her, too. The violent incidents were increasing in frequency and in intensity. Her injuries were getting worse, less easy to hide. Sally was afraid, and her fear reached nearly unbearable proportions the night Bill got drunk and broke her nose.

She herself had stopped drinking months before, after her doctor had warned her that it was bad for her failing health. But one night, with Bill drinking excessively again, ranting and raving more than he usually did, she sensed danger in the air and allowed him to fix her a drink, too. Afraid of getting another beating, she left the living room for their bedroom to read. Bill's mother had done that with his own father sometimes, to avoid a beating. But the technique failed to work on Bill this time. He followed her, incensed that she'd dared to leave him alone, continuing to verbally threaten and degrade her. Then he seized her by the arms and began shaking her, throwing her down on the bed, pounding her torso and face with his fists. Later Sally wouldn't remember exactly what he'd been saying, though it sounded like the familiar litany: how stupid she was, what a bitch she was, how she never could seem to do anything right or to his satisfaction.

Bill staggered to his dresser, opened a drawer, and took out a handgun. He began to pistol-whip her.

"I'll kill you, bitch," he said, holding the gun to her head.

But all he'd had to drink that night got the better of him then. At that moment, he slapped her once more, placed the gun on top of the dresser, and headed for the bathroom, warning her not to move or she'd "really get it."

Sally wouldn't remember what happened next. She must have stood, seized the gun, and walked the few feet to the bathroom door. Bill soon lay dead, several bullets lodged in his body.

The prosecutor assigned to this case accused Sally of murdering her husband out of anger, shooting him while his hands were otherwise occupied, while he was urinating drunkenly, claiming that he had been helpless at the time.

When I interviewed Sally, I sensed a genuine terror in her recounting of the story that was similar to the terror I'd become used to hearing in other battered women. On the night of the homicide, the alcohol she had consumed herself had probably dulled her own sensations, distorted her perceptions, and contributed to her later amnesia concerning the circumstances of the killing. Afterward, she said, she remembered being scared that he'd come after her for the gun and start to hit her with it again, so she'd hidden it under the mattress in their guest room. Then she'd had a few more drinks, called his mother, then her daughter, and finally the police.

Her first attorney, Jim Wagner, asked me to read through three boxes filled with witness statements, medical records, and the state's discovery materials. By the time I was finished reading, it dawned on me: no one had asked Sally the truly critical question.

"What did you hear while you were lying on your bed waiting for Bill to come back?" I asked her, during our interview.

"He was yelling at me."

"But what was he saying?"

"I don't remember. That same stuff about how I'd better not move or he'd kill me, and more like that."

Then I asked the question: "What was he doing in the bathroom?"

"Why, he was peeing."

"How do you know?" I asked, breathlessly awaiting what I hoped would be her answer.

"I could hear the sound of it hitting the water in the toilet bowl," she said, and I wasn't disappointed. I pressed on.

"Then what did you hear?"

"He flushed the toilet." She paled. Then began to cry, the pain overwhelming her. "I don't remember anything after that."

But Sally had remembered enough for me, and for her defense team. If she had heard Bill flush the toilet, she would have known that he was on his way back to continue brutalizing her; she would have believed that if she did not act immediately to save her life there would be no chance of escape. In addition, she'd been ill that day, unable to move quickly.

Now her case had all the elements of a good solid self-defense plea.

I called Jim Wagner and asked if the contents of the toilet

bowl had ever been analyzed; there had been no mention of that in any of the laboratory reports I'd read.

"Yes," he remembered, "but they didn't find anything useful."

"Wait a minute, Jim. Nothing in the toilet bowl means he flushed it. It means that he was on his way back into the bedroom to beat her."

Over the phone, I could hear Jim laughing with glee.

The fact that Bill had been found with his pants unzipped but his genitals in his underwear seemed to lend further credence to Sally's reasonable perception of imminent danger on that night. The facts of this case, along with her history of increasingly bad abuse, the broken bones she'd suffered, and her own declining health, should have sufficed, in my opinion, to acquit her. There was no doubt in my mind that it had been fear, not anger, that had motivated her to kill her husband.

Unfortunately for Sally, justice was not immediately served in her case. The jury found her guilty of second-degree murder. Despite the subsequent discovery that one of the jurors had lied on *voir dire* (falsely denying that she herself had ever been a battered woman), the judge refused to call a mistrial. Sally was sentenced to eighteen years in prison.

Sally appealed the trial. Almost three years later, she won her appeal and was granted a new trial. An appellate court had ruled that the fundamental due process guaranteeing a trial by unbiased jurors had been violated in her case. Just recently, I testified again at Sally's second trial. This time the judge refused to allow any misconduct, carefully protecting Sally's rights along with her new defense attorney, Rowan Kline. Sure enough, justice prevailed, and this jury found Sally not guilty. It couldn't make up for the three years she spent in prison, but Sally says she relishes her freedom now.

But alcohol is not always a factor in isolation. It can exacerbate other abusive behavior until the violence goes out of control.

MARIE'S STORY

Bud's alcoholism interfered with his sexual habits. A heavy drinker whose abuse of liquor had increased with time, he could no longer have an erection.

Marie had married him after they'd dated a while, when both were in their fifties. She'd known then that he worked at a local porno shop in downtown Portland, Oregon, but thought that after they were married he would give up that job for another one she had in mind: they would manage apartments together. When they married, Bud did give up his job.

But, unknown to her at first, he never gave up his obsession with pornography.

In the basement of the apartment complex they managed, Bud fixed up a room for himself where he stored trunkloads of blow-up dolls, vibrators, X-rated films, and sex toys. He'd spend hours down there splicing film together, first one way, then another, watching the sequences before going upstairs to demand sex with Marie. At the time, she had no idea what he'd been doing downstairs. But later she would remember his unreasonable, seemingly sudden demands.

One day, after several years of marriage, the police appeared at their apartment door asking for Bud. He wasn't home, but Marie let them in. They told her they needed to search the premises for an unregistered handgun. She accompanied them down to the basement. When they found Bud's private room and his cache of pornography, she was right there with them.

Marie was shocked. With this new find, her feelings toward her husband changed overnight.

Bud, on the other hand, felt oddly liberated. Now he could, and did, demand that Marie watch his pornographic movies with him; he demanded that she use his sex toys. Horrified, she refused at first. But he continued to demand her participation and eventually began to enforce it, beating her whenever she demonstrated reluctance. Along with his increasing obsession went his increasing use of alcohol.

Eventually just the whirring sound of the film projector was enough to make Marie sick with anticipation of another beating. If she went along with Bud, she was invariably forced to submit to sex she found disgusting and abusive. But whenever she refused he'd beat her black and blue. Even with his movies and his vibrators, Bud was having more and more difficulty becoming aroused. He'd become so sex-obsessed that he often walked around their apartment naked, one hand fondling his limp penis, while he did household chores.

Sick for years with a variety of illnesses, Marie became increasingly depressed. She felt she could no longer live with such a "dirty old man," as she called him. But she didn't know what the alternative was. She grew more and more desperate.

One rent-collecting day, always a time of tension in the apartment complex, Bud got very drunk, then increasingly noisy and violent. Marie tried hard to calm him down, afraid that one of the tenants would hear. When he finally passed out in front of the door, frail Marie had to drag him to the sofa. Then he stood, suddenly awake, and began to hit her.

Later, Marie would have no memory of stabbing him to death. She must have gone to the kitchen, taken a steak knife out of a drawer, and returned to the living room, where she stabbed him repeatedly, too many times to count. Many of the wounds were in the groin area. He died from a wound in his heart.

Kathleen Payne-Pruett, the state's attorney in Portland, originally charged Marie with first-degree murder.

A thin, sickly woman, Marie chose not to go to trial. Instead, she pleaded guilty to the lesser charge of manslaughter; her attorney, public defender David Falls, requested a sentencing hearing. The prosecutor was asking that Marie serve the full five-year term in prison. Although Payne-Pruett herself believed that the lesser charge was appropriate, she fought hard for Marie to do jail time; some of her behavior, probably, was to impress her male-dominated department with how "tough" she could be. During the sentencing hearing, I was brought in to testify on behalf of the defense.

Falls had done all his homework. After every piece of pornography Bud had owned was introduced as evidence, the judge sentenced Marie to a five-year term but immediately suspended the sentence, placing her on probation.

Falls had gotten Marie a place to live in one of downtown Portland's old renovated hotels, a facility for senior citizens. He and his paralegal assistant, Suzanne Singleton, helped her complete the necessary applications for medicare so she would be able to obtain the medical treatments she desperately needed.

They arranged for Marie to receive counseling at the nearby YWCA, first in individual therapy, and later, hopefully, as part of a battered women's out-patient group.

Marie began to make friends, something she hadn't done in years. Slowly her health improved. She began to emerge from the terrible fear and isolation she'd lived in for so long.

7

THE TERROR OF
SEXUAL VIOLENCE

PORNOGRAPHY, mentioned in the previous chapter, is one aspect of sexual abuse; there are many others. Sexual abuse often plays a major role in the cases of battered women who kill. Some have been raped with such force that their genitals and internal organs have been torn or irreparably damaged. As a result, many have had to have hysterectomies when still very young, and venereal infections and disease are not uncommon among these women. In one study of those who had attempted or completed homicide of their abusers, 87 percent of the 90 women evaluated had been sexually abused by those men. Several had been so brutalized that they were unable to have sex again.

Can a husband rape his wife? For many, this concept is new. Until the last ten or fifteen years, it was commonly accepted that a marriage license gave a man permission to have sex with his wife whenever he wanted it. But that is no longer the case. According to Laura X, director of the National Clearinghouse Against Marital Rape in San Francisco, legislators in thirty-six states have passed laws specifically making husband/wife rape a criminal act. In other states, prosecution is possible on more generalized assault charges, even where marriage is deemed an exemption from prosecution under sexual assault laws.

Researchers have found a relationship between coercive sex acts and a general preoccupation with sex itself. This correlation is true for married men who hold down respectable jobs, as well as for unemployed criminals. Frequent masturbation to violent sexual fantasies and use of "stimulants" (including pornography, physical abuse, and arousal response to inappropriate others, such as children) are frequent with known sex offenders. For most of these men, as for batterers, sex and coercion go together, along with a desperate need to control. In these cases, the batterer's need for power, his need to dominate women, gets expressed in his unusual level of sexual aggression. But it is really desire for control and power, not normal sexual desire, that is the motivating principle. And that makes rape the violent act it is, differing so dramatically from sex that is engaged in as an expression of love and intimacy.

Still, many battered women we interviewed spoke about their batterers as being good lovers at least part of the time. Many of them experienced and expressed confusion concerning sex and love. Many expected sexually stereotypical behavior of all men. They never learned how to make appropriate judgments in their relationships with men, either. Some who did engage in sex before · marriage felt guilty about it once they were married. They, too, had unintentionally absorbed our society's message that women who desire a fulfilling sexual relationship are "bad." And some were likely to confuse a man's abnormal sexual preoccupation with sexual freedom.

But battering relationships are like quicksand: once they go beyond a certain point, it is impossible to turn them back or even sometimes to get out alive. Most of the battered women in our samples cannot remember when they finally realized that the man who'd started out as a wonderful, sensitive lover was really a sex offender practicing at home. Looking back, all could see that the warning signs had been there for quite a while, but none recognized them at the time.

Irene, a petite, pretty, middle-aged woman from a small town in northwestern Montana, is one of these women. Her story is significant, not only because it points out the shocking brutality that is the inherent potential of any battering situation, but be-cause—luckily, and thanks to a system of justice well applied—it had a more or less fortunate ending.

IRENE'S STORY

Recently divorced after twenty-six years of marriage and terribly lonely, Irene met Ken while he was working on a construc-tion project in the Kalispell-Whitefish area of Montana. Ken, in his late forties, about her age, was a lumberjack from the Northwest. Irene found him charming. When he asked to move into her house, a rustic property outside of town, she said yes. A tradition-alist, Irene wasn't particularly comfortable with their nonmarried status, but she was delighted to have a man in her life again.

Irene attributed Ken's heavy drinking to his sorrow over the recent breakup of his own long-term marriage. She figured it would stop once they lived together. Ken complained a lot, too, about his former wife. But Irene knew that she was different; he wouldn't have anything to complain about with her. It did bother her that he beat his young children when they came to visit, for minor infractions, she thought.

"Do you have to use straps and sticks?" she asked. "They're just little kids."

"Mind your own business," Ken told her. Then he threat-ened her with the straps and sticks he'd used on the kids, telling her she had no right to interfere with him disciplining his own. She guessed he was right. She tried to comply.

In fact, Irene tried to comply with Ken in every way for two and a half years. But his violent behavior increased. He never stopped drinking heavily. As time went on, his outbursts became more frequent and totally unpredictable. The man whose charm-ing presence had once brightened her lonely life was progressively turning her daily existence into a hell.

The worst part of it was when his once-gentle, playful love-making became a ritual of torture. It was as if another person took over, she thought: his facial features would change so that he didn't even resemble the man she knew. He would grab her brutally, throw her on the bed, then threaten her with his gun before finally putting it aside to rape her, shouting obscenities all the while.

One night, he approached her with pointed gun, demanding sex. Before she had the chance to respond, he threw her on the bed, beating her with his fist, yelling foul obscenities at her. Then he shoved the barrel of the gun into her anus. He began describing, in painful detail, just how the bullet would travel through her body after he'd fired it. Pushing the gun barrel further and further into her, he continued to talk, becoming sexually aroused. Irene lay there, certain she would die.

Pull the trigger and get it over with, she prayed silently. If I'm going to die, let it be.

But Ken wasn't finished with her yet. He removed the gun and placed it by her head. He ordered her to her knees. Irene obeyed, sure she'd die any minute, and wishing now for the peace that would come with death. Without warning she felt a sudden, intense pain and heard her own flesh tearing. She was in shock; it took her a while to realize what was happening: he was raping her anally. Her insides were being ripped apart.

Oh, my God, she thought, please just let me die.

The pain was worse than any she'd ever experienced. She passed out for a while. When she became vaguely conscious again she could still hear him calling her obscene names as he thrust into her torn body repeatedly, finally reaching orgasm. He stood then and walked into the next room, setting his gun on the coffee table. Irene lay as still as she could, bleeding onto the bedsheets.

"If you move, bitch," said Ken, "I'll kill you."

After a while, she asked for permission to get a glass of water.

"Sure," he said.

She hobbled in a trancelike state to the bathroom, dripping blood. On her way back to the bedroom, she noticed the gun on the coffee table. As if on impulse, she picked it up and stared at him.

Irene wouldn't remember aiming or pulling the trigger. At the time, she didn't even realize she'd shot him.

Ken managed to stagger to the telephone and call the sheriff for help. Bleeding profusely, he stumbled outside. Irene thought he was going to get another gun—she knew he kept one in his truck—and shot him again.

The next thing she'd remember was seeing headlights coming up the road to her home. She was in a state of extreme confusion; what went through her mind was that some friends must be coming to visit, and she would be unready to receive them. She took off her soiled, blood-soaked nightgown. She picked a blood-spattered rug off the floor and threw it in the washing machine along with her nightgown. When the sheriff entered he found her swishing a mop around in a puddle of blood. The blood was going nowhere but in circles.

Later, a prosecutor would insist that Irene's use of the mop had been a calculated attempt to cover up her crime. The sheriff and his staff knew differently. Irene was a local; Ken had been a noticeably hard-drinking guy from out of state. They were willing to believe her side of things.

Nevertheless, she was charged with first-degree murder. The district attorney was determined to prosecute vigorously.

The trial judge, a good-looking local politician who, some said, had been elected more for his name recognition than for his knowledge of the law, was expected to be prejudiced against defense attorney Steve Nardi's presentation of either expert witness testimony or Battered Woman Syndrome. (As a matter of fact, I have been told that this same judge later informed a class of law students in nearby Missoula that I was nothing but a radical feminist who wanted all men to die!)

Steve Nardi and I talked on the telephone frequently as he prepared to go to trial. Irene had received permission from the court to leave Montana for a few months beforehand to stay with her daughter in Alaska. She was becoming physically and emotionally stronger as time went on. Both Steve and I believed she'd be able to withstand the pressure of the trial, even testifying about her sexual abuse. I'd been worried about her mental health. During the two days she'd spent being interviewed and evaluated at our Denver offices, she'd shaken all over, vomiting as she retold the story of her rape. At that time, in her damaged and fragile state, even remembering had seemed too difficult.

Steve's main concern was finding the right jury in that small Montana town. Would the sexual abuse be too terrible for them to believe? he wanted to know. Would the jury wonder why Irene hadn't just left Ken? Would they wonder why on earth she'd ever loved him in the first place? Could we make them understand?

"Yes," I told him, "it's been done before, and we can do it again."

Personally, I harbored a belief, born of experience, that people in small western towns are more likely to sympathetically understand battered women who kill than are people from large metropolitan areas. Maybe it is the ethic, sometimes inherent in small-town settings, that women don't give up easily on the men they love, even when their men hurt them. Within the context of that loyalty ethic, if a woman has to kill her man to protect herself the homicide somehow seems more justifiable. It's my sense, too, that frontier justice has much in common with Carol Gilligan's theories of women's justice.* Or maybe the common concern with survival shared by country dwellers creates a common

---

*Carol Gilligan, Harvard psychologist and author of *In a Different Voice*, has extensively studied men's and women's concepts of justice. What she calls the "male model" is based on an agreed-upon standard and applied equally to everyone. Any exceptions are rationalized in some way. But Gilligan points out that for women the preferred model is different: it includes the same agreed-upon standard but is expected to be tempered by compassion. Thus each case is evaluated for its own unique nature, and justice is administered accordingly. Exceptions to the rule are not necessary, since allowance is normally made for individual needs and circumstances.

understanding: that compassion must sometimes temper mere rules for true justice to be delivered.

Steve did his best in selecting a jury.* Considering both he and Irene to be my clients, I did my best to calm his nerves in the weeks leading up to the trial. I was busy preparing myself, too, reading the pertinent materials he'd sent me and sensing that Irene's chances for acquittal were probably good.

Then Steve called me with news neither one of us expected. Irene had gotten married in Alaska.

"Oh, no, Steve. How could she do that before the trial?"

"I had to," Irene insisted, when confronted. "This man is so good and kind. He treats me so well. Now I can stand anything, even the trial."

Neither Steve nor I had the heart to remind her that she was facing a sentence of life imprisonment if convicted, and that this particular judge was unlikely to mitigate the expected life-in-prison sentence on a first-degree murder conviction.

All of Irene's children came into town to be with her for the trial. So did her new husband, Joe. He was a kind and delightful man, and he did keep her spirits up. But Steve and I were very worried about how her marriage would look to the jury.

Irene and Joe confessed to me that their marriage had never been consummated. Joe said that, no matter what he did, Irene found herself unable to relax sufficiently to have sex. Joe feared that she had been permanently, irremediably scarred by Ken's brutal rape. He loved her, he said, and was committed to being with her anyway. But both of them wondered if any therapeutic measures could be taken to alleviate her mental suffering.

*On the final jury were a woman who had worked with a battered women's task force and another who was head of a local rape crisis volunteer group. Years later, I met this second woman, who had been elected foreperson of the jury at Irene's trial. She told me how important the Battered Woman Syndrome testimony had been in determining the jury's deliberations and final verdict. Now studying to be a psychologist, she said that her experience sitting on Irene's jury had been the catalyst in her decision to return to school.

"Give it time," I suggested, thinking it wise for them to get through the trial first before dealing with any other issues.

Steve thought otherwise.

"Let's put Joe on the witness stand!" he suggested. "The jury will see what a decent guy he is. And he can testify as to Irene's inability to have sexual intercourse, which will support her version of what happened."

By then the trial was under way. Ken's former wife and children had already testified for the prosecution, the children each saying under oath, "My father never hit me, except when I needed discipline," despite the fact that other independent witnesses had verified Ken's physical abuse of them. I wondered how the state's attorney could let the children testify like that. Did he realize how profound the psychological risk was for them, to witness and experience violence at home and then be encouraged to deny it? Ken's former wife stated that Ken had hit her "only once, and I deserved it." In fact, she walked with crutches, having lost a leg from an unknown injury; it is possible that the jury believed her loss of limb was a result of Ken's violence to her in the past.

In view of this testimony, Steve Nardi encouraged Joe to go on the witness stand.

Joe was willing. "If you think it will help Irene, I'll do it. I'll tell the truth."

"I don't want to put you through all that," Irene protested. "This is my problem, and you don't need to share it."

"Nonsense," Joe replied steadily. "I married you for better or worse, knowing all about these problems, and I'm not going to give up now. If Steve thinks it will help, I'll do it."

He did. His testimony was wonderful and convincing. So was Irene's.

I testified last. As I spoke, I sensed that the jury was following every word sympathetically. A good sign. I had to leave immediately afterward to get back to some business matters in Denver. As I rushed from the courtroom, hoping to catch the last flight out, the bailiff, a small, elderly man who had full control of his court-house, approached me, grinning widely. He shook my hand.

"You know what I think, Doc? She should have done it sooner!"

I knew then that Irene would be acquitted. Jurors and bailiffs have a special connection; even though they never communicate verbally, they experience the trial through similar eyes.

Sure enough, with a minimum of deliberation, a not-guilty verdict came in the next day. Steve and Irene called with the good news. I was sorry I couldn't be there to celebrate it with them as I listened to their merry laughter in the background.

The last I heard, Joe and Irene were still happily married. (Proof, again, that even the most severely brutalized women can thrive after their batterers are gone.) Hopefully Irene will go through a healing process, as other rape victims have done, and will one day be able to engage in normal sexual relations again. Time and unpressured understanding from a truly loving mate is thus far the best cure.

Irene had a very good experience with the legal system. Justice was served in her case; the system itself did not force her to endure more suffering than was absolutely necessary for the completion of her trial. Not so for Paulette, whose story follows.

PAULETTE'S STORY

"My Jacques was a romantic and great lover, until we were married," Paulette would later remark. "Then he could no longer be a man. He needed to get dirty magazines and rub himself. Still, he could do nothing. He made me feel like I wasn't a woman. I complained, and he told me I had to let him fuck me in the ass."

Raised by French Catholic nuns, Paulette believed that non-procreational sex and extramarital sex were "bad," sinful. She had never been able to live up to those standards of morality, having had a relationship with a man out of wedlock for fifteen years before marrying Jacques. Although she'd loved this man, claiming that he treated her well most of the time, she had felt devalued because their relationship had never been legally sanctioned. So when she and Jacques were married and he immediately became impotent, Paulette believed that something was wrong with her, not him. Maybe, she reasoned, this was her punishment for living in sin all those years. Still she was unhappy with the situation. She often acquiesced to his increasingly violent and perverse demands, in an attempt to somehow make things better.

Paulette's focus on her own share of blame, imagined or otherwise, in the downward spin of their relationship rendered her unable to see that Jacques was cruel and violent to others, too. His constant heavy drinking, his refusal to get a job, his insistence on keeping her isolated in the primitive cabin he called home were not perceived by her as having any connection to the sexual abuse he inflicted. Suspicious that Jacques was seeing another woman— which, to Paulette's way of thinking, would have made a perfectly good explanation for his inability to perform sexually with her in normal ways—she gave vent to her anger and jealousy. The jealousy was more easily observed than her heartbreak that the man she loved was causing her so much pain.

Isolated, unsure of herself, Paulette knew only instinctively that the kind of sex Jacques demanded of her, brutal anal intercourse after he'd become aroused by reading pornography magazines, had nothing to do with sexual pleasure between intimates, nor was it the kind of sex she expected between husband and wife. It was degrading, humiliating violence and violation, the kind women are often too ashamed to discuss.

On the night he died, Jacques raped her with special brutality, throwing her up against a table, ripping off her bathrobe and turning her over. As he penetrated her anally, Paulette experienced such intense pain that she thought she'd pass out. She felt her body becoming limp. Jacques lost his erection and withdrew. But moments later, he became aroused again and picked up where he'd left off. When he'd finished with her, she was in agony, sobbing and shaking. He yelled at her to stop crying. It was keeping him awake, he said.

Since there was no running water in their cabin, Paulette staggered down to the nearby lake. There, she put some water in a basin to wash with. It immediately turned blood red.

Some time after she returned to the cabin and before getting into bed next to him, she must have shot Jacques to death. She would later have little memory of what had happened.

Arrested two days later, Paulette was still bleeding.

The prison doctor who initially examined her noted in the records that she had bleeding hemorrhoids. She was too embarrassed to correct him.

Several months later, in jail, she was subjected to a routine body cavity search. When the woman warden told her to bend over, Paulette became hysterical. The memory of that final rape had flashed immediately through her mind. It still does now and then, as would be expected in someone suffering from Post Traumatic Stress Disorder—causing her instant, uncontrollable panic, even without any physical stimulus.

In some states, the law permits prosecutors to take the depositions of defense witnesses prior to trial. The prosecutor accompanied the public defender to our offices in Denver in January 1986, a month before Paulette's trial was scheduled to begin. He wanted to begin to depose me as an expert witness.

While answering his questions, I tried to be as clinical as possible. The prosecutor made it clear from the beginning that he had trouble believing Paulette could have endured that kind of sexual abuse without somehow "wanting" it. His explanation was that she'd been exaggerating the story all along in order to make everyone feel sorry for her. It became obvious very quickly to all of us on the defense team that Paulette's most intimate and private moments would have to be exposed in detail at the trial, in order to make the jury understand why she had shot and killed Jacques. She was afraid he'd rape her like that again.

Jacques's friends were prepared to testify as to Paulette's

angry and jealous nature. (There was evidence that she had yelled at and threatened several of them.) But I remained totally convinced, and was willing to try to convince the jury, that Paulette had not killed Jacques because of anger or jealousy. She had shot him out of fear, after experiencing a savage rape that occurred as the culmination of years of being beaten, half-starved, and forced to live in isolation in extremely primitive surroundings. She had shot him after becoming convinced that she could expect nothing from him but more of the same. Paulette was terrified that he would rape her again, causing her further physical injury and maybe even death. She had shot her husband in self-defense.

I never was able to tell this to the jury.

Paulette decided that she was too embarrassed to talk at a public hearing about the terrible things that had been done to her. She chose to plead guilty and stay in prison, perhaps for the rest of her life, rather than expose her experiences of degradation and violent sexual abuse.

Paulette, I feel, has been victimized doubly by a society whose norms are sometimes impossible for even strong, privileged women to live up to. Although she had no social privilege, no wealth or power, and perhaps no great capacity to understand the ramifications of what had happened to her and the ramifications of her own silence, Paulette sensed intuitively that she would have had to give up her cherished identity as a "good" woman if she were to publicly admit to being a sexual one.

8

THE CHILDREN:
PHYSICAL ABUSE
AND INCEST

Physical Abuse

IN BATTERING SITUATIONS, it is often the helpless, the weakest, who are victimized most. About one-half of batterers batter their children as well as their wives.* The batterer's violence often increases when the woman is pregnant, when children in the family are very young, and again when they become teenagers. Men who batter are extremely dependent individuals, constantly demanding a woman's undivided attention. Such a man is guaranteed to experience extreme frustration when his woman's attention is diverted from him and his needs; the presence of infants and children in the home ensures that this will happen. Infants and children, the most helpless and dependent of people, force the batterer to share his woman with them while teenagers usually challenge many of their parents' views. Intolerant of the adolescent's developmental task, which is to separate and become an

*This statistic comes from psychologist Carol Newberger and pediatrician Eli Newberger, who direct several research programs in family violence at Harvard University's Children's Hospital, in Boston. It is also reported by the women interviewed for my book *The Battered Woman Syndrome* (Springer, 1984).

independent individual, the batterer reacts badly when he feels emotionally abandoned, resulting in even greater conflict with teenage children.

Children reared in violence bear psychological scars for life. Our society condones some use of physical violence against children as a means of discipline and control; thus children can learn that those who love you also have the right to inflict pain on you. Women likewise are infantilized on many levels. And a man who batters tends to view the battered woman, at least in part, as a child of sorts, one who deserves the punishment he metes out to her to "teach her a lesson." It is no surprise, then, that children raised in a battering situation learn dishonesty, secrecy, silence, manipulation, denial of tension and anger, and avoidance of problems in general, early on. They learn to live in a fantasy world, because it is so much nicer than their real world. They learn that their own needs will rarely be consistently fulfilled, that confrontation is to be avoided at all costs.

Children who grow up in battering households usually identify with one parent or the other by the age of around ten or twelve. It is not uncommon for children in the same family to be divided along different lines in this regard. (If they come from a family in which a homicide has occurred, especially one in which the battered woman has killed the abusing husband/father, the father-identified children may be furious and embittered, the mother-identified children relieved.) Sometimes, tragically, these children witness violent incidents and actual homicide; sometimes they are then used as witnesses for the prosecution, to testify against their own mothers.

Nevertheless, children who have lived with battering fathers or with any kind of domestic violence, *universally* prefer to live in peace, nonviolence, and comparative security, even if that means living with only one parent.

The batterer is adept at using people and precious objects as pawns, to coerce his woman into doing whatever he wants her to do at the moment. When there are children involved, she is often held hostage to the batterer emotionally. She may try to placate him at almost any cost, in order to save her children from harm.

But the batterer's physical abuse of a child is often the catalyst for battered women who kill—the final straw, the thing they can no longer tolerate without going mad. In many cases, knowledge of child abuse is the thing that prompts a battered woman to kill in self-defense, to protect the child and herself from a violence that knows no bounds.

NADA'S STORY

Nada's husband Mussafir beat their six-month-old infant with his fists one day, threatening to use a belt the next time.

Nada had put up with his physical abuse of her for quite a while. But she wouldn't let him hurt her son again, she decided. She was angry that day but also terribly afraid that the child would be subjected to more battering and that she also would be, afraid that Mussafir would kill them the next time. She found the handgun they kept in a bedroom drawer. In the middle of his ranting, she shot and killed him. She was seventeen years old at the time.

Terrified by what she'd done, Nada dragged Mussafir's body into a hallway closet, which locked automatically when the door was shut, hoping, in her state of shock, that his corpse would freeze in the winter cold, that no one would find it until the summer thaw. She wrapped her son in warm blankets and fled their place by car, heading for the airport. There, she left the car in a no-parking zone (where it was bound to attract attention sooner or later). She and her child boarded a plane headed to where her family lived. She planned to stay with them.

But, back in the apartment where Mussafir's dead body lay in the hallway closet, a stray bullet had pierced the wall, traveling into her next-door neighbor's place. This neighbor notified the police.

By the time they'd found the body, Nada and her child had left the state. Extradition proceedings were initiated a few days later.

Because Nada had been a juvenile at the time of the homicide, her attorney, Meg Greene, argued that she be tried as one.

Meanwhile, Nada was locked up in a juvenile detention facility for one and a half years before even coming to trial. Her son, whom she'd tried so hard to protect, was being raised by her parents.

When Meg Greene lost the motion to have her tried as a juvenile and had to put a difficult adult defense together, she contacted me. By this time, Nada had been moved to the jail in her hometown. I traveled there with an associate to interview and evaluate her.

Nada had been an angry, troubled teenager, with a prior juvenile record for running away and truancy, and juries tend to react adversely to such records. In her home state, the penalty for first- or second-degree murder is harsh. When our evaluation was complete, the state offered to plead down to manslaughter, which carried a fifteen-year sentence. Meg thought it a comparatively good deal, especially considering the lack of witnesses available to testify about the abuse suffered by Nada and her baby.

After listening to the history of abuse and how it had affected Nada's state of mind at the time of the shooting, the judge found that in her case there were mitigating circumstances and cut the sentence nearly in half, to eight years. With the time she'd already served awaiting extradition and with the several months she'd spent in jail prior to the sentencing hearing, Nada would have about one more year to serve. After that, with good behavior, she'd be eligible for parole. At that time, she would be twenty-one years old.

An outcome like this is sometimes the most "just" face the law can put on.

Like their battered mothers, children are often doubly victimized: first by cruel and abusive fathers, then by the state, whose legal and child-care bureaucracies too rarely take into account the truths of the human heart and psyche, as the following story shows only too clearly.

SHERRY'S STORY

Sherry shot and killed her husband trying to protect herself and her five-year-old son, Kevin, from his physical abuse.

The child, a victim of violence and a witness to the homicide, understood what had happened. The state decided to use his testimony for the prosecution, as evidence that Sherry had indeed shot her husband, a fact she was entirely willing to admit to anyway. Her bail was granted *on provision that she not see or speak with Kevin until the trial was over.* The boy was placed in a foster home, and their long wait began.

As could have easily been predicted by any reputable child psychologist, Kevin became more and more emotionally distressed. His severe depression worsened, and he displayed typical failure-to-thrive symptoms. Now this child, who had been terribly abused, who had witnessed repeated incidents of violence, and who had watched his father die, was being deprived of his mother's love so that a state might win a trial conviction. Sherry, devastated, was further traumatized by the loss of her son.

Her defense attorney, Steve Thayer, thought she had a very good chance for acquittal. After hearing the facts of her case, I agreed. There was no doubt in my mind that Sherry had shot her husband in the middle of an acute battering incident, to protect herself and her child from further harm or death.

But Sherry, knowing that juries are never predictable, wouldn't take any chances. She did the only thing she could do as a mother: she refused to cooperate with Steve Thayer in preparing for the trial; when a plea bargain was offered by the state (assuring her that she wouldn't have to serve time in prison, and that she and Kevin would be reunited), she demanded that her attorney accept. The separation was simply more than she and he could bear.

Both mothers and children may also be victimized by a system of law enforcement that acts either too slowly, too ineffectually, or not at all, failing to ensure their safety from further abuse even when they have left the batterer. The law may limp along at a pace insufficient to effect the delivery of real justice. When time is of the essence—a matter of life or death in some cases; in others, a matter of safety or harm, sanity or being driven to the point of madness—the amount of time the law spends spinning its wheels before the batterer is effectively dealt with is often much too long.

The following story is typical.

JENNIE'S STORY

Jennie became pregnant with Doug's child while they were living together. Seriously ill from two earlier terminated pregnancies, she decided to bear this baby to term, but to give her or him up for adoption. She'd witnessed the terrible abuse Doug inflicted on Jeff, her son from a former marriage. Doug, she reasoned, just didn't like children. Beyond that, she was afraid he'd go too far one day and actually kill the infant.

During her pregnancy, Doug's abuse of Jeff became much worse. Finally, Jennie sent the boy to live with his father.

This left her feeling better about her son's well-being, but she became increasingly afraid of Doug now that she was alone with him. He'd already beaten her several times before; she was terrified that he'd beat her again before she gave birth, damaging the fetus. The combination of factors—her own ill health and physical incapacitation, plus the stress of trying to keep Doug reasonably calm—took its toll. Jennie was depressed and feeling terribly isolated by the time she gave birth.

Her emotions were mixed, too: she felt relief and joy at the beauty of her healthy new daughter, grief at the thought of giving her up. As she filled out the adoption papers, Jennie wept. But she knew she couldn't care for the child. She would never be able to ensure her daughter's safety as long as she lived with Doug; she couldn't even protect herself from Doug's unpredictable, brutal assaults. In a way, she'd resigned herself to living with him; she believed she'd never be able to leave. But maybe she could help her child escape. She wanted desperately to give her an opportunity for a decent life.

Jennie had begun to feel much stronger in her resolve when Doug's mother visited her in the hospital, volunteering to raise the child herself. She urged Jennie to give the baby to her "instead of to strangers." She'd already lost a granddaughter, she said, when Doug's first wife had fled the state (to escape his abuse). She pleaded with Jennie to reconsider, promising her that she'd be able to see her daughter whenever she wanted.

Jennie weakened, and finally relented.

Doug's mother had her lawyer draw up the appropriate papers. Jennie signed them. By now, she was getting nervous again; she just wasn't sure that her husband's mother would do right by the baby.

Jennie returned home to Doug, and another year of terror began. He became instantly jealous of her feelings for her daughter. He beat her, often and seriously. Jennie rarely visited the child, for fear of starting another battering incident. Finally, after a beating that put her in the hospital, she sought counseling at the local shelter for battered women.

With the help of the shelter staff, Jennie left Doug, filing civil charges against him for damages and pressuring the city until they prosecuted Doug on criminal charges of assault. When Doug's mother refused her visitation rights, Jennie sought to regain custody of her daughter.

But Doug's mother proved obstinate.

"Drop the charges against my son," she threatened, "or you'll never see your baby again."

Jennie struggled painfully with the decision to proceed legally. She was afraid that neither she nor her daughter would ever really be free of the threat of Doug's violence. She received a lot of support from the professionals working at local battered women's facilities, as well as from her battered women's support group (which I led at the time). Still, the decision was hers alone to make, in the end; no matter which path she chose, it was sure to be a lonely and difficult one.

Eventually, she decided to press charges. She'd taken too much abuse from Doug, she said, for too long. She was unwilling to live with the threat of more.

Jennie won her civil suit, although collecting the money awarded for damages proved extremely difficult. But, as of this writing, she is still entangled in a legal web.

Doug was found guilty of criminal assault and sentenced to six months in jail. However, because of overcrowding in the local jail and his "sincere" promises to seek counseling, he spent a total of only nineteen days there.

His mother, meanwhile, still refuses to let Jennie see her daughter. The judge assigned to this case repeatedly threatens to hold Doug's mother in contempt of court but consistently fails to follow through with any real action.

Jennie is broke. She can't afford to keep going back to court. For her, the nightmare has continued. Sometimes, she says, she thinks it would be better for them all if she just gave up and got out of her daughter's life for good.

Even after divorce and separation, even after the batterer has lost custody of his children, he may still use them as his vital link to the battered woman. The batterer often manipulates visitation rights as a way of continuing to harass and harm her.

The following story is not unusual.

HEIDI'S STORY

Each time Heidi's ex-husband, Mark, exercised his visitation rights and came to pick up their young son for the weekend, he used the opportunity to beat, harass, or molest her. On more than one occasion, he hid in her darkened apartment waiting for her to come home from work, raping her when she finally arrived.

He'd often bully his way into her place, then sit and watch TV with the boy even after she'd demanded that he leave. It didn't seem to bother Mark that his own son witnessed his continual abuse of Heidi or heard the obscene things he said to her.

One day, Mark threatened to go to court and gain full custody of their son. He planned to remarry, he told Heidi; since she was a single mother, chances were good that the court would award him the custody he wanted.

Heidi was afraid that she wouldn't be able to stop him this time. She was afraid that the terror would never end.

She was working full-time and going to school part-time, hoping to get a degree that would qualify her to make a good living and to become financially independent of Mark. As she got closer to graduating, Mark's beatings and harassment escalated. Neighbors reported hearing strange sounds coming through her apartment walls, like a body being slammed, hard, against furniture.

Mark began threatening to kill her. But she was too frightened, by this time, to call the police. A friend gave Heidi a gun.

One day soon after, Mark forced his way into her apartment to pick up Danny for his visitation and was in a violent mood. He began to beat Heidi in front of their son. She ran from him into the bedroom, screaming that she'd call the police, hoping that would scare him into leaving. Once there, she didn't call the police at all. She opened a drawer and picked up the gun. Mark was yelling at her from the living room, threatening again to kill her.

Heidi went into the living room, pleading with him to leave. She pointed the gun at him.

Mark laughed. He told her she'd never to able to shoot him.

Then he grabbed for her. Her hands flew up self-protectively; the trigger got pulled. Heidi shot Mark twice: once in the head, once in the chest. He died instantly.

The Covington, Kentucky, prosecutor charged Heidi with murder in the first degree.

He failed to understand, he claimed, how she could have

permitted Mark's abuse of her to continue even after their divorce. (In fact, divorced women are often subjected to abuse from their ex-husbands.) During Heidi's trial, the prosecutor tried to convince the jury that the crime had been committed in cold blood; the motive, he stated, was that Heidi had wanted to prevent Mark from seeing his own child.

Heidi's defense attorney, Bob Sanders, had asked me to evaluate his client and to testify at her trial as an expert witness. I spent nearly an entire day on the stand, answering questions, trying to speak directly to the jury whenever I could, explaining my professional point of view about the psychology of battered women, how Battered Woman Syndrome affects a woman's state of mind at the time she kills her abuser. Since I was not permitted by the judge to use the term "self-defense," I literally had to teach the jury to understand all the pertinent concepts; hopefully, they would then be able to put the pieces together themselves.

Heidi's family and friends also testified on her behalf. And, like other juries before them, this jury was able to put the pieces together as we had hoped. After deliberation, they rejected the prosecution's argument and found Heidi not guilty.

But even when a battered woman who kills her abuser is fully acquitted, the damage done to the children in the family, who may have witnessed horrible abuse or suffered abuse themselves, can be and often is permanent.

No other kind of legal case causes me as much anguish and terror. Divorced battered women with children often are not taken seriously by law enforcement agencies and the courts. The batterer's violent behavior is often denied, minimized, or declared irrelevant in determining his parenting ability. The stated legal standard—the best interests of the child—is rarely given more than lip service. (In 1986, Dr. Phyllis Chesler, psychologist and author of the books *Women and Madness, About Men,* and *Mothers on Trial,* organized a speak-out in New York City, the purpose of which was to provide the public with details regarding the subtle and not-so-subtle sabotaging of women's rights by the same courts in which we are supposed to receive justice.) I have had firsthand experience of the court system's sometimes insidious abuse of women; in more than one case, I have been accused of causing the violence between husband and wife through therapeutic intervention, and ordered by the court to stop treating the woman!

Don't make a big deal out of it. The abuse will just go away somehow. That is the wish of this country's divorce courts as well as its criminal justice system when it comes to dealing with battered women, and of the family courts when it comes to dealing with child custody and visitation issues; that is the wish at the root of all denial. But our data clearly shows that this is not what happens. Domestic violence escalates and escalates, often until it reaches the point of homicide. Terror and brutality will not go away simply because professionals turn their backs on it.

Children who witness their fathers beating their mothers are at greater risk of being beaten themselves than children who do not witness such events. Yet, in divorce cases, even when the children have testified about their father's abuse, they are expected to be shuttled back and forth between parents for visits. Only their fragile survival skills can keep them safe. Mothers are sometimes accused of causing their children's dislike of being with their fathers. A new disorder called Parental Alienation Syndrome parades as the latest cover-up of battering situations involving children. Psychological coercion, physical violence, and fear fill these children's lives. Even when there is no physical or sexual abuse, the fear remains. Neither the appropriate professionals nor the courts are yet ready to measure the toll such terror takes on a child. Anxiety disorders, conduct problems, school failure, and depression—these are among the more obvious symptoms, as is lack of ability to empathize with others. Children who grow up in abusive families are more likely to be on the giving or receiving end of abuse in the families they create as adults. In short, we are producing another generation of batterers and battered women.

Some battered women even voluntarily give up their children to the batterer as a way of protecting themselves. These women reason that their men have never physically abused the children, only them, so they think their kids will be safe from abuse after they leave. Others, harboring extremely low self-esteem, believe that their children are stronger and more capable than they are; they believe the children will be able to somehow "take better care of themselves" than they saw their battered mother doing. (These women see themselves as the catalyst for their men's violent behavior.) In some cases, in which the children have learned an abusive father's lessons of violence, a mother may need to escape being beaten by both her husband and her children.

But walking out on a family, especially when there are children, is a terribly difficult decision to make. Women who have actually done it still bear a heavy burden of guilt. They may talk of drowning their pain in alcohol or other substances, self-destructive behaviors that may have caused them to be inadequate parents in the first place. Mostly, though, they speak of missing their children. They speak of how much they love them, of how they have never stopped loving them.

Yet, rarely do they go back to visit. Years later, they remain absolutely terrified at the mere thought of reentering the world of violence in which they once had lived.

And too often it is the child in a battering situation who winds up paying, sometimes with her life.

HEDDA'S STORY

On November 2, 1987, Hedda Nussbaum was arrested in New York City with her live-in partner, Joel Steinberg, who eventually was charged with the murder of their illegally adopted daughter, six-year-old Lisa Steinberg.

Charges against Hedda were never filed, with the agreement that she would cooperate with the prosecutor in what became one of the most publicized murder trials in United States history. A year later, after extensive medical and psychiatric treatment, Hedda testified in court about the life of horrifying, brutal abuse she had endured with Joel. Television viewers across the nation had the opportunity to watch her live testimony.

A public debate formed around Hedda's testimony. Some wanted to hold her equally responsible for Lisa's death; others (myself included) understood that Joel's abuse of Hedda had caused her major psychological as well as physical damage— damage that rendered her incapable of acting to save Lisa's life as the child lay unconscious on the floor for twelve hours after being beaten by Joel.

Like so many other battered women, Hedda spoke of being too terrified to summon help, afraid that it would show disloyalty to Joel if she disobeyed him. In the end, brainwashed by her abusive partner, irreparably damaged physically by the terrible beatings she had endured and the drugs she'd abused in her attempts to please him and perhaps blot out pain and reality, she could make no reasonable attempt to save the life of her child.

Hedda's story is not much different from that of many battered women. She grew up in a middle-class New York City home, attended college, became an editor of children's books in a major New York publishing house, met Joel, a nice-looking lawyer, and fell in love. They lived together in his small Greenwich Village apartment. At first, Hedda would later say, Joel had demonstrated intense interest in her; he talked to her about her feelings, thoughts, and plans for the future. He became her therapist; his goal was to take control of her mind, to make her a better person. She liked his interest and his program for her self-improvement. Then, in subtle ways, his attitude toward her began to change. The intensity remained, but Joel began to choose all the topics of discussion, and if her responses weren't "correct," he'd get abusive. The abuse was verbal at first; he would push or slap her once in a while. After several years, the abuse escalated into major battering incidents. Both used marijuana and cocaine, experimentally for Hedda at first, but after a while, when Joel began to freebase, Hedda's drug use also increased.

Joel Steinberg had charisma, was a smooth talker, and seemed to always know how best to make a deal. The people for whom he practiced law were reputedly involved in organized crime. He pulled strings to illegally obtain Lisa, and later an infant boy, Mitchell.

At first, they'd had friends they shared. But eventually people stopped coming around; Hedda stopped calling others. This isolation was encouraged by Joel, whose intrusive and possessive behavior took her over completely. Their apartment had once been clean and well cared for. When police entered on November 2, 1987, to find Lisa unconscious on the floor, it was indescribably filthy. Two-year-old Mitchell was found tied to a playpen. The place looked like a war-torn battle zone. It was.

Hedda Nussbaum and I are the same age. I, too, grew up in New York City; I, too, was a well-educated girl from a middle-class Jewish family, looking for a Joel Steinberg to marry and make a family with. Earlier in my life, I found myself making some of the same choices Hedda made. When I decided to give up my career as a teacher of emotionally disturbed children in 1964, the year my son was born, I never considered the long-lasting consequences to my own self-esteem. Within a few months of staying home with my child full-time, I recognized that there was something terribly lacking in my life. My first husband (whom I later divorced, and who could have been described as psychologically abusive, had we known of such labels back in the 1960s) had too much power and control over me. I realized that I needed to develop an identity of my own and to work for my own mental health. After some rocky times, I returned to work and later went on to school for graduate degrees.

But I could easily have been in Hedda's place. It is possible for any woman to make decisions that, in retrospect, will turn out to be irrevocably wrong. Life provides so few recognizable warning signs about the quicksand that may lie ahead.

I believe that those who blame Hedda for the death of her child may be secretly afraid that what happened to her could have happened to them, too. The truth is that any woman is in danger of becoming a battered woman, of losing control over her destiny, until such time as she is free of violence again.

But Hedda's case is different from those of other battered women in a number of ways. First, it was her child, not her husband or she, who died. The social taboo against mothers who fail to protect their children is far worse than that against women who kill their abusive husbands. Hedda lived; Lisa died; and many will never be able to forgive her. She paid more attention to what was happening between herself and Joel than to anything else in her environment. However, as we have seen, battered women really do believe that, if they can keep the batterer calm, everyone will be safe. This view is not totally distorted, either. When the batterer is on "good" behavior he is often kind, generous, and loving to everyone around him; when he is "bad," his violence tends to be directed, at least initially, toward the woman. Many battered women react in ways similar to Hedda's. It is simply a matter of luck that, in their cases, their children are not killed.

In Hedda's case, she eventually could not tell the difference between her own thoughts and Joel's. He had literally taken over her mind. In that condition, she was unable to kill anyone, but she was unable to protect anyone, either.

The truth is that Lisa Steinberg died at the hands of a violent and abusive man, one who was able to fool the world with his veneer of education, professionalism, good looks, and fast talk.

But Joel Steinberg, despite his three-piece suit, was dangerous; he chose not to control his violence. Because he was a smooth talker, because he appeared socially successful, he was able to hide his criminal nature. Joel killed Hedda Nussbaum's mind long before he killed Lisa's body. He was found guilty of manslaughter for the death of Lisa. But, like most batterers, he will suffer no legal consequences for what he did to Hedda.

Murder by omission, that is, doing nothing observable to protect the child, is the name given to cases in which mothers are indicted for murder when their husbands or boyfriends kill their children. Frequently, these homicides occur after a short period of intense "discipline" that really is abuse of the child for failure to conform to an inappropriate standard set by the man, who also beats the child's mother. Often these battered women are young, poor, uneducated, and with little access to resources. Frequently, they are so badly beaten and scared of the batterer that, like Hedda Nussbaum, they are rendered incapable of better protecting their child. Most agree with other battered women: seeking outside help, especially from authorities, makes things worse. Seeking such help raises the risk that the woman or child will be more seriously harmed or killed by the batterer.

Those who criticize Hedda Nussbaum believe that she should have taken six-year-old Lisa for emergency medical treatment.* But maybe that would have been ineffective also. Imagine two equally possible scenarios that could have occurred at the hospital, had Hedda gone there when she discovered Lisa lying on the bathroom floor. In scenario one, the medical personnel recognize that Lisa's injuries were not naturally inflicted and alert child protective services to take custody of both children. Joel comes home and finds them gone. It could be predicted that, in his rage, Joel would beat Hedda, perhaps until she was dead. In scenario two, medical and child protective services personnel would have treated Lisa without becoming aware that she was a battered child—not an implausibility considering their ignoring other warning signs from earlier reports. Joel would have concocted another story and then used his charm to get it believed. Hedda and Lisa, had she survived, would have been even more unprotected from Joel's brutality. Next time, perhaps Hedda as well as Lisa might have been killed. In either of these scenarios— and there are others I have not even described—the outcome is more abuse, not the protection sought. And that, of course, is the point that often guides a battered woman's behavior.

*Susan Brownmiller, feminist author of *Waverly Place* (1989), has led the critics in being unable to understand Hedda's inability to protect Lisa.

Incest

Many batterers also display seductive sexual behavior toward their children, especially their daughters. Many studies indicate a strong connection between battering and incest, a connection that exists on more than one level. Just as there is a high statistical incidence of boys who witness fathers battering their mothers growing up to become batterers themselves, so there is a high incidence of fathers *and brothers* having incest with female children in those families where the father is a batterer. It is my firm belief that rape, battery, and incest are strongly interrelated; all are crimes against women or young children, committed by men who want power and control.

We know that a high percentage of battered women are incest survivors. While there is a great deal of controversial new research going on now in the study of incest—and while I am somewhat loath to jump into the theorizing fray until more facts are brought to light—I have long hypothesized a connection between the early oversexualization of an incest survivor and her ability, later in life, to become seduced by a batterer.*

Incest survivors often have missed out on learning human intimacy during the preteen "same sex friendship" stage of childhood. Because the incest survivor often has no experience with developing emotional intimacy as a prelude to sexual intimacy, she often has little ability to differentiate between different types of intimacy. Later, there may be no period of intercession between emotional and sexual love with her battering partner. These relationships very quickly become inordinately intense, with sexual attraction intimacy's only conduit. The payoff, as in all battering relationships, is a great amount of shared nurturance during the "good" times. There is no realization on the part of the woman that this intensity is not normal; she has nothing

*But it is also entirely possible that so many battered women are incest survivors simply because both incest and battery are highly prevalent forms of abuse against women.

"normal" in her own past, her own childhood, with which to compare the adult relationship.

If it is obvious to a trained observer that she is living in great danger, it must be remembered that safety is something the incest survivor has rarely known. What she has known well is violation and invasion, and living in constant fear of suffering violence at the hands of someone she loves. In this sense, then, it is no surprise that a high percentage of battered women are survivors of incest. For the incest survivor, being hurt by those who are supposed to love and protect her is nothing new.

It is easier to develop compassion for a woman whose children have been sexually ravaged when her own history of sexual abuse is better understood. These women are placed in a no-win situation (especially now, with the reliability of young children's allegations of incest being challenged by fathers' rights groups). If a mother suspects that her child is being sexually abused by her battering husband and reports it, she must be prepared to immediately seek some kind of safe shelter. More often than not, the abuser will be filled with homicidal rage toward her when he learns that his secret is out in the open. And if the sexual abuse is revealed during a hotly contested divorce, with child custody at issue, a mother's chances of being believed are much less than are the chances of her abuser's allegations being believed; she will often be accused of lying to keep her husband away from his own children. Courts do not like to deny a man access to his child.

This problem is one whose seriousness cannot be overstated. An abused child may be too frightened to reveal the truth of the molestation until the batterer is out of the home for good. These same dynamics are at work in the case of the mother, the battered woman, who finds herself also unable to reveal the extent of the abuse she has suffered until she feels reasonably safe from retaliation.

The current trend toward awarding joint custody of children, even in families with a history of violence, places both the battered woman and her children in continuous, grave danger.

MAGGIE'S STORY

Although she had long been battered by Chuck and knew the violence of which he was capable, Maggie wouldn't believe her fifteen-year-old daughter's complaints at first. Carol kept telling her that Chuck was coming on to her sexually.

Teenagers are always trying to put a wedge between mothers and stepfathers, Maggie thought, echoing Chuck's complaints to her. *My daughter's just jealous of the time and attention I'm giving him; she just wants to start trouble.*

When Carol failed to stop complaining and her behavior began to deteriorate, Maggie had her placed in an adolescent treatment center. As Maggie went for counseling with the staff there, her thinking changed. She found that she was able to stop blaming her child and to begin considering her husband's real behavior.

It's true, she finally concluded, in horror. *I'm sure she's telling the truth. He has molested her.*

Maggie was flooded with difficult emotion. Fear for her own safety was now mingled with fear for her daughter's. Mixed in with the terror, too, was a deeply felt rage. *How dare he!* she kept saying, silently, to herself. *How dare he touch her!*

She realized that she could no longer bear to live with Chuck, a realization that battered women commonly come to, given time, after they learn of their husbands' incestuous behavior. Maggie worked up courage and decided to confront Chuck with what she knew, and she did. But Chuck denied it.

Maggie wouldn't back down, though. When he continued to deny it, she told him to get out.

"No," he pleaded with her. "Don't throw away our love just because that juvenile delinquent daughter of yours is lying about me. She's just jealous—she wants you to choose her over me—and now you're giving in to another of her whims."

Maggie held her ground. While she had finally come to believe her daughter, Chuck's protestations only convinced her more. She insisted that he get out, feeling strong now—even, for once, righteous in her demands. She told Chuck that she would be gone for a few hours, during which time she'd pick Carol up from the treatment center. By the time they returned home, she said, she wanted him gone. She had the right to demand this; the house was in her name, having been awarded to her when she'd divorced Carol's father.

Maggie left for several hours. She picked Carol up. Together, they returned to the house to pack some clothes. Chuck had gone, it seemed; they planned to leave town for a few days together, though, until he really understood that Maggie had meant it: the marriage was definitely over.

Some time later that afternoon, in between packing and setting the house in order, Maggie stopped at a K-Mart to buy bullets. She wanted them for one of the guns Chuck normally left in the house. She didn't really need any; there were bullets for his guns all over the place, in every drawer. But Maggie was becoming terrified that Chuck wouldn't leave quietly; she wanted to feel protected and prepared. While Carol was busy packing, she kept watch outside the home. Sometimes, she cried. She was so afraid of Chuck, and at one point that afternoon expressed her fears to her daughter.

"He's going to come back," she said, desperately, "I just know it."

Finally, frightened herself, Carol went to a neighbor's house to arrange for help should they need it. Meanwhile Maggie paced back and forth, sinking deeper and deeper into terror, finding herself unable to make decisions about packing anything. Until the terror came true—Chuck drove up. He got out of his car and starting walking toward the front door, toward her.

"Don't come in here!" she warned through the door. "I told you to get out. Just go away!"

"No!" he yelled. "This is my house, and I'll do what I want!"

"You know it's my house," she responded, panicking. "Just go away! We're leaving anyhow."

Her last comment must have set off all his worst fears of

abandonment. Without warning, he came storming toward the door.

"Get away from me!" Maggie yelled. "I've got a gun and I'll shoot you if you try to come in!"

She and Carol had put a chain on the door. They'd stuck a kitchen chair up under the doorknob.

Why don't those friends of mine hurry? Maggie thought.

But no one came to stop Chuck as he burst into the house, smashing through all barriers. No one was there to protect Maggie.

Except Maggie herself, who kept shooting the gun she held, again and again, as he came toward her. Finally, he fell.

"She just stood there and lay in wait until her husband came home," the prosecutor told a jury.* "She led him into ambush. She and her daughter plotted this poor, innocent, law-abiding citizen's death."

Ignored by the state's attorneys were the long histories of battering and sexual abuse in this case. Hospital records had reflected Carol's disclosure of her stepfather's molestation several weeks prior to the homicide; she could not have simply concocted such an accusation of incest on the spur of the moment in order to protect her mother.

The defense attorney showed all the pertinent records to the jury. He described Maggie's long history as a battered woman in this relationship and was able to make use of my expert witness testimony to persuade them that all the family violence described by the defendant had occurred.

As embarrassing as it was for her, Maggie's daughter got on the witness stand and told the jurors exactly what Chuck had done to her. Her mother's ability to finally believe in her, to take actions

---

*In most states, those who purchase ammunition must sign a special form, which is kept on file. Maggie's form was later brought into the trial and brandished dramatically by the prosecution as intended proof, no doubt, that the homicide had been premeditated.

to protect her, had helped her begin to heal from her trauma. Now, she said, it was her turn to protect her mother if she could by telling that jury the truth.

Maybe the jurors really did understand the full implications of Chuck's brutal and despicable behavior. It does seem to be the case that most women who kill a man guilty of committing sexual abuse against their daughters are judged favorably. The prosecution sought a first-degree murder conviction, but the jury found Maggie not guilty.

Maggie was lucky. Justice was done in her case. Also, because of the strong bond of belief, trust, and mutual protection established between mother and daughter, Carol exhibited signs of becoming a strong, cognizant survivor of sexual abuse, rather than just a victim.

But the following story describes two women, also a mother and her daughter, who were not so fortunate.

LINDA'S STORY

Linda knew there was a strange bond between her husband, Joe, and her oldest daughter, Angela. Even though there was something about it that had never quite felt right to her, she found that despite herself she would let Angela go off with Joe alone. At least that way she could grab a few peaceful moments with her younger daughter and son. When Joe was off alone somewhere with Angela, he could be counted on not to beat and abuse the rest of them.

Like many incest victims, Angela hated her mother openly by the time she'd reached adolescence.* She ran away from home

---

*For the victim, incest is a double-edged sword comprising her conflicting wishes to be saved from further victimization and to hide the terrible secret. Many daughters who are victims of incest expect their mothers to know, to protect them, despite the fact that they go to great lengths to cover up the incest themselves (sometimes to protect their already abused mothers); they are thus

for the first time at the age of fourteen (a common way for a girl to attempt to terminate incest).

Although Linda's friends kept telling her that it looked as if Joe was sexually abusing Angela, both Joe and Angela denied it when Linda confronted them. They accused her of having a filthy mind. Linda handled this new round of family conflict poorly; she was growing more angry with her daughter, less capable of mothering her. Accusations flew back and forth between them. Linda finally sent Angela to live with her aunt in Mississippi, away from the mess of her own life, she hoped.

But with Angela gone, things kept getting worse, and more violent, between her and Joe. She became more and more depressed. She began to contemplate suicide. She even began keeping a loaded gun, just in case she finally decided to kill herself.

The day arrived when, during another one of their violent battering encounters, Joe came at her in their driveway with a tire iron. Linda took out the gun she'd been keeping ready (for shooting herself) and shot him instead.

She kept shooting long after he'd fallen dead by the side of his car.

When she learned what had happened, Angela was heartbroken.

The prosecutor appointed to Linda's case located her and paid her travel expenses (plus a cash living allowance) to bring her back home for the trial. On the witness stand, Angela denied her

---

left in the untenable position of being both family scapegoat and guardian of the family's self-protective denial. Professionals often perpetuate this stance by continuing to blame mothers for not taking positive action against their men. This attitude relieves the incest perpetrator—who is often a batterer, too—from taking ultimate responsibility for his actions, at the same time perpetuating unfortunate woman-blaming stereotypes. From the point of view of the therapeutic process, it also perpetuates the emotional distance between victimized mothers and daughters, a distance that must be addressed if a child is to heal from her incest experience.

own incest vehemently. "My mother's always hated me," she testified. "Everything I've ever wanted, she's taken away from me."

Somehow, the necessity of winning this case took precedence, in the prosecutor's mind, over the necessity of saving Angela, then sixteen years old, from a life filled with irreparable emotional scars that come from having been abused sexually and psychologically, from having been exposed to violence and homicide, from lying in order to testify against one's own mother.

Like other members of families living in the shadow of violence, Linda and Angela were ripped apart. The state and its system of so-called justice exacerbated the violence already done to them. Rather than using its authority to ensure that the survivors go about the process of healing and getting on with their lives, it used misguided notions of law to perpetuate a dead man's abuse.

Linda was convicted of manslaughter, sentenced to prison, and released after spending three years in prison. She proved willing to work, to attempt to put together the shattered remnants of her life. But Angela, by that time a severely disturbed teenager, had had two babies out of wedlock, one of whom died in infancy. Unable to work, she lived on welfare. Her parenting was supervised by social service agencies; her surviving child was shuffled in and out of foster care homes. And she herself may never recover sufficiently to live a reasonably happy or productive life.

What justice has been served here?

Children in battering situations, sensing the mother's inability to protect herself and them from continued harassment and violence, learn to protect themselves as best they can. They may even become their mothers' protectors at times, learning to "parent their parents" as a way of keeping everyone as safe as possible.

Sometimes, too, other family members will intervene.

DIANE'S STORY

Diane knew her husband was acting oddly around her ten-year-old daughter. She thought she'd go crazy every time he hit her. But the child said he did "worse things" when he took her into the bedroom alone to punish her.

Only the child knew exactly what went on, but she was too frightened to tell Diane. And Diane was afraid to confront her husband directly. He'd beaten her severely in the past and, she knew, he would have no qualms about doing so again. She was afraid that the next time he'd kill her.

Diane did tell her brother, though.

Together with a friend of his, her brother took Diane's husband for a car ride into the hills above Portland, Oregon. Her husband's body was later found up there, bludgeoned to death. There were still blood stains in the car.

Rather than go to trial—where, to save herself, she would probably have to testify against her brother—Diane pleaded guilty to the comparatively lesser charge of soliciting murder. She was sentenced to nine years in prison. I was asked to testify on her behalf at the sentencing hearing.

"Don't you think this woman has a responsibility," said the judge, "to stop protecting her brother?"

"No, your honor. In a family already tarnished by betrayal, such loyalty may help all of them, including the child, to heal."

"But, Dr. Walker. This is murder. Don't you think murderers should pay for their crimes?"

"Well, your honor," I replied, "my moral views aren't relevant here. Only my professional views are important, and I've already stated them." I crossed my fingers silently then, hoping that the judge wouldn't be too annoyed at my brazenness. Hoping, too, that he wouldn't push me any further.

I was lucky. He allowed me to get back to safer ground; under defense attorney Larry Matasar's questioning, I was able to tell what I could about Diane's state of mind as a battered woman, how it had caused her to accurately and reasonably perceive physical danger to herself and her children. In a conspiracy case, it is more difficult to testify effectively about the perceived imminence of danger, since the typical acute battering situation isn't always present. However, it's important to make it clear that battered women always feel endangered and, furthermore, that it is reasonable for many of them to perceive ever-present danger.

After her initial confession to the police, Diane never again implicated her brother or anyone else in her husband's death. But her brother was subsequently convicted and sentenced to life in prison (on the same circumstantial evidence used against Diane), while the man who had actually inflicted the fatal blows was never tried, due to lack of evidence.

I had never met a family more relieved to have the batterer dead. His behavior had been relentlessly brutal. But judges, like juries, want to see remorse in a homicide defendant and are likely to reward a display of remorse with a lighter sentence. They do not understand that, by the time actual murder has occurred in a violent family, the surviving family members may simply be so emotionally exhausted that all they are immediately capable of feeling, or of expressing, is relief that the abuse and terror have finally ceased.

According to Oregon law, Diane would have to spend only about two and a half years in prison, because she had no prior record. (Actually, she was released after serving sixteen months because of good behavior, and because of other circumstances that warranted her presence with her children.) It was a pretty good deal for her, and no one, including me, wanted to spoil it.

As further justification of my belief in Diane, today she holds a responsible job working on behalf of abused and neglected children.

In the next case, incest also played a major role. But the legal outcome was different.

NELLIE'S STORY

In Nellie's family, the incest victim was her stepdaughter, Sue (her husband's daughter from a former marriage). Nellie had always thought that the little secrets they seemed to share between them and the excluding behavior they demonstrated when together were strange; she had trouble understanding her own feelings of jealousy when she was around the two of them. For a while, she tried to pretend that her feelings didn't exist. She was a little ashamed of herself for resenting Hal's relationship with his own daughter, a common problem for many stepmothers.

But when the girl told Nellie she was pregnant with her father's child, Nellie came unglued. She confronted Hal, and he denied it vehemently; but she knew that his daughter had not lied. For quite a while, Hal had been beating her, and her love for him had been diminishing all along. Now, she knew, she could never feel love for him again.

Soon after Sue's disclosure, another argument between Nellie and Hal instigated an acute battering incident. In the midst of threatening her and abusing her verbally, Hal stopped to pick a knife up from the dish drainer. That was when Nellie ran to the sofa and pulled out the gun she'd hidden there, just in case.

Hal turned to her, holding the knife. When he saw the gun in her hand, he ran into the bedroom, slamming the door shut behind him.

Nellie emptied the gun through the closed door. Later, she'd remember hearing him fall as he yelled out her name.

More than one of the shots could have killed him. But she had been so victimized and beaten by this man that she was still terrified he'd get up somehow and come back after her. So she reloaded the gun as quickly as she could, then emptied it by shooting through the closed door again.

Nellie waited a while, until she heard no more sounds. Slowly she pushed the bullet-riddled door open. It was hard to move; her husband was lying right against it. The movement upset his still body; his hand, still clutching the kitchen knife in a death grip, flew up toward Nellie. She jumped back screaming, certain that he was still alive and coming to get her.

Finally, after a long wait, she worked up enough courage to look back into the bedroom and see that he really was dead.

At Nellie's trial, her stepdaughter testified for the prosecution. She portrayed Nellie as a jealous bitch and recited every fight they'd had. The death of her father had successfully erased from her memory any hint of the genuine loving relationship that had at one time existed between her and Nellie. She denied, too, that she was pregnant with her father's child.

But Ivan Lebanoff, Nellie's attorney, mounted a spectacular and successful defense. Knowledge of her husband's incest with his own daughter, Ivan said, had proven to Nellie once and for all that he was a man who set no limits on his own behavior. Would she have been as frightened of Hal during her own beatings, had she not found out he was also a perpetrator of incest? At one point in the trial, Ivan showed Nellie the knife Hal had threatened her with. Nellie jumped out of the witness stand, shaking with terror.

The jury found that Nellie had committed justifiable homicide. They delivered a verdict of not guilty.

The average person very often protects himself or herself from experiencing the battered woman's terror by participating in its cover-up. If a battered woman can be labeled as "passively not caring about herself," as "hysterical," as "making much ado about nothing," or characterized as a "provocative, angry bitch who stirs up trouble and only gets what she deserves," then others will not have to acknowledge her genuine pain. Victim-blaming makes those who fear that they, too, could be victims feel temporarily safe.

As explained earlier, the most dangerous time in a battering relationship is at the point of potential separation. Yet this is also the time when our entire judicial system—and, very often, the professional community—turns out to be the least helpful.

Judges and child custody evaluators may mistake the love that abusive fathers have for their children (and these fathers' willingness to spend time with their children) as evidence of adequate parenting skills. Undoubtedly, if motivation and good intentions were the cure, many batterers would stop their abusive behavior immediately. But that doesn't happen with the women they love, nor will it happen in their relationships with their children. I fear that judges who assign custody to the father, or joint custody, are creating a new generation of batterers and thus of battered women. Children often identify with a father's coercive behavior. Seeing it as a method of gaining power and control, they begin to model their own relationship patterns along similar lines. In battered women's shelters, it is not uncommon to see children as young as two years old controlling their mothers by using the same language and mannerisms they've seen their fathers use. By the age of five, many children, particularly boys, want their father's approval so much that they will do nothing to jeopardize it. By allowing them as much exposure to the batterer's behavior as is allowed in joint custody situations, our system aids and abets these children—in their own victimization, in mimicry, or in both.* Exposure to the batterer even after divorce convinces the child that he or she is truly unprotected, that there is no place to hide; it forces innocent children to negotiate the complex and frightening world of adult violence without a guide.

The result of a child being raised in violence without any help or guidance is that the child will become an adult living in, and sometimes perpetrating, violence. The next story is a tragic illustration of this syndrome.

*Dr. Geraldine Stahley, a psychologist at California State University at San Bernardino who works closely with battered women's shelters in southern California, has begun to develop programs to intervene with these children in hopes of preventing the continuing development of their abusive behavior patterns. She believes that these children need to learn to develop empathy, the ability to feel what another person feels, particularly their pain upon being abused.

DEBBIE'S STORY

Debbie Gindorf was nineteen when the public defender assigned to her case asked me to come to the jail in Waukeegan, Illinois, where she was in custody. She was charged with the murder of her two children: a two-year-old daughter, and a three-month-old son.

The state had added special circumstances to the charge and, claiming aggravating factors, seemed determined to pursue the death penalty. None of the usual forensic psychiatrists or psychologists were willing to work on the case; the lawyers said everyone was too appalled at the nature of her crime.

When I entered the jail's interview room, I was immediately struck by the childlike appearance of the dirty, disheveled young woman sitting there. It was hard to get her to smile, but when she did she looked even younger than her nineteen years.

Debbie told me she had been abused her entire life—first by a mother who neglected her and her brothers and sisters before abandoning them, then by her father and his new wife. When she met and fell in love with Paul, she said, even his neglectful, violently abusive behavior was better than what she'd known. When she found out she was pregnant, they got married. But she was young and lacked any parenting skills whatsoever. Paul left her alone a lot; she became more and more depressed. Finally, when she became pregnant a second time, he deserted her for another woman.

Never fully recovered from the depression she'd suffered after the birth of her first child, Debbie fell into a severe postpartum depression after the birth of her second. All alone with two young children and desperate, she looked for help at a local mental health clinic, where she was assigned to a male psychology intern who performed a complete battery of standardized psychological tests but failed to help her. Getting two infants dressed and to the clinic with her was difficult. To top it all off, Paul kept stealing her car. Still, she tried the best she could. Neighbors later remarked that her children always seemed well fed and well dressed, and that their home was always clean. Debbie was determined that the kids have a better life than she'd had; still, she felt so tired and depressed all the time that she doubted her ability to keep functioning. As time wore on, she became suicidal.

Finally she reached a point where dying seemed preferable to living. One day she sat down and composed letters to both her children so that, when they grew up, they would understand why she'd killed herself. She paid the gas and electric bills for their small apartment, put some money in two envelopes for them, then got a friend to drive her to a local drugstore, where she bought some over-the-counter sleeping pills. Back home, she suddenly remembered her last conversation with her mother. In her mind, she heard her mother repeat the words, over and over: "Don't think you can leave your children with me. They're your babies and you'll find a way to raise them. I'm not going to raise your own children for you." Alone in the apartment, these words seemed to take on a life and a meaning to Debbie; it was then that she decided that the only way to keep her babies safe was to take them with her. God, she thought, could take care of her babies in heaven. But no one would take care of them here on earth.

Debbie bought a bottle of scotch to go along with the sleeping pills. She picked the children up from the neighbor who'd been watching them and returned to her apartment.

Then she took out the sleeping pill capsules and poured all the powder into one large pile. She divided it up into a larger amount for herself, a smaller amount for her two-year-old, and an even smaller amount for her three-month-old infant. Then she straightened the room up so that God would look favorably upon them all. She added the baby's portion of sleeping pill powder to his formula, and the two-year-old's portion to her juice bottle. She fed it to them, singing them to sleep. Then she took the powder she'd saved for herself, washing it down with scotch.

Instead of dying, though, Debbie became violently ill and began vomiting. Retching, disoriented, she lay on the floor expecting to die.

When she awoke the next morning she found the dead bodies of her children lying next to her. Horrified, she tried to smother herself with a pillow. Then she slit her wrists with a knife. She tied a rope around her neck, turned on the gas oven and lay down again next to her children, passing out momentarily. But she awoke again some time later and, shocked at still being alive, tried to put her head in the oven.

Then she walked in a daze to the nearest police station and told them what she'd done.

Armed with my findings about the battering, neglect, and abuse Debbie had suffered in her own childhood, I determined that she was a battered woman with an observable case of Post Traumatic Stress Disorder and that she also suffered severely from postpartum depression. Her attorney entered a plea of not guilty by reason of insanity, and decided to present the evidence in closed hearing before a judge rather than take his chances with a jury trial. If found insane, Debbie would be sent to the state hospital, where hopefully she would finally receive treatment until she was competent and then some day be released.

Debbie Gindorf's trial took only a few days. But the outcome was as strange as the rest of her young life had been.

The judge agreed with both prosecutor and defense attorney that Debbie had been mentally ill at the time she had killed her children. But instead of finding her not guilty by reason of insanity, the usual verdict in such a case, he found her *guilty, but mentally ill.* This unusual verdict saved her from a death sentence, but it forced the judge to sentence her to the state hospital for the criminally insane until such time as she might be found competent, *and then to prison for the rest of her life!*

Debbie did go to the hospital for the criminally insane. With the care she received there, she improved rapidly and recovered from postpartum depression and PTSD. From the state hospital, though, she went immediately to the state penitentiary.

Since then, all her appeals have been denied. She is in prison, hoping for a clemency pardon from the governor.

Such are the wages of child abuse and domestic violence: an unending cycle of further abuse and violence, mental illness, suicide, and murder. The helpless are victimized most. And sometimes, in these cases, it is difficult to determine where the victimization stops and the perpetration begins.

9

"CRAZY LADIES"

C LINICAL PSYCHOLOGY, the branch of psychology in which mental disorders are studied, explains only a very small part of the field of human behavior, although it is this part of psychology with which the general public is most familiar. This fact can be a problem when professionals with no expertise in the field of battered women, but with impressive professional psychological or psychiatric credentials, testify in a court of law, and it is one reason why only a qualified expert witness should testify in any trial involving a battered woman who kills.

The behavior of battered women who kill their abusers needs to be understood as *normal,* not abnormal. Defending oneself from reasonably perceived imminent danger of bodily harm or death ought to be considered a psychologically healthy response. Most battered women who kill do so in self-defense, not because they are mentally disordered. And the expert witness who can provide judges and juries with a genuine understanding of this fact can have a critical role in changing our criminal justice system's inadequate response to the entire problem.*

*A battered woman's rights are tenuous when it comes to mental health evaluations, and should be strenuously protected by both legal and clinical

169

Psychoanalysts who believe that internal mental conditions alone, and not external circumstances, cause mental illness ought to take note of this contradiction. The symptoms of mental illness displayed by many battered women tend to quickly clear up once they are able to live without fear of further violence. Given the

---

professionals. Many victims of violence who file civil actions to recover damages are required to sign release forms, allowing the defense to look into any previous mental or physical condition they may have had. (This occurs when the victim of violence has put her mental health at issue in suing for personal injury.) The defense is permitted to research how much, if any, of the individual's current mental health disorder is due to the litigated trauma and how much might have existed prior to the violent incident. Some states, however, now insist that the presiding judge apply a "balancing test" between the victim's right to confidential treatment and the opposing side's right to know. Personally, I never release raw test data or records of therapy sessions without first asking the presiding judge to make such a ruling. (In Colorado, this is referred to as a Bond hearing; most attorneys in the state are, unfortunately, still unfamiliar with its ability to provide protection for victims of violence.)

I've found that, in those cases in which I've filed an affidavit with the court—stating my professional opinion that to turn over any such records would jeopardize my client's treatment—the court has rarely ordered me to turn over the records. I do sometimes disclose much of what is contained in certain clinical records during a deposition, but this does not have nearly the same impact on ·a client as does the sudden discovery that her most personal confidences with a therapist have been exposed and attached to any number of legal documents, blatantly violating trust and damaging the therapeutic process. As a rule of thumb, no record should be turned over to *any* investigator without first discussing it with the client. Likewise, it is important for shelter workers to obtain legal opinion from a representative lawyer before turning over any records to the court (even with the woman's permission). In some communities, legislative rulings protect victims of violence from having their therapy records turned over to any attorney to be used against them in a court of law. As more and more victims turn to litigation to redress wrongs done to them, this issue of control of confidential records becomes a critical civil rights issue.

I will stress here, as a note to mental health professionals, that if a therapist believes a woman really *is* about to kill someone, that therapist is both ethically and, in many states, legally obliged to notify the police, and maybe even the intended victim, of the danger. On the other hand, if the woman's statement is not thought to be a serious threat, then it does not belong in the records in the first place. In all cases, the professional must exercise careful judgment.

facts that 70 percent of out-patient psychotherapy clients are women and that a majority of institute-trained practicing clinical psychiatrists are men, maybe it's true that women have been "bamboozled" into thinking they are insane for men's economic gain.

A lot of "crazy" ladies aren't so crazy, after all.

A battered woman often adopts unusual behavior that earns her a diagnosis of insanity, of being "crazy." In fact, many of her seemingly bizarre actions may have purpose and logic when viewed within the context of the violence and terror in which she lives.

In context, the "crazy" actions of battered women may be effective survival techniques. Diagnoses of mental illness, delivered by uninformed medical personnel and mental health professionals, are often wrong. And, as we will see in the stories told in this chapter, these women usually abandon their abnormal behavior when they are finally free of the insane, terrifying circumstances that produced such behavior in the first place.

ROBERTA'S STORY

Roberta's marriage to Jay had been a long-term battering relationship. The physical abuse had stopped for about a year; after an acute battering incident in which Jay had actually stuck his hand up Roberta's rectum and tried to rip out her intestines, leaving her to die. Luckily, Roberta's sister found her and took her to the hospital. After several operations, including a colostomy, Roberta managed to survive.

A year later, when Jay hit her and threatened to rip out her windpipe, she knew that he meant it. In reasonable fear for her life, she entered what in psychological jargon is called a dissociative state—going into a sort of automatic-pilot mode in order to survive. Roberta experienced a flashback of the previous brutal incident in which she'd almost been killed; then she had an out-of-body experience.

Roberta saw herself escape from Jay's grasp.

She observed herself walking into the bedroom, and finding and loading the shotgun they kept there.

She watched herself walk back into the living room, where Jay sat, momentarily absorbed in some TV program.

She watched them both then, as if in slow motion: Jay stood and moved toward her; she raised the gun calmly, without aiming. She shot him, and he fell.

Then, just as slowly and calmly, she walked back into the bedroom and put the gun away, right where it belonged.

Jay managed to stagger to his feet again. Bleeding profusely from the mouth, he got to the telephone and dialed for help. A police dispatch tape recorded his gurgled, unintelligible plea.

After he dropped the phone, Roberta picked it up. The dispatch tape recorded her then, alternately yelling at him to die and whispering how much she loved him. She also sobbed frantically that she couldn't find the site of the wound to apply pressure to it, as the dispatcher was instructing her to do. (The bullet had entered through Jay's open mouth, and the site of the wound was inside his head, a fact that, in her traumatized state, Roberta could not have known.) Most of the dispatch recording was filled with her screams of anguish and terror.

As Roberta would later describe it, none of this behavior had seemed under her control at the time. It was, she said, as if she'd been a bystander at the scene of a crime or somebody watching a movie. She even used third-person language when telling her story. The trance was broken, she said, when she'd heard her five-year-old son come into the room screaming.

The prosecutor assigned to the case had a transcript of the police dispatch recording typed up, and it got published in the local newspaper. (He used it during his cross-examination of me, after I'd testified about my opinion that Roberta had shot Jay in self-defense.)

I sat up throughout most of the following night with Roberta's attorney Caroll Multz, trying desperately to figure out how to help the jury understand Roberta's state of mind at the time of the homicide. Insanity could not be an issue here, despite the fact that she had indisputably been in a dissociative state at the time, because in Colorado a separate plea must be entered to prove an insanity defense. We had our work cut out for us: we'd have to demonstrate, in no uncertain terms, that, even though Roberta had been under terrible stress that had altered her behavior to the point where it was well outside of so-called "normal," she still had been able to reasonably perceive Jay's dangerous behavior. His behavior had caused her to go into a dissociative state, but she had killed him in self-defense.

Caroll and I listened to the police dispatch tape over and over. Finally, it occurred to us to compare it to the prosecutor's transcript copy that had been printed in the newspaper. Sure enough, there were many discrepancies. The published version had omitted Roberta's soft pleas ("Don't die, Jay, please don't die" and "I love you, Jay") but had left in the more incriminating quotes ("If you die, I'll kill you" and "Goddamn you, die already").

The next morning, back on the witness stand, I played the dispatch tape for the jury. Starting and stopping it to make sure they heard the parts that were missing from the typed transcripts they'd been given,* I explained as clearly as I could what the recorded tone of Roberta's voice indicated about her emotional state. My years of teaching stood me in good stead. Apparently, the lecture format was so convincing that one of the jurors raised his hand to ask a question. Forgetting momentarily that I was in a courtroom, not a classroom, I called on him!

The day before, I had explained the meaning of the term "dissociative state"; now I reviewed it. In trial after trial, I had found that explanations are most effective when accompanied by familiar examples. At this trial, too, I tried to make the concept easily comprehensible. When people are preoccupied with thinking about one thing, I told the jury, their focus narrows and

*The state's clearly intentional omission of crucial transcript evidence was, to my way of thinking, itself a prosecutable offense.

they don't remember paying attention to other things around them.

"For example," I said, "if you're preoccupied with solving a business problem while you're driving home from work, you may arrive in front of your house without actually recalling anything that happened during the drive. Obviously, you drove home properly—you got there safe and sound—but you probably don't remember stopping at any lights, passing any particular cars on the road, or other details of the trip. You've made that same trip so many times before that you're on automatic pilot. The memory loss you experience because of this is due to a mild form of something we call *selective psychogenic amnesia,* which occurs during a *dissociative state.*"

The intense concentration used to think about the hypothetical business problem, I explained, caused all those other details of the trip to recede from a person's awareness. Although that individual might not realize it at the time, he or she had been paying careful attention to all those other details on another level of consciousness. This situation, I told them, was similar to being in a state of mild hypnosis. If something demanding the driver's full attention were suddenly to occur, such as a road block, he or she immediately would have automatically snapped out of it.

I could tell, that day, that the jury was fully involved in the testimony; each one of them had fully comprehended the impact of dissociative states and would keep it in mind when attempting to reach a verdict. Even the judge seemed impressed.

This was the turning point Caroll and I had hoped for; Roberta's future seemed less uncertain. It seemed to us all that we had gotten beyond the hurdle thrown in our path by the prosecution's seemingly malicious omission of recorded evidence. And, in fact, justice prevailed in this case. Roberta, who had suffered at the hands of a brutal husband for so long—sustaining permanent physical injury and illness, and being pushed nearly over the brink into a state of insanity—was acquitted.

Unfortunately, Roberta died from cancer a few years later.

Perhaps the delicate, healthy balance of mind and body gave way under the severe stress of repeated abuse.

Dissociative states are common among all victims of abuse and trauma. Victims learn this mild form of self-hypnosis in order to protect themselves from terror and physical pain; in short, they learn to separate their minds from their bodies. Like Roberta, many victims of violence describe out-of-body experiences, times during which they observed themselves acting without apparent voluntary control.

The intense concentration battered women develop to protect themselves from physical danger can itself cause this kind of dissociative state. During an acute battering incident, the abused woman often does not feel the blows. Later, though, she may be able to describe what happened in great detail. And, like Roberta, she will often use third-person language, as if describing the actions of someone else.

But does a dissociative state meet the legal definition of insanity?

Or is it a normal reaction, in a way, "normal," at least, for someone who experiences repeated physical, sexual, and psychological abuse without seeing any way to escape, "normal" for someone suffering from Battered Woman Syndrome?

Legal Definitions of Insanity

The M'Naughten Rule was this country's original measure of legal insanity.* Essentially, it stated that the crucial test of legal insanity was to determine whether or not the accused understood the difference between right and wrong.

Finding this definition too restrictive, legislators added a

---

*M'Naughten 8 Eng. Rep. 718 (1843) was the original case in English common law from which we adopted our own insanity statutes.

rider to it as stated in the *Model Penal Code* (1982): was the accused capable of conforming his or her behavior to the community standard? In other words: not only did accused individuals have to know "right" from "wrong" to be considered legally sane; they also had to have community-approved control over their overt actions.

Sure enough, in many jurisdictions the conjunctive definition (the M'Naughten rule plus the rider) was seen as too restrictive, and either part was then recognized as an operational definition of legal insanity. Thus, if a person knew right from wrong but nevertheless could not stop from behaving impulsively in "abnormal" ways, an insanity defense would be possible. In this sense, a dissociative state, in which a person might know right from wrong but be unable to conform behaviorally because her mind was temporarily out of conscious control, would fit that definition of insanity. (It is my opinion, though, that in some dissociative states, the individual does not even "know" the difference between right and wrong, since the legal definition of "know" often presumes mental control, which is not present.)

Legal definitions of insanity have changed a great deal since the early 1980s, many of these changes the result of the nation's outrage when John Hinckley (the man who shot then-President Ronald Reagan) was found legally insane and judged not guilty. In the Hinckley case, teams of eminent doctors were put together by lawyers on each side, each team providing expert witness testimony to contradict the opposing team's expert witness testimony. (Ironically, the law firm of Williams and Connolly, the same firm with which I'd worked on the Beverly Ibn-Tamas case, a case that helped pave the way for battered women's use of the self-defense plea, provided Hinckley with the successful defense that caused a nation-wide reexamination of our insanity laws.) As the arguments of these various professionals were made public, demonstrating how differently mental health professionals think and how differently they may evaluate the same client, the question of diagnostic accuracy became a national issue.

Legislators and professional groups alike began clamoring

for change in the system. New laws, they said, would "weed out" and lock up the dangerously insane before they committed acts of mayhem; then we'd all be safer.

But no one was willing, yet, to look inward: at the dangerous currents of violence running through so many areas of American culture, at the largely unremarked physical and sexual abuse taking place every day in the supposed sanctuary of our homes.

Prior to the Hinckley trial, the established definitions of legal insanity worked quite well. They were so difficult to meet that fewer than 5 percent of defendants ever used them. And rarely did anyone claiming legal insanity have to endure a trial by jury; most forensic psychiatrists work so closely with the courts that judges often use their conclusions to make the final decisions. Rarely, too, did psychologists, who are the best-trained in objective assessment methods of all mental health professionals when it comes to making diagnoses, get the chance to present their more systematic evaluations to the courts.

Since the Hinckley debacle, a series of confusing new judicial rulings have attempted to define when someone is both guilty *and* mentally ill*—an unusual and contradictory situation in a legal system that prefers to define criminal responsibility according to the *mens rea*, or actor's intent. By definition, mentally ill people cannot form intent, so how can they be considered legally guilty? Many of these new laws are so complicated and so unsupported by any legal precedent that they have been

---

*The federal Rules of Evidence differ from many state's rules; they do not permit trying an insanity defense and a factual defense together. Rather, if an insanity defense is raised, the government must proceed and prove that there are no grounds for it before going on to a separate trial on the facts. Some think this is a good system, since it does not confuse the two issues and also gives the defendant two chances for acquittal. Some states, like Colorado, follow the federal Rules of Evidence and bifurcate insanity trials. Even there, it is rare for a defendant to actually go on trial. Usually, psychologists and psychiatrists agree on a diagnosis and present their findings to the presiding judge, whereupon a verdict of not guilty by reason of insanity is adjudicated. Sentencing usually includes either in-patient and/or out-patient counseling.

used only infrequently in trials where I've testified as an expert witness.*

My personal feeling is that it is patently unfair to expect that lay people on a jury will be able to make diagnostic decisions that mental health professionals go to school for years to learn how to make. (Just because we mental health professionals often disagree on the meaning of various pieces of data doesn't mean that untrained people can be expected to do better.) And if it is unfair for lay people on a jury to be expected to make professional diagnoses, giving them that right is more than unfair to the person standing trial, and to our society at large. I realized long ago that an insanity defense really works well only when mental health professionals are allowed to battle it out with an enlightened judge as a referee. The confusion of new laws and regulations obscures the root of the problem: in most cases, defense by reason of insanity simply does not work, and attempting to determine sanity or insanity via a unanimous lay vote is one of the reasons why.

All defendants are victimized by the law's lack of clarity in this area. Especially victimized are those defendants who are already victims: including battered women, violated and silenced, mistakenly diagnosed as "crazy," mistakenly believed to be vindictively "angry," when they are really in fear for their lives, in fear for their own mental stability, which our society has already implicitly called into question.

Making a Diagnosis

The proper application of Battered Woman Syndrome can make many things clear in cases in which the sanity of a battered woman defendant is in question. Because it is a subcategory of

---

*The self-defense plea is still most common in those cases I have been involved in, although insanity or diminished capacity is appropriate in some cases.

Post Traumatic Stress Disorder, four specific criteria must be met, clinically measured, and evaluated for Battered Woman Syndrome to be assigned as a psychological diagnosis.*

The first criterion is the presence, in the life of the individual being evaluated, of a recognizable *traumatic stressor,* a source of extreme stress outside the normal experiential boundaries of most people, one that would be expected to evoke major symptoms of mental illness in those victimized by it. Spouse abuse is considered such a stressor.

The second criterion is the individual's *reexperiencing of past traumatic events* without willfully thinking of them. This reexperiencing can take the form of recurring nightmares, sleep disorders, daydreams, intrusive thoughts that the abuse is reoccurring, and flashbacks catalyzed by some reminder of the previous trauma. It involves the individual's experiencing a sense of powerlessness, a loss of control. The involved professional should note that it is not just what the patient describes, but how she describes it, that will confirm the presence of this particular criterion. In many cases, healing can be facilitated by allowing the victim to continue retelling the story of her trauma until she feels a sense of mastery over it.

The third criterion is *a numbing of emotions and avoidance of reminders of the abuse,* frequently resulting in a *disturbance in interpersonal relationships,* including a lessening of interest in other people and activities. For the battered woman, her abuser's possessiveness and pathological jealousy contribute to her isolation. She may become depressed, and is less and less likely to participate in social activity as time goes on. Along with her sense of isolation comes a belief that the batterer, intrusive and seemingly omnipotent as he is, can find out about everything she does and can somehow know everything she thinks.

The fourth criterion involves a combination of various

---

*According to section 309.81 of the American Psychiatric Association's *Diagnostic and Statistical Manual of Mental Disorders,* 3rd ed., revised (DSM-III-R).

symptoms indicating a *heightened arousal response,* only two of which need be present to complete a diagnosis of Battered Woman Syndrome. (Frequently, though, more than two are present in a battered woman.) These symptoms include *generalized anxiety, panic attacks, fears that evolve into full-blown phobias,* and, in the cases of battered women who have been sexually abused, certain *sexual dysfunctions.* Along with these symptoms comes a *hypervigilance to cues of further violence* (the woman may respond in a startled manner when touched or approached) and a heightened suspiciousness that often resembles certain types of paranoia. Sometimes she demonstrates sleep problems and becomes irritable, with outbursts of anger. (Any professional involved in evaluating a battered woman must keep in mind that the battered woman has every sane reason to act in such so-called insane ways.)

Although they are not included as official Post Traumatic Stress Disorder criteria, the presence of battered women's coping skills—such as minimization and denial of serious violence, dissociation, appearance of compliance and willingness to please, fear of confrontation or its opposite, frequent confrontations—are also diagnostic for Battered Woman Syndrome.

It is essential that we learn to recognize Battered Woman Syndrome for what it is: a terrified human being's *normal* response to an abnormal and dangerous situation. Psychiatrists and other helping professionals tend to confuse the effects of domestic abuse with "masochism," "borderline personality disorder," or any number of other inapplicable diagnoses. Those involved in diagnostic procedures must remember that, in the case of battered women, lives depend upon proper, knowledgeable, and accurate evaluations and conclusions.

We must also break through our denial about the severity of the sadistic manipulation and psychological control—amounting, in some cases, to real brainwashing—that a batterer may exert over a battered woman. The case of Hedda Nussbaum, described earlier, is an excellent example. Hedda's mind, however, was more seriously damaged than are the minds of most battered women I have worked with. In the end, she was truly unable to recognize reality from fantasy. Yet her ability to testify cogently at Joel Steinberg's trial is an equally powerful reminder that battered women are capable of functioning again, at least on some recognizably normal level, when they are far enough removed from the batterer and his terrorizing physical and psychological violence, especially when they get good support and professional help and intervention.

When free, once and for all, of the battering circumstance, most of these women cease to manifest any so-called behavioral disturbances or personality disorders, a fact that proves, to this professional, at any rate, that their previously abnormal behavior was directly caused by their victimization. When they are no longer victimized, the bizarre behavior disappears.

The following story provides a good example.

AGNES'S STORY

Agnes married Charlie after meeting him in church one Sunday, when she was a girl in her teens. The marriage would last more than thirty years. Hard-working people, Agnes and Charlie both held factory jobs at a Western Electric plant near where they lived. With their savings, they managed to buy a home. Together they raised two sons and a daughter.

As the years passed, Agnes noticed that Charlie's occasional psychological cruelty toward her and his verbal abuse of her were becoming more frequent. Once in a while, he'd even hit her. She began to suspect that he was sexually molesting their daughter, Linda. After one suspicious incident, Agnes never again allowed the girl to be alone with her father. She and Linda became very close. Their closeness increased as the boys grew into men and began to act more and more abusively, like Charlie.

Meanwhile, Charlie's threats became more serious. He told Agnes several times that one day he would kill her.

When Charlie's mother died (and Agnes believed that her death had been the result of an overdose of two antagonistic medications prescribed for her by one of her sons-in-law) Charlie's behavior deteriorated further. His threats became more frequent and more vicious, his psychological cruelty more acute. Naturally a worrier, Agnes agonized over her situation. Slowly, she began to develop private rituals, ways of acting that she hoped would somehow keep her safe.

Certain that he'd find some way to poison her, Agnes began refusing to eat any food that she hadn't personally prepared or watched being prepared. If she opened a can, then remained in view of the food in it from that time until the time it was served to her, it was all right; if, however, she turned away for a moment or left the room or refrigerated the left-overs, she could not eat it.

Soon her vigilance spread to cigarettes. If she put an opened pack on a table and left the room, she'd insist on getting a fresh, unopened pack.

She eventually developed a fear of germs. Agnes began to wear gloves to touch things Charlie had touched.

Charlie inherited a small home in a nearby town after his father's death. He and Agnes moved there; their son and daughter and their families continued to live in the house they grew up in. When Charlie refinished the floors in their new home, Agnes began to wear a surgical mask. She figured he might have let poisonous fumes loose into the air.

Agnes's fears became more powerful with time, especially her fear that Charlie would kill her. She tried to obtain relief by locking herself in her room and reading the Bible. But the obsessive thoughts became so omnipresent that her memory was affected. She stopped being able to concentrate while driving, so she stopped and therefore stopped going places. When she was laid off from her job, Agnes's isolation became truly complete. She'd spend entire days and nights in her room, which by now had several locks on the door. There, she felt sheltered in the dubious safety of her private world.

She and Charlie had stopped sharing a bed years before. Agnes knew he had girlfriends. And she suspected (rightly) that, in addition to Linda, he had sexually molested two other young relatives. Any love she'd felt for her husband had died a long time ago, but divorce was at first unthinkable for her, as she was an intensely religious person, utterly devoted to the concept of family. Throughout her life, nearly all of Agnes's socializing had taken place with members of her large, extended family.

Finally, though, the pain of isolation and of her own diseased thoughts became too much for Agnes. She decided that Charlie's worsening sadistic abuse left her no choice but to divorce him. The entire extended family, traditional though it was, accepted the fact that Agnes was getting divorced and, in their .own way, seemed to support her. She and Charlie even began discussing how to split up their property. But while these discussions were going on, his physical abuse of her increased. He didn't display any affection to her when he wasn't being abusive, nevertheless making it clear that the idea of separation was intolerable to him.

The summer before he died was an explosive time for this family. After several serious violent incidents initiated by Charlie, Agnes asked their youngest son, John, to move in with them. It seemed to everyone who knew them that something terrible would happen, yet no one did anything to intervene.

On Labor Day weekend, John went away for the holiday. Charlie and Agnes fought off and on throughout the holiday morning. At one point, Charlie locked himself out of the house. When Agnes let him back in, he pushed her down a flight of stairs. She crawled to a telephone to call the police. But at the moment she picked the phone up, she could hear no dial tone. She thought the wire might have been cut.

Agnes retreated into her room and locked herself in. This time, though, her rituals couldn't calm the rising terror. He was going to kill her, she thought; she just knew it.

Agnes got an old loaded gun out of the closet. Just having it near at hand, she thought, would make the panic go away. She crept out of the room and quietly secreted the gun in the kitchen cabinet. Then she returned to her room.

As the day wore on, Agnes found that she could barely tolerate the anxiety, the unrelieved tension. Charlie had gone downstairs, she knew; that was where he usually spent most of his time. But what was he doing? Was he making plans to kill her now? She thought she might feel safer if she knew. So she picked up the telephone again and, this time, heard a woman's voice.

Agnes unlocked all the locks on her door and went back into the kitchen. Charlie was there fully dressed, getting ready to leave.

"How dare you pick up the phone and listen in on my conversations?" he yelled.

Agnes noticed a familiar look in his eyes. She noticed that his face was beginning to distort, and there was a strange tone to his voice. These signs meant that he'd start beating her soon, either now or the moment he returned home.

She went to the kitchen cabinet, opened it, and took out the gun. She and Charlie struggled briefly over it.

The next thing she would remember was the sound of a single shot. Charlie turned and ran outside. Agnes followed him, the gun still in hand.

She wouldn't remember firing two more shots. But those shots missed him. He'd already fallen dead. The first bullet had pierced his heart.

My associate Bobbie Thyfault and I traveled to her hometown to perform Agnes's evaluation. (She was not physically strong enough to come to our Denver offices.) We spent two days interviewing first Agnes, then her daughter Linda.

From my preliminary interpretation of the evidence, it seemed to me that there were four possible defenses: insanity, self-defense, accidental homicide, or diminished capacity.

Before flying back to Denver, Bobbie and I met to discuss our findings with Agnes's attorneys. Had Charlie really intended to kill Agnes that day? We couldn't know for sure, but we only needed to know how *reasonable* her *perception* of imminent danger had been. If her perception had been based on reality, then she'd shot Charlie in self-defense; if her perception had been tainted by mental illness, she would have to plead either insanity or diminished capacity; if the fatal bullet had been fired by accident during Agnes's struggle with Charlie, she could plead accidental homicide. In any case, we would have to explain why she'd felt the need to bring the old gun out of storage in the first place. Agnes had said she'd placed it within easy reach in the kitchen cabinet because she was afraid Charlie would start beating her again. But if a jury believed the homicide had not been accidental, she could still be found guilty of voluntary manslaughter, which in her state could carry a fifteen-year prison term.

I recognized that it would benefit Agnes to bring another local psychologist in on her case. First, it would allow the jury to hear evidence provided by psychological test results from another professional, allowing me to concentrate my testimony entirely on how those results impacted on Battered Woman Syndrome. Second, it would be good to have another psychologist arrive at an opinion similar to mine but from a different clinical perspective, adding credibility to the defense. Third, I believed that Agnes needed supportive counseling to reduce her anxiety during the long wait for a trial. I could not offer this long distance; furthermore, I was afraid that her mental condition had deteriorated to the point where she might attempt suicide.

I asked my sister-in-law, Dr. Anne Auerbach, a licensed clinical psychologist, to work with us. At first she was hesitant, not sure she'd know how to work with a "murderer." But she'd heard me talk about my work for a long time and was intrigued, despite her fears. Ultimately, her compassion and her intellectual curiosity won out.

Anne agreed to see Agnes, and began by administering several basic standardized clinical tests: the Wechsler Adult Intelligence Scale (WAIS-R), which measures intellectual ability and cognitive performance; the Rorschach (the famous ink-blot test); the Thematic Apperception Test (TAT), an unstructured personality test that uses pictures, from which people make up stories; the

Minnesota Multiphasic Personality Inventory (MMPI), a true/false structured objective personality test; and other less-familiar tests that helped her evaluate Agnes's level of emotional functioning. When she'd ended her evaluation, Anne felt sure that Agnes was genuinely not responsible for her behavior. All the test results supported an insanity defense.

Agnes's profile on the MMPI clinical scales were consistent with others demonstrating symptoms of Battered Woman Syndrome. But they also indicated that some of her confusion was the result of a thought disorder; Agnes reacted to incidents she imagined, as well as to things that really happened. On the unstructured Rorschach (where creativity is rewarded) she had had trouble responding normally. Instead, she had become quite confused, demonstrating how her emotions kept her from using her otherwise good thinking skills. When Agnes became emotionally upset, her mind literally "shut down," as if she had mentally retreated back inside her room and fastened all the locks on the door.

When Bobbie and I had finished our evaluation (one conducted separately from the psychological tests administered by Anne), we found that Agnes did indeed have a Post Traumatic Stress Disorder—Battered Woman Syndrome type. We concluded that she'd shot her husband in self-defense. Agnes's responses on the Battered Woman Syndrome assessment materials did not indicate thought disorder on her part; instead, she responded like many other battered women who are terrified that the escalating violence in their homes will result in their deaths.

The result of all this testing was that we now had two complete, albeit different, possible defenses for Agnes's attorneys to consider: insanity and self-defense. Agnes's perception of Charlie's potentially imminent use of force had been reasonable; it had been based on the legitimate fear that, on the day of his death, he had been about to cause her bodily harm. On the other hand, he hadn't actually threatened to kill her that day; Agnes carried that belief around in her tortured mind.

Her "insane" behavior, though, may also have been the

very behavior that saved her life, which is what makes it sane as well.

The defense turned our reports over to the state, which, in turn, sent Agnes to their own experts: one a psychiatric nurse with experience in evaluating battered women, the other a forensic psychiatrist who specialized in diagnosing insanity. Both experts concurred with our assessments: Agnes was a battered woman who had killed, in self-defense, while temporarily insane.

The prosecutor knew that she could not proceed to full trial. She did the entirely appropriate thing: a nonjury trial was held before a judge. Only one witness, Dr. Robert Latimer, the state's psychiatrist, was called. He testified that Agnes suffered from Battered Woman Syndrome and had been legally insane at the time of the homicide; he went on to state that he found her to be perfectly sane now. Then, in a statement unusual from a professional trained to relate insanity to an individual's severe emotional problems in childhood, he stated that he found her insanity to be the result of the battering and abuse she'd suffered during her thirty years of marriage to Charlie. Since the death of her husband, he testified, the mental state that had created her psychosis was no longer present.

To be on the safe side, he recommended that Agnes continue in therapy with Dr. Auerbach until such time as the psychologist determined that she no longer required treatment. The judge concurred.

Today, Agnes is picking up the pieces of her life. She is working again, and she has found some inner peace, too, as a volunteer spending time with chronically ill children.

As Dr. Latimer testified in court, Agnes's psychosis is no longer present at all. She no longer performs any of her obsessive-compulsive rituals to stay safe. She eats whatever she likes, whenever she likes. There are no locks on her bedroom door. She is free of mental illness because she is free of the situation of violence and terror that caused it. Agnes's long-term insanity was "cured" by Charlie's death.

Stereotypes

When we speak of the insanity defense, it is also appropriate to explore some of the common myths and stereotypes that our society has of women. The common cultural image of a woman gone crazy from the pain of a broken heart is so much a part of our folklore that it's natural for people, including people on a jury, to believe that any woman who kills a man she loves does so because of jealousy or out of a sense of betrayal.

This stereotype feeds into the cultural myth of women being biologically predestined to greater emotional instability than men, in more ways than one the "weaker" sex.

Not enough is said, however, about the absolutely "crazy-making" behavior of the batterer. And battered women, who tend to be filled with self-doubt and extremely low self-esteem anyway, often develop a real fear that they, not their men, are going crazy.

But if being a little "crazy" or "unstable" is expected of a woman in our society, what is patently unexpected is that a woman will use violence in a rational way to save her own life. I believe that there is a tacit understanding, in Western culture, that violence lies in the province of male prerogative. A woman adopting "male" survival techniques is likely to be punished.

But the standard of *reasonable perception of danger* is the legal standard. And that a woman could kill her own husband, yet still meet this standard, is a reality few people want to acknowledge.*

If a defendant doesn't fit the stereotype of a crazy woman, jurors are more apt to view acquitting her as allowing her to "get away with murder." They want tangible proof that the battered

*Another fact unlikely to be acknowledged publicly is the statistically verifiable one that women, in general, are mentally healthier when they are *not* married. The opposite is true for men; their mental and physical health improves in marriage (despite the commonly held cultural belief that a wife's incessant "nagging" presence is somehow injurious to her husband). Lenore Radloff's work at the National Institute of Mental Health's Center for Epidemiology provides data from large-scale studies to support these facts.

woman defendant really has had some sort of "nervous break-down," which is difficult to demonstrate, unless she is still quite psychotic at the time of the trial. The "catch 22" here is that, if she is still psychotic, she will be considered incompetent and not be allowed to go to trial until such time as she is considered competent to assist in her own defense; however, when finally declared competent, she will not likely appear "crazy" to the jury.

If a battered woman is genuinely mentally incompetent, or if she is found not guilty by reason of insanity, she will most probably be assigned to a state mental hospital for an indeterminate period of time, at least until the doctors there say she is well. These doctors are usually male psychiatrists, some trained in psychoanalysis and many others from foreign cultures with limited and stereotyped views of American women. Organized psychiatry, in general, has displayed an appalling ignorance about the psychology of women in general, and of battered women in particular. A homicide conviction brings a time-limited sentence, but not guilty by reason of insanity brings a hospital sentence of potentially unlimited duration.

The first insanity case on which I ever consulted posed many of the standard problems.

ROXANNE'S STORY

Roxanne slit the throat of her husband, Philadelphia Eagles star Blenda Gay, one day in 1977 when he was sleeping (or temporarily passed out, depending on whose version of the story you believed).

Being married to a famous athlete had made Roxanne's life no different, in many ways, from the lives of other battered women. The beatings she endured had become so bad over the years that, on a number of occasions, she'd called the police. (Typically, the records of those calls were nowhere to be found when it came time for her trial, although several policemen did remember going on domestic violence calls to the football star's home.) In the meantime, Roxanne had managed to contact several feminist advocates of battered women's rights, who later helped her attorney prepare for a defense trial. They contacted me and I agreed to perform a professional evaluation of Roxanne.

Before I could do so, though, the families pressured Roxanne and her attorneys not to expose Blenda's shameful secret.

The families won. Roxanne was found incompetent to stand trial and was locked up in the Vroom Building for the Criminally Insane at Trenton State Hospital for six long years.

Finally, in 1983, she was declared competent. She went to a trial before a judge and was found not guilty by reason of insanity *at the time of the homicide,* but competent now and released into the community. For a period of time following her release, Roxanne lectured and worked within the battered women's movement.

She was free in the end, after all. Still, six years of life in a mental institution, after years of marital abuse, seems a harsh sentence indeed, especially when there is any chance at all of acquittal—when there is any chance at all of self-defense being proven.

It is in the nature of psychological self-defense that a battered woman may kill to stop herself from *going* crazy. She may sense that she is finally being driven over the edge, killing to preserve the inviolability of her psychological boundaries.*

Some women, though, are driven over the edge by a batterer, as in the case of Agnes and, more tragically perhaps, in the case of Hedda Nussbaum. The untenable psychological position of being abused by someone you love certainly can create a condition of temporary insanity. The next story is a good example.

*Charles Ewing, an attorney and psychologist, has developed a theory to support a justification defense for battered women who kill in psychological self-defense. He explains it in his book *Battered Women Who Kill* (Lexington, 1987).

PATTIE'S STORY

Prior to their marriage, Pattie and Tom had both been married to others. Tom had gained custody of his two youngest boys (his oldest son was a grown man and married himself). Pattie devoted herself to raising them, along with her own son and daughter. In addition to raising the four children, Pattie, a pretty, light-skinned Hispanic woman, maintained an immaculate home. She was also a successful local businesswoman, owning and managing a popular downtown bar. Her expectations of herself had always been extremely high.

Tom, a salesman, was often on the road. When he was home, they fought frequently. Sometimes, Pattie wound up getting a beating. Still, she loved Tom, pretending that everything was all right.

One of Tom's young sons had asthma, a condition that, in his case, was exacerbated by emotional stress. A school teacher, sensing that problems at home were affecting him adversely, suggested during a parent/teacher conference that they go for family counseling. Eventually, Pattie was able to talk Tom into going. This forced them both to reexamine their relationship.

Using standard systems theory techniques, the family therapist they consulted urged Tom to take over more family responsibility so that Pattie wouldn't have to do everything. But this changed the balance in the tenuous system they'd devised; instead of relieving the stress in their relationship, it actually made Pattie feel unloved and unwanted. Even the children began joining in with Tom's anger at her when, at the therapist's insistence, she refused to do the things they'd come to expect of her. Pattie began to feel that her life was "upside down."

Her behavior began to change, becoming bizarre at times. Eventually, she became suicidal.

Concerned that therapy seemed to be making their situation worse and concerned that Pattie posed a danger to herself and to others, their therapist filed a "hold and treat" petition, asking the police to commit Pattie to the mental ward of a local hospital for a seventy-two-hour period of observation and evaluation. Pattie successfully evaded the police but voluntarily went to a community mental health facility. There, however, she felt that the other patients were "too crazy" to be around. After several days, she checked out and went to stay with her stepson and his wife.

Pattie was right: her behavior was different from that of the others in the community facility. Most of them were chronically ill; Pattie's emotional distress and seemingly bizarre behavior were circumstantially induced. She was afraid of the man she loved, afraid that he would continue to beat her whenever they argued. With the changes in family structure recommended by the therapist, they argued more frequently than ever, so she was getting beaten more than ever.

She tried to take refuge in a battered women's shelter. But the shelter refused to let her in; with her recorded psychiatric history, they didn't think they'd be able to handle her. (Ironically, had Pattie gone to the battered women's shelter first, she would surely have been admitted immediately.)

Away from the house and the children she loved, away from the job that had provided her with so much self-esteem, Pattie felt isolated indeed. When Tom called one evening, inviting her to come home and cook dinner for him and the children, she quickly agreed.

The family had a wonderful dinner together and shared a peaceful Saturday. That Saturday night, though, Pattie and Tom went out, stopping in at the bar she owned. They had an argument, which culminated in Tom getting drunk and beating her in front of all the customers. Then, still drunk, he sat next to another woman and began making overt sexual advances.

Physically and psychologically abused, Pattie was nevertheless grateful for the opportunity to be with Tom again. She suppressed her rage and humiliation that night, driving him home at the end of the evening. They went to bed together and even made love for the first time in a long time. He spoiled it, though, by suggesting that next time they bring another woman home to join them in bed. Pattie didn't sleep at all that night.

The next morning Tom went off for the day without telling her where he was going. He did say he'd call her later and made a date for them to go out that evening. Pattie, wanting desperately to make their marriage work, continued to suppress her pain over his humiliating behavior. Tom called later, telling her when and where to meet him. When she got there, though, he arrived with another woman on his arm. Then he and the other woman drove off, leaving Pattie standing there.

Already in a fragile emotional state, still bruised physically and psychologically from the night before, Pattie got into her car and followed them.

Tom pulled up in front of a motel.

Pattie parked her car, got out, and confronted him angrily. Laughing, he invited her to join them for a threesome.

Pattie was horrified. She drove back immediately to her stepson's house, stopping off long enough to get bullets for the gun she kept in her car.

"I only wanted to scare him," she would say later.

It was a game they had played before.

When Pattie caught up with Tom and the other woman, they were in a parking lot outside her bar.

Pattie walked slowly toward Tom's car. He rolled down the window and yelled at her, threatening to beat her. Then, while she watched, he reached for the woman sitting next to him.

Pattie took out the gun. She told the woman that she was "history"; she told her husband to "get rid of the bitch."

Tom made a sudden move then, as if to get out of the car.

Later, Pattie would remember the smirk on his face.

She would remember shooting only once, aiming at the ground, intending just to scare him.

The next thing she'd remember was the sight of Tom, lying dead before her on the parking lot. The gun Pattie held was empty; all the bullets had been fired.

There was no sign of the other woman, who had managed to escape, unharmed, as soon as she'd heard the first shot.

* * *

Bill Fritche and Mort Davis, two Denver lawyers called in by Pattie's family to conduct her defense, were the ones who contacted me initially.

Right after her arrest, Pattie had tried to kill herself. She'd engaged in behavior that was sufficiently bizarre for jail officials to request her immediate transfer to Ward 16 of Denver General Hospital (a locked psychiatric facility for those accused of criminal acts). By the time I interviewed her, ten days later, she'd begun to come out of her suicidal depression and wanted to live again.

Her two teenaged children were visiting her when I arrived; after they left, she and I talked for a couple of hours.

Pattie had, indeed, been angry with Tom. But from the history she gave me, and from my own clinical impressions, I had no doubt that she'd been a battered woman in that relationship. It wasn't anger that had motivated her to pull the trigger, but pain, fear, and a terrible sense of grief. (I wasn't at all sure that the facts of the homicide, or even of her current psychological condition, supported an insanity defense more than a plea of self-defense, although her recent history documented her impaired state of mind.)

Released from prison on bail, Pattie began a long round of required mental health interviews. Her attorneys decided to file an insanity plea, based on the fact that she had no memory of the homicide and seemed to have had no voluntary control over her actions that night. When an insanity plea is filed, the state is usually allowed to examine a defendant with its own appointed mental health experts. Chris Cross, the Denver Deputy D.A., selected Dr. Jeffrey Metzner, a soft-spoken forensic psychiatrist well-known for his thorough and conservative opinions. Pattie also came to our office to complete the Battered Woman Syndrome Questionnaire and evaluation. Afterward, I agreed to see her for supportive therapy. All the psychotherapeutic intervention she received helped her become a great deal stronger emotionally. Jeffrey Metzner understood what had happened, too; his findings indicated that she had simply been pushed too far by her abusive, sadistic husband and that, under stress, her mind had temporarily snapped. Both Metzner and I agreed that the facts of the case and our professional evaluations regarding her state of mind at the time of the homicide would support an insanity plea.

In the Denver area, this consensus of professionally evaluated information is usually sufficient for most prosecutors and judges to accept. The common sentence is to order the defendant into treatment.

But prosecutor Cross was a young man, behaving like others, trying to build a reputation as a "tough" attorney in hopes of eventually leaving the D.A.'s office and moving into private practice. Some lawyers don't trust their own legal abilities, augmenting their practice of the law by playing dirty. In my opinion, Cross was one of those lawyers. Instead of sticking to the facts of this case, he attempted to introduce clearly erroneous material as evidence, in order to discredit both the defendant and her expert witness.

Cross and I had faced each other in court on two previous occasions. In both cases, the jury may have been turned off by his seemingly sneaky tactics, and had delivered verdicts in favor of the defense. Two losses for Cross were enough; he was apparently determined to "beat" me this time.

"No pleas!" he insisted. He asked Judge Martin to appoint another psychiatrist for a third opinion on Pattie's mental state. Unable to legally refuse the request, Judge Martin acquiesced. Dr. Seymore Sundell was appointed.

Every jurisdiction has a forensic expert like Dr. Sundell—a professional, often called for expert witness testimony, who has been around long enough to develop a good deal of arrogance. Sundell, who is smarter than many forensic psychiatrists, sometimes makes decisions based on very brief interviews that sometimes last only thirty or forty minutes. (Most health professionals spend many hours arriving at an opinion, especially when that opinion will affect the rest of a person's life.)

Sundell is known to rely heavily on supplementary reading materials for an individual history, rarely attempting to verify their reliability or validity. Memorizing what he has read, he delivers opinions that almost always turn out to be what the state wants to hear. His testimony is generally extremely convincing. Sundell can't be bothered attempting to gain a special understanding of the psychology of women; more than once, in fact, he has stated that abuse of women as a social fact is irrelevant to his forensic opinions. When testifying, he is known for his lack of visible warmth. Perhaps his need to insulate himself from the impact of the thousands of cases he's worked on has alienated him, in a way, from his own humanity. In Pattie's case, he and prosecutor Cross were a deadly team.

Pattie had been coming to my office regularly for supportive therapy (fulfilling a promise she'd made to the authorities when she was released on bail). She was becoming emotionally stronger, closer to the feisty, capable self that had almost been destroyed by Tom. When Sundell interviewed her, though, she said that she "froze up inside," and began, again, to have recurring feelings of inadequacy and terror.

Sundell, who did remember her from her two-week stay at Denver General's Ward 16, kept bouncing his final decision back and forth between a diagnosis of insanity and a diagnosis of diminished capacity. Pattie's defense attorneys kept hoping his qualifying "maybe" would, along with the other evidence, persuade a jury to acquit her. They decided to take the case to trial. Let the jury listen to what all the experts had to say, they figured, then decide whether or not Pattie's behavior fit the legal definition of insanity. After all, they had two experts "for" insanity, and only one "maybe."

Just before the scheduled beginning of Pattie's trial, it turned out that Judge Martin was still presiding over another courtroom trial. Instead of making us wait until he was finished, he asked a young judge, Sandra Rothenberg, to hear Pattie's case.

This seemed a great stroke of luck for the defense. Judge Rothenberg was one of the first feminist women to have been appointed to the bench. A former president of the Colorado Women's Bar Association, she was well-attuned to gender bias in the courts. We could not have hoped for a fairer judge. Throughout the trial, she could and did keep Chris Cross from getting too far out of line. In addition, she ruled that I could stay in the courtroom and, as Pattie's therapist, serve as consultant to the defense as well as offering my expert witness testimony.

For the first time, I found myself involved in the selection of the jury. Pattie participated, too; if she wasn't comfortable with a potential juror, her attorneys wanted to know about it. It was exciting to see her taking an active part in shaping her future. Sharing in crucial decision making can help battered women heal from the scars of abuse, regaining much-needed self-esteem after years of being beaten, manipulated, and socially controlled. Of course, the jury candidates that I instantly liked, thinking they would be sympathetic to my client, were dismissed quickly by the prosecution. Each side had the right to exercise up to twelve peremptory challenges; all the Hispanic women were challenged by the prosecution. It was obvious that, if Chris Cross had his way, he would try to make ethnic bias work for him.

Finally, though, twelve jurors and two alternates* were selected. The trial was ready to begin.

In an insanity trial in Colorado, at that time, the defense had the burden to "go forward," in other words, to demonstrate that there was good and sufficient reason to raise the insanity defense. The state, on the other hand, had the burden of proof, to prove that the defendant was not insane at the time that the alleged crime was committed. (A hard task for any lawyer, it is even more

---

*One of the alternates worried me, an engineer who seemed nonpsychologically minded and struck me as unfriendly. I thought that, in case he had to stand in for one of the regular jurors, he might prove detrimental to Pattie's case. But Bill Fritche liked him, explaining to me that a seemingly unfriendly loner is often good in a difficult case because such a person will sometimes hold out for a proper decision, refusing to yield to peer pressure. (All you need to win a trial is a hung jury; and all you need to hang a jury is one holdout. For this reason, defense lawyers try to hedge all their bets. A new trial may be better than a conviction.) As it turned out, in the middle of my testimony one of the jurors, a man, and the only Hispanic on the jury, became violently ill and asked to be excused. The engineer became juror number twelve. When the trial was over, we learned that he had, in fact, been the last holdout—on our side. This experience taught me a valuable lesson in legal humility.

difficult today, when the burden of proving insanity falls on the defense, not on the prosecution.)

Dr. Sundell was the state's strongest expert witness. He testified that he believed Pattie had been mentally "disturbed" at the time of the homicide, but not quite insane.

Cross put Tom's girlfriend on the witness stand to testify that she and Tom had had only a platonic friendship. Pattie was portrayed as a jealous and angry wife who'd shot her husband in cold blood. Most damaging of all, perhaps, was the testimony of Tom's oldest son, who, on the witness stand, stated that Pattie had seemed "perfectly normal" when she'd stopped off at his home to pick up bullets for her gun that night.

"She was angry and jealous," Cross maintained. The jury, watching a subdued, sullen-appearing, and no longer crazy Pattie, believed him. Despite the preponderance of the mental health evidence presented, they reacted like the lay people they were, armed only with their own common sense, lacking the knowledge of trained professionals. They found Pattie sane.

Despite the fact that the prosecution's evidence supported nothing beyond a charge of manslaughter, Cross made it clear that he would try to win a conviction of first-degree murder. After hearing the evidence presented at the insanity trial, another judge might have directed the dismissal of all murder charges, and allowed the case to proceed only on manslaughter. But Judge Rothenberg was trying terribly hard not to appear biased. She knew that she was being carefully watched by the press, as well as by the rest of the Colorado judiciary. So she allowed the charges to stay as they were.

Negotiations between the prosecutor's office and the defense took a serious turn for a while. But Cross agreed to settle for a plea of manslaughter only if he could demand a six-year prison sentence. Most judges refuse to be bound by sentence recommendations of either side in a case; Judge Rothenberg was no different in this regard. When his demand was refused, negotiations broke down. Pattie would stand trial for murder in the first degree.

"Pattie shot Tom in a fit of jealous rage," Cross told the jury.

Jealousy. Rage. These accusations say a great deal about our society's view of women, especially in light of the generally tacit (and, in some states, legally explicit) social rule that permits a husband who has found his wife in bed with another man to murder them both, without fear of punishment. The implicit assumption here is that men are the rightful owners of property, and that women are their property; that men have an absolute right to protect or avenge the usurping of their property as they see fit. However, the reverse is never true: women are not seen as being the rightful owners of property or of men; they possess no socially condoned right to dictate the actions of men. For these reasons, Cross felt he had a chance at winning a first-degree murder conviction.

When the second trial was over, Cross had failed to win the first-degree murder conviction he'd sought. Pattie was convicted, instead, of voluntary manslaughter. Judge Rothenberg sentenced her to three years in prison, then suspended the sentence.

Pattie was ordered instead to the Lakewood Community Responsibility Center (CRC), a community corrections facility near Denver. There she would receive job training, counseling, and alcoholism screening, and would also be able to supervise her son and daughter, who were still in a nearby high school.

Cross couldn't let this one go. Furious that Pattie was to serve no prison time after all, he took it upon himself to watch her every move. Whenever it was reported to him that Pattie had been sighted "at large" in the Denver community, he would call the community corrections facility to lodge a complaint. Sometimes, he complained directly to Judge Rothenberg.

Fortunately, Judge Rothenberg and Nancy Campbell, the CRC director, had a good working relationship. Nancy insisted that Pattie's whereabouts were known and approved by her at all times; Rothenberg believed her. It was clear to all concerned that Cross was way out of line. Nevertheless, he continued to complain about alleged sightings of Pattie throughout her stay at the CRC, even up to the day of her discharge.

Pattie spent a little more than a year in the CRC rehabilitation program. She received training to be a long-distance trucker and now drives huge tractor trailers across the country. She has remarried and settled back into the community.

Like other battered women who kill, she has never since been involved in any acts of violence. I predict she never will be.

Perhaps it is the ultimate irony of this case that, had Pattie been found not guilty by reason of insanity in her first trial, she might still be in a state hospital. Instead, perhaps, the jury's perception of her as Cross portrayed her, as a somewhat unstable, predictably hot-tempered, jealously angry Hispanic bitch worked to her advantage, but only because her ultimate conviction was balanced fairly by the knowledge and compassion of a clear-headed judge.

Part of the reason for Pattie's induced state of temporary insanity was her suppressed pain and rage at being abused, beaten, and psychologically taunted and tortured by the man she loved. But anger suppressed has a different effect from anger expressed, as we shall see in the next chapter.

10

ANGRY WOMEN

BATTERED WOMEN WHO KILL eventually experience anger. In fact, anger is an emotion felt, sooner or later, by nearly all victims of abuse or violence. But, in my many years of professional involvement with battered women, it has been my experience they are not motivated to kill the abuser solely out of anger. As I've stated time and again: *battered women kill out of fear.* And, as I've also often stated when testifying as an expert witness in battered women's self-defense cases: If every battered woman who was angry were to kill her batterer, there'd be a lot more dead men around. When a battered woman recognizes her own anger, this recognition generally coincides with a realization of all the grave injustices she suffered at the hands of the abuser. Some battered women, particularly those with "street smarts," learn not to show their fear, instead pretending to be tough so that men do not know they are afraid of them. This toughness is often misinterpreted as anger. The anger a battered woman experiences, after the homicide, is actually an intrinsic part of her own healing process. But—and I cannot stress this enough—the battered woman is able to feel the true depth of her anger, and work it through to resolution, only after she is free of her all-encompassing terror.

In our society, men experience emotions differently from women; they are trained to do so from an early age. It is also true that men are socialized to express their emotions in different ways than women.

In general, men are trained not to feel or express terror. From boyhood on, they are taught to transform all their "bad" feelings, such as fear and pain, into action or rage. This training is one reason why men who work in the criminal justice system or are on a jury have a difficult time believing that women who have suffered terrible abuse at the hands of men do not kill out of anger. To kill out of anger would be a male response. In the minds of men, anger becomes the most likely motivation; furthermore, it seems the only reasonable motivation. The irony of this perception is that, on the other hand, men do not like to see women expressing anger in violent physical ways (physical violence also falling into a distinctly male behavioral province in our society). And, if they perceive a battered woman defendant to be truly angry, they are likely to judge her more harshly than if they perceive her to be "merely" afraid, but more on that later.

When a woman kills, it is common for her self-perceived level of terror to be more acute than normal. Still, women hardly ever kill as a first response. A woman will emote, plead, and endure great suffering before resorting to physical defense of her own life and well-being. When a woman does kill, she has almost always been horribly, irrevocably hurt, physically and emotionally.

Because they are generally in positions of greater power and economic privilege than women, it is often difficult for men to truly understand women's psychological and material needs. For instance, men sitting on juries and male judges presiding in courtrooms often cannot understand why a woman who is terribly afraid of her battering husband or boyfriend would voluntarily run after him or approach him. In some cases, women have followed a battering husband or boyfriend, even after an acute battering incident, in order to obtain money promised them. In each of these cases, the money promised her by the batterer was money she desperately needed, to make necessary household payments, to buy food, to support her children. We have on record the cases of several battered women who actually shot their abusers as they were leaving, but in no case was this because they were angry. In every case, the woman feared what would happen when her batterer did return home, as she knew, from experience, he inevitably would. Each woman knew that, when her man returned, he would beat her again. In each one of these cases, the battered woman who killed did so because she felt she could not, under any circumstances, endure the agony of waiting for more abuse.

Addressing Anger

In general, women, and especially battered women, tend to live in denial of their own anger. (Battered women tend to live in a state of denial most of the time, period.) When I prepare a woman for trial, I believe it is necessary to address her feelings of anger, whether those feelings are conscious or not. It is essential to explain to her how dangerous it would be to express anger during the trial.

Often, a defense attorney will decide not to put a battered woman on the witness stand, fearing that if she should prove unable to control her emotions and appearance she will be misunderstood by the jury.

The following story provides an excellent example of how a battered woman defendant may suffer at the hands of a jury if she is perceived by them to be angry.

DOROTHY'S STORY

Late on a spring evening in May 1982, Dorothy and Ray, the man she'd lived with for more than two years, were arguing in a local bar. Ray began to scream and hit her, the way he usually did when they fought. This time, though, people saw him doing it. A few of them actually came to Dorothy's aid, holding Ray back as she ran outside.

Dorothy was a little drunk herself. She got to her car as quickly as she could, stepped in, and started it. But before she could drive away, Ray was there, trying to open the doors, banging on the windows as hard as he could, pounding on the windshield with his fists. He even climbed onto the front hood, yelling at her.

Dorothy began to drive. Trying to smash through the windshield, Ray flailed wildly and then slid right off the hood. He fell under the car wheels, which crushed him to death as Dorothy, terrified, sped away.

"I didn't know he was there," Dorothy told the police later.

"Where did you think he went?"

"I assumed he just went back into the bar."

"Well, didn't you hear anything?"

"Nothing except a crunch, crunch, crunch, crunch. That must have been his body, huh?" she replied, not knowing at the time that with that statement she had just about done herself in.

A middle-aged hairdresser living in Vale, a small community in eastern Oregon, Dorothy had been arrested while driving intoxicated. She was known as a drinking woman who hung out a lot in bars. She had neither privilege nor prestige in that small town; people generally thought the likes of her were "white trash," better off eliminated. When she was charged with manslaughter, it was obvious to her attorney that it was going to be extremely difficult for her to be fairly judged by a "jury of her peers."

Not only did unanswered questions permeate this trial from the beginning (had Dorothy known that the crunching noises were her car's wheels crushing Ray's body, and had she then driven off, leaving him there on purpose?), but Dorothy was an outsider in Vale, and looked it. Her lawyer knew that her appearance could damage the outcome of the trial; he tried to get the trial delayed so Dorothy's one-inch-long punk hair style, dyed carrot red, would grow long enough for her to appear somewhat more like the other, "normal" (that is, socially accepted) women in town.

Rightfully, perhaps, Dorothy became even more furious.

"Why can't I just look like myself?" she asked me once, as we discussed preparing for the trial.

"Dorothy, how many other women in town are wearing British punk hair styles?"

"None that I know of."

"Well, that's just the point. You've got to persuade your jury that what you did was justifiable because you were scared, not angry. Any one of those jurors needs to believe that, in the same situation, she or he would have done the same thing you did. If you go in there looking so different from all of them, how are they going to identify with you?"

"I really don't like it," Dorothy sighed, "but I understand what you're saying. How come my lawyer didn't explain it like that? He just told me to lose a few pounds and dye my hair back to brown." She'd thought, she confided, that her lawyer was trying to control her, the way any man would try to control her, the way Ray had tried to control her. She reacted with anger to his demands that she listen to him just like she had been angry with Ray when he tried to force her to do what he said. But she killed him out of fear, a feeling she also had, not anger. Although she realized now that her lawyer had only been trying to help the case, her experiences again caused her to immediately mistrust his motives.

"He's just a man," I said, trying to connect with the almost universal sense of humor most women display when discussing the foibles of most men. "And he doesn't really have the sensitivity to explain it to you, because he himself doesn't understand that he's expressing a sort of bias against women. But he does know the way it is in court."

I bit my tongue then, stopping myself from launching into one of my own feminist diatribes about how the law enforces social values. It wouldn't have been appropriate. Dorothy was too engrossed in her own situation, and rightfully so; her future was at stake. I felt, though, that whatever the trial's outcome, it was bound to be a radicalizing experience for her. When her brush with the law was over, she would be more sensitized to social politics, in her own way.

The outcome of this particular incident was that Dorothy agreed to let her hair grow and to color it back to its original shade of brown. But, she warned, when the trial was over, she intended to let her hair and her body "go back to the way I like it!" To the best of my knowledge, she did.

The jury eventually found Dorothy guilty of manslaughter, which surprised me, considering Ray's responsibility in jumping up threateningly on the hood of her car (after beating her in public).

I am convinced that Dorothy's social status as an outsider in this small western town counted strongly against her. Dyeing her hair and changing the clothes she normally wore did not quite do the trick. She still appeared angry and somehow "unacceptable" to the jurors, and paid the price. However, the judge used his discretion to apply justice by granting her a sentence that amounted to the time served awaiting trial. After eight months in custody, Dorothy was released on probation.

Racism and Anger

The ratio of Black women to white women convicted of killing their abusive husbands is nearly two to one in one of my studies. My feeling is that this is the result of our society's misperceptions of Black people in general, of women in general, and of Black women in particular. The "angry Black woman" is a common stereotype in many white minds; subtly, but no less powerfully, white society in America fears "Black anger." There is also the probability that whites in America perceive many normal Black cultural modalities, such as speech patterns and gestures, as telltale signs of anger and as personally threatening to whites. In this atmosphere, being racially different from the white majority may put a defendant at risk in an American court of law, whether or not she takes the witness stand in her own defense.

Race also makes a difference in a woman's chances for acquittal (or, at least, for serving no jail time). Fully a third of the first hundred women I've evaluated have been non-Caucasian, yet they represented only 25 percent of those found not guilty; although 21 percent of the women were Black, Black women represented only 10 percent of those acquitted.*

The same liability is noted for really impoverished women with no job skills. While they constituted 25 percent of the entire group, only 5 percent were found not guilty. Not only were these women totally dependent upon a court-appointed attorney to represent them legally, they also had difficulty finding witnesses and persuading them to testify honestly in a system that, because of its exclusion of the poor, creates mistrust among the very groups it is most likely to persecute.

Racism and economic discrimination are inextricably linked to sexism in our culture, creating an ugly nexus in our courts of law. Poor women, occupying the lowest end of the economic and social totem pole, are often familiar with government bureaucracies, most frequently through social service agencies designed to aid them. Strangers to the inner workings of the bureaucratic maze that often victimizes them, they see themselves (rightly) as outsiders to the inner workings of this government's system of justice as well. When a woman appears confused, defensive, or hostile in court—especially when she is poor or Black—there is a great likelihood that she will be judged severely, and punished severely, too.

*This obvious racial discrimination was less evident where other minorities were concerned. Nine percent of these women were Hispanic, and this group represented fully 10 percent of the acquittal group. Other minorities, including Native American and Asian American women, represented too small a part of the sample to make meaningful statistical comparisons.

GLADYS'S STORY

The night before she killed her husband, Ernest, Gladys Kelly had lent him money when he'd demanded it, in fear of her life. Ernest had always hit her. Sometimes, he'd beat her badly.

But the money she'd lent him that last night was money Gladys had set aside to buy food for herself and her seven-year-old daughter, Janice. She knew from past experience that Ernest would drink it away. She knew, too, that she desperately needed to buy food for the house; otherwise Janice would go hungry that week. But Ernest was dangerous. When he demanded the money, she gave it to him. She knew she had no choice.

The next day, after he got his paycheck, she demanded that he give the money back, as he'd promised. They had a fight. Even when he began to hit her again, she continued to demand it loudly. Gladys was beaten this time, but not silenced. Finally, in a rage, Ernest stormed out and went to a friend's house for dinner.

Gladys followed him there.

She sat in his friend's house quietly—respectfully, she thought—while Ernest ate dinner. When he'd finished, though, she began to ask for her money again. This demand started another fight that continued as Gladys followed Ernest down the street. Ernest attacked her again, and had to be dragged away from her by people on the street who saw the incident. These people told Ernest to leave while they protected Gladys, still without her money, from further harm. Then Gladys couldn't find Janice in the confusion. Gladys was terrified that he'd taken Janice, as he had previously threatened to do. She grabbed a pair of scissors from her purse and ran after him screaming for her child.

Ernest heard her and turned around, then approached her threateningly. That was when she stabbed him with the scissors, as he rushed at her. Ernest fell down, apparently having a heart attack. Both were taken to the hospital by ambulance. Records show the doctors ignored the small wound made by the scissors, believing it was a surface wound, and instead treated him for a possible cardiac infarction. In that busy Newark city hospital, no one noticed that the stab wound had pierced the myocardium surrounding the heart. Within the hour, Ernest bled to death internally while lying in the emergency room supposedly being medically monitored.

Would this homicide have occurred if Gladys hadn't needed the money to buy food for her child?

Were her actions justifiable? Were they in self-defense?

What role did the doctors play in Ernest's death?

In Gladys's first trial, the presiding judge refused to allow any expert witness testimony on her behalf. The prosecutor (an economically privileged white woman who wore magnificent clothes and expensive jewelry in this Newark courtroom, and who, in my opinion, had no understanding whatsoever of the needs of an impoverished Black woman struggling to keep her child fed) tried to convince the jury that Gladys had killed Ernest because she was angry that he was about to leave her. In the absence of conflicting testimony, the jury agreed; they convicted Gladys of voluntary manslaughter, and she was sentenced to five years in Clinton State Prison.

But Gladys appealed her conviction.

In a precedent-setting opinion written by the New Jersey Supreme Court, she was granted a new trial. (Her appeal, in fact, resulted in the New Jersey courts allowing many more battered women to present expert witness testimony concerning their state of mind at the time of the homicide.)

Gladys Kelly was retried. On the witness stand and in the open courtroom, though, she appeared angry, which by this time, having suffered at the hands of both an abusive husband and an abusive state, she might well have been. But she also had an uphill battle against stereotypes of the angry Black woman. A second jury convicted her again of manslaughter.

The expert witness testimony presented offered a strong case for acquitting her on grounds of self-defense. But the trial court judge did not permit continuous testimony and cross-examination, as is customary, in order to accommodate to the prosecutor's request to cross-examine at several intervals, as the testimony was too "confusing" for her and therefore perhaps for the jury. Nonetheless, Gladys's angry appearance was what the jury really believed, so she was reconvicted and returned to prison to fulfill her sentence.

I doubt that it would have happened had she not been Black and had the jury not believed her to be angry.

In Gladys's case, and in many other cases, I believe that racism plays a major role.

The following story is another illustration of these racial dynamics, and of the legal dilemmas they pose.

JESSIE'S STORY

Jessie Belle, a large Black woman living on the edge of Philadelphia's Mainline suburbs, had been married to Israel for nearly thirty years. Both had been born in the South, where they'd met each other. After marrying, they'd headed up North together.

Israel was a dedicated worker; he held the same factory job all his life. Jessie raised their three children and kept a home for them all, a home of which she was extremely proud. Life would have been good indeed, had Israel not beaten her so often and so badly.

But Jessie had never really done anything about it. She wasn't a complainer. In fact, she never told anyone outside of the immediate family. Only her children knew, and as adults they all tried to convince Israel to stop brutalizing their mother. Israel's response was to bar them from the house.

This situation was intolerable for Jessie and her children. The oldest daughter, Jessie Mae, had recently given birth to their first grandchild, whom Jessie adored. She refused to obey Israel, insisting that Jessie Mae and the child could visit whenever they wanted. But Israel continued to beat her when they argued about this or any other issue.

He and his children, too, fought verbally. Recently, their

quarrels had escalated to the point of his physically assaulting them, especially Jessie Mae and the younger daughter, Diane. The day Israel was killed, Jessie Mae ran from the house after a particularly brutal battle, Israel chasing her with a shotgun in his hand, threatening to shoot and kill her if she ever returned.

After this incident, Jessie and Diane conferred. Both had been physically injured by Israel; so had Jessie Mae. Israel's threats to kill her if she came back home suddenly seemed real to them. They decided they couldn't let it happen. Things had gone too far. Israel was getting more violent and unreasonable by the day. He was trying to divide the family, they thought. The two women were in a state of despair.

Israel went upstairs to his bed, saying that he was going to lie down and take a nap. There may have been a short period of calm.

Jessie and Diane found the shotgun he'd used earlier that day. They crept quietly upstairs to the bedroom where he slept. Then, as if they were one person, both women raised the gun and pointed it at Israel.

Later, their stories would differ. Jessie would say that she had pulled the trigger while Diane held the gun; Diane would say that she was the one who'd pulled the trigger while her mother held the gun. Each woman obviously tried to protect the other. But neither mentioned aiming the shotgun at the sleeping man who had beaten and tormented them for so long.

Israel died instantly from a single first shot.

A few minutes later, Jessie went into their garage and found a can of gasoline.

She poured it over Israel's dead body. Though she would not later remember doing it, she bound his feet together with twine, perhaps, as other battered women have believed, still thinking that the man was alive. Then she lit a match, setting him and the house she loved on fire.

She and Diane walked a while then, up a steep hill to the nearby hospital. Jessie frequently visited the emergency room there with a variety of illnesses. The medical records would later show that, on that particular night, she was out of breath and in great pain.

While she was undergoing treatment in the emergency room, hospital personnel learned of the fire at Jessie's house and told her. From her reaction, it was clear to them that she was in a state of shock. They contacted social services personnel, who helped Jessie and Diane get a temporary place to stay. Jessie had lost everything she'd ever owned, except Israel's wallet, which they had taken; it was filled with money, although, in their state of shock, they had not bothered to look through it at the time. Jessie Mae joined them.

Jessie, her two daughters, and her granddaughter were together at last.

Four days later, after giving the inquiring police investigators several different stories, Jessie and Diane were both arrested. To keep them from concocting another conflicting story, the authorities saw that the mother and daughter were put in different jails in different parts of the state, both too far away from Jessie Mae for her to visit either one of them. These three women, who had fought so hard to be together, were bitterly separated. It was a genuine tragedy for them all.

When my associate and I went to evaluate Jessie in her jail cell, we found a quiet, passive, extremely depressed woman who cried constantly and stated that she felt she'd lost all reason to live. She missed her children deeply. They had been the joy and the focus of her difficult life. She was a simple woman, probably of borderline intelligence, but extremely loving, loyal, gentle, reliable, and hard-working.

At the time of our interview, she simply could not remember large portions of time during which the homicide and burning of the house had taken place.

Kami Smith was the compassionate public defender assigned to Jessie. With the help of her boss, she put together an excellent defense. She included a well-known Philadelphia psychiatrist and a psychologist, both highly respected for their expert witness testimony, on the defense team. It was exciting for me to work with such knowledgeable and compassionate professionals. Together, we coordinated our findings and planned a trial strategy.

Diane's attorney, though, refused to work with us. No doubt he believed that his client had a better chance for acquittal if Jessie took the rap. Originally Jessie had been willing to do just that, but some of Kami's fighting spirit rubbed off on her. She began, slowly, to want to live.

To hear her story told by the state prosecutor to an all-white Philadelphia Mainline jury—obviously not a jury of her peers—Jessie was a manipulative, conniving, angry (that is, Black) bitch who had plotted with her angry (that is, Black) daughters to kill their hard-working, saintly husband and father because they simply did not like him anymore.

During the trial I often asked myself: can men really believe that women will kill them just because they have stopped liking them? Or was there something else going on there, something over which I and the defense team had no control? Despite the evidence, did the jury judge Jessie to be guilty—guilty of being angry (guilty, in other words, of being Black)? Maybe, I thought, if she'd been white, and had committed the homicide alone, she would have been perceived as she really was: a simple, frightened woman who was afraid of being hurt again and of seeing her children hurt; a simple, frightened woman who had been beaten hard all her life, but who refused, in the end, to be separated from the children she loved.

The all-white jury found Jessie Belle guilty of murder in the first degree. They also found her not guilty of arson, by reason of insanity.

To my mind, this verdict seemed absurd. Did the jury really believe that Jessie had gone from a state of sanity to a state of insanity in the period of time between killing Israel and burning down the house, a period of several minutes at most? Mental health experts testified that this would have been highly unlikely, at best; more likely, the thing that had caused her to snap had been her husband's abuse and his threats to kill her eldest daughter and grandchild. Or maybe she had never really snapped at all; maybe, in a subconscious way, she had knowingly set Israel's body and her beloved home on fire in order to symbolically terminate that no-longer-tolerable chapter of her life. Only Jessie knows for sure.

In the end, Jessie Belle proved less despondent over her conviction than the rest of us on her defense team; she received a sentence of life in prison. Diane, who pleaded guilty to a lesser charge, received a ten-year sentence. Mother and daughter were reunited in the same prison.

Jessie Mae visits them both as often as she can, usually bringing her child with her, so the family is together again, in a way.

And it is testimony to the terror bred in them by all the years of living with Israel's abuse that both Jessie and Diane believe things are better for them now than they were before. Prison is a terrible place. Yet, for these women, it proved a place of comparative freedom—freedom from violence, freedom from relentless tension, emotional pain, and fear.

Again, racism has an overwhelming effect on the tactics of any trial. Almost inevitably, this is to the detriment of a Black defendant, as the following story again illustrates.

CECILE'S STORY

Cecile, a Black woman in her early thirties, mother of three children, had long been beaten and abused by her husband, Henry. A bright woman, she was in the process of completing her final year of undergraduate work at prestigious Colorado College when she and Henry finally agreed to divorce. The children, who bore no love for the stepfather who abused them too, were pleased with their mother's decision, and looked forward to the day when they would all finally be free of him.

Cecile and Henry began working together on legal do-it-yourself divorce papers.* But Henry's behavior became even more abusive than it had been before. Even when batterers claim to want a divorce, they appear to have great trouble in letting the woman go. He seemed literally unable to stop beating her.

After one especially brutal incident, Cecile recognized the danger of her situation. She fled to a local battered women's shelter, taking the children with her. There, she told a counselor how angry she was with Henry; among other things she confided to the counselor that night, she said that she was angry enough to kill him. The counselor put Cecile's statement into the record. (Had Cecile not eventually killed Henry, these statements would have remained unimportant. Most battered women express a wish, at some point in their relationships, that their batterers die.) Eventually, Cecile and the children went home.

After another acute battering incident a few weeks later, Cecile became truly terrified that she and the children would be killed. That was when she bought a gun.

One night Cecile and the children returned home from an evening at a friend's house to find Henry in an inexplicable rage. He began to beat Cecile as soon as she walked in. When she managed to escape into the bathroom and lock the door behind her, he turned on her teenaged daughter and began to choke her. Henry's father, who was living with them at the time, intervened. The three of them collapsed, struggling, on the living room floor.

At that moment the teenager ran from the house, terrified. Henry stood up and ran after her. Witnesses later reported seeing Cecile run out of the house after them, gun in her hand.

Henry caught up with the child and grabbed her around the neck, starting to throttle her. He saw Cecile and let go of the girl. That was when Cecile fired the shot. It took just one to kill him.

* * *

*In Colorado, as in many other states, couples who have no disputes about division of property or issues around custody and visitation with children can follow the directions to prepare and file dissolution of marriage forms.

In an appalling subversion of the rules of confidentiality, the staff of the battered women's shelter where Cecile and her children had fled gave in to the state prosecutor's subpoena and turned over their records without a fight. Even worse, two of the shelter's volunteer counselors, without Cecile's permission, violated confidentiality and agreed to testify on behalf of the prosecution.

Their testimony was damning. They supported the prosecution's contention that Cecile had killed her husband out of anger. Even testimony from her college professors as to the exceptionally fine academic work she'd managed to produce consistently, except during the periods when Henry was beating her, did not help to overcome the jury's impression. Neither did my expert witness testimony. To the mostly white jury Cecile appeared angry, not terrified.

Her attorney, Mike Warren, decided not to put Cecile on the witness stand, even though she probably could have testified eloquently on her own behalf. He was afraid that she looked too angry. (Maybe, I thought, he was afraid that she looked too Black.) The result was that the jury was able only to watch her in court, but never to hear what she herself had to say about these events. (Later, Mike defended his decision; he explained that he hadn't wanted her to be cross-examined about another relationship in which she was involved.) And it was true, in a way, that Cecile's expression at rest sometimes made her appear angry. The mostly white, conservative juries in Colorado Springs are unlikely to acquit an angry-looking Black woman who has killed a man. Cecile was convicted of second-degree murder.

To his credit, the presiding judge understood Battered Woman Syndrome. Perhaps it helped that he had heard my testimony in previous trials. He also recognized the prejudicing racism underlying this case. Although he had no choice but to sentence Cecile, he gave her the minimum time allowable: twelve years and six months in prison. However, while Cecile's appeal was pending, the judge allowed her to remain free on bail. The bail had been raised by community battered women advocates, who were horrified by what their colleagues at the local shelter had done.

News that a shelter had betrayed one of its battered women flew quickly around the state. Emergency meetings between attorneys and battered women's shelter staffs were held in many locales. The attorneys provided staff members with critical legal advice. All hoped that such a betrayal of a battered woman's rights would never happen again.

For Cecile, of course, it was a little bit late in the day.

Cecile lost her appeal. She was finally ordered to the state prison to serve her original sentence. Before sending her there, however, the judge tried to gather all available statistical data in an effort to determine whether or not Cecile had been judged more harshly by the jury because she was Black. Little such data was available in Colorado at the time.

Ironically, Cecile had been studying prison reform on the day she was arrested.

She delivered another child while in prison. There, she spent a great deal of time trying to organize other battered women. Within a few years she was placed on "honor" status and offered a job in the governor's office. As I write this, she has just won her struggle to get her sentence reduced. After four years in prison, the governor has granted her early parole. She is now at home with her three daughters, one of whom she had not seen since the child was four days old.

Cecile was one of the women who did not benefit from my expert witness testimony, although she was not convicted of first-degree murder as the prosecutor asked. Most of the women I've seen convicted appeared to be angry. Many of those who appeared angry were also Black. Their palpable fear and terror were somehow obscured. Or, perhaps, the mostly white juries that convicted these women were unable to see them as being vulnerable or terrified because the racism rampant in our society implicitly denies Black women the right to manifest a full range of emotions. It is clear to me, as I write this, that Cecile, Jessie, Gladys, and many, many other battered women are being punished because they were perceived as angry. In the minds of many white people, anger and color may intertwine.

Anger and Feminism

In her book *Women Who Kill* (1980), Ann Jones describes how social norms influence the severity of judgment that jurors impose on a woman, especially when she kills a man. Women who kill are feared (as feminists are feared) because of what is widely assumed to be their overt "anger" at men.

Psychoanalytic theory would maintain that men fear women's anger because they have internalized their childhood fears of their mothers' anger, and that, simultaneously, they have internalized the child's resentment of a mother's power to control.

Social-gender analysis would maintain that men fear women's anger because of their collective guilt at the oppression under which they have forced women to live. (Much like a Southern plantation owner during the Civil War or a cruel dictator about to be overthrown, men know that oppressed subjects can eventually unite to rebel against those in power.)

The feminist movement does have the capacity to unify women, and, in a collective sense, it does express anger toward men. It is entirely possible, albeit entirely unproven, that women who kill their batterers are subconsciously perceived as expressing a collective message from all women to all men: *your days of controlling us are over.*

Battered women who kill have dared to appear angry; they have dared to adopt an attitude that men are likely to condone only in other men. Conviction is the male juror's way of responding to these women, of saying: "You will pay for my brother's death." Women jurors may even be more harsh in their judgment of another woman, especially when they know of others, perhaps including themselves, who have been battered but do not kill prior to getting divorced. When a woman is perceived by the jury as being angry, a self-defense plea becomes less convincing. This bias is held by judges, prosecutors, and defense attorneys, as well as by jurors. It also permeates psychological evaluations done by uninformed health professionals.

It is true, in our society, that women constitute the largest and fastest-growing poverty group. It is true that women still earn only about 62 cents for every dollar a man earns. It is true that those women who choose to work at home run the highest risk of being physically, sexually, and psychologically abused by the men they love. And it is a rare woman who hasn't been touched by women's daily struggle to survive in our sexist world.

This knowledge, consciously or unconsciously, rightfully makes women angry, but feminism, and the women's movement, merely validates that anger—it does not cause it. And anger does not cause battered women to kill the men who beat them nearly to death. Anger is the emotion that *follows* homicide, the emotion that is allowed to exist freely only when terror and pain, shame and grief, are washed away.

Anger and Power

During the writing of this book, I was invited to Chicago to present some of my research findings on battered women at a meeting of the prestigious American Family Therapy Association. Neil Jacobson, a psychologist at the University of Washington in Seattle, had put together a panel of experts for the event; our job was to present our findings and discuss their implications for family therapists. (The other two panelists, psychologists Gayla Margolin from UCLA and Robert Geffner from the University of Texas at Tyler, Texas, were involved in research into more traditional forms of couples therapy.) Jacobson had asked us all to be provocative and to stress our different points of view.

The group of professionals attending this meeting, several

hundred family therapists from all over the world, had been getting a fairly heavy dose of gender-and-politics programs during the conference. Many of them, the men in particular, were restless and somewhat defensive. During the question-and-answer period that followed our panel's presentation, I found myself the focus of a good deal of anger.

"Dr. Walker," asked one man, "isn't it true that feminists are so angry that their anger spills over onto their clients? And isn't that why so many women in therapy, especially battered women, are angry today?"

"Of course not," I replied. "The data I've just presented indicate that a woman is much more likely to be angry in an abusive relationship than she is with a nonabusive partner. Dr. Geffner's data and Dr. Margolin's data bring us to the same conclusion. Feminists do validate women's anger at being oppressed, but they don't cause it. In fact, feminist therapy allows a woman to work through her anger so that she doesn't get stuck with it. Only after she works through anger can she move from being a victim to being a survivor. Sometimes battered women experience so much rage that it frightens them—they want to be free of it. Women therapists are generally more able than male therapists to let the client feel her rage and work through it without becoming afraid of its intensity. Well-trained feminist therapists are often much more useful for a battered woman client than are family systems therapists who see the couple together."

As I finished speaking, I looked at the questioner and realized that he was standing with his hands alternately gripping and releasing the microphone. His face seemed distorted; it was obvious that he himself was quite angry. I found myself reacting, silently but instinctively, with a moment of fear. Was he a batterer, too? Was I really in danger, either professionally or personally? How easy it is for outspoken feminists to become the target of men's anger when their patriarchal values are challenged, even with empirically sound scientific data.

Argentine-born psychiatrist Teresa Bernardez* talks of how unfortunate it is that there is only one term in the English language for all kinds of anger. She feels that causes a problem in the perception of victimization; the anger of the victim, she believes, is different from the anger of the abuser.

One difference is that the abuser, often a male, does not always acknowledge the *other*. The victim, usually a female, almost invariably does. Recognition of the true sanctity of the *other* may, in fact, fall more into the province of the female in our society. In battering situations, it always does.

Bernardez talks of the "anger which liberates." This anger is an emotion to be uncovered in therapeutic situations, the goal being that the client can utilize anger in a positive way, working through it to facilitate the ending of her suffering.

When understood and used positively, anger is not a punitive emotion; rather, it can provide the energy to move toward empowerment. As an undeniable force, anger stands in direct psychological contrast to powerlessness. When women in therapeutic situations begin to get in touch with anger, they often experience a direct increase in self-esteem and in clarity of purpose.

Through this type of anger—so different from an attitude of scorn, defensiveness, or contempt—it is possible for an individual to truly reveal herself. The angry person can still hold others in respect, and respect of the other is the true beginning of relationship. Angry in this positive, creative way, people speak to each other as equals. This anger feeds the flames of esteem for others and for self, of love for self and love for others. It is an individual version of the collective anger exercised by oppressed groups when they fight against unfair laws. It is exemplified by

---

*Bernardez, who is in private practice in Michigan, was a member of the Committee for Women in Psychiatry during the discussions preceding publication of the *Diagnostic and Statistical Manual of Mental Disorders*, 3rd ed., revised (DSM-III-R). She is a Menninger Foundation-trained analyst who has moved toward a feminist therapy approach in her understanding of women's anger and women's issues in therapy.

those who fight for peace in nonviolent ways or who use their anger at injustice to energize their struggle. It is part of the loving indignation that in the end can transcend personal rage, an anger that will fight for advocacy and for justice.

This is the emotional potential of every battered woman who survives: the positive force that lies beneath many destructive manifestations of pain and rage. Moreover, this anger is the emotional potential of every woman, and of every man.

Perhaps it is this creative, constructive anger that is most feared by corrupt people in power. For it is this anger that most threatens the injustice of any social order, having, as it does, the power to challenge, to redeem, and to transform.

11

WOMEN IN PRISON: RESISTANCE AND REFUGE

T HE BARS SLOWLY CLOSED BEHIND ME, clanging automatically across the small opening. Ahead lay another set of bars that would open after the ones behind were firmly shut. Closed-circuit TV cameras recorded my movements from every angle.

I felt panic rise in my throat. I prize my independence with great ferociousness. Just thinking about strangers controlling my movements even temporarily flooded me with fear. Nevertheless, I found myself obediently walking forward as the rolling bars parted for me.

Ahead lay another station, the guard there ready to check my credentials. Finding them in order, I was told to follow another pleasant but clearly "no nonsense" guard to the small, windowless Contact Interview Room, as it is called, equipped with a table, two chairs, and a paper ashtray. The furniture took up so much of the space that every piece touched another. On the wall hung a telephone without dial mechanism. Huddled in the back corner on one of the chairs was my client, a woman I had never seen before.

"Just pick up the phone and call us when you're through," the guard instructed, turning to leave us alone.

223

As soon as the heavy steel door with no handles slammed shut, the small, frightened woman dressed in shapeless prison overalls looked at me and in a reassuring tone said, "Don't worry, they really will come and let you out. It's not as bad as you think; it just takes some getting used to. I know, I went through it at first. All of us do."

Get used to this? I thought. *I just couldn't.* I took several deep breaths and calmed down enough to become acutely aware of the role reversal going on.

"How do you get used to it?" I asked, trying to regain my professional composure.

"It's better than the hell I lived with," she said calmly. "There are rules here, every day's predictable. I don't worry anymore about doing something wrong to make him angry. You can't imagine what a relief that is. I feel better now. At least I know what to expect."

The profundity of her statement—that she felt better in jail—seemed, for a moment, to widen the gulf between her life and mine. With its loss of freedom, jail simply terrified me. But this realization brought home an important truth about those who live in violent relationships: they are not able to exercise free will because they are not free. Violence creates a psychological prison, from which escape is sometimes impossible. Real prison may be a less noxious form of bondage than a battering relationship, at least for some women who kill.

Statistically, very few women (as compared to men) have ever spent time in jail or prison.* Jails are generally run by individual cities or counties and hold people charged with crimes and awaiting trial, including people who have committed serious crimes as well as crimes such as prostitution, disorderly conduct, and misdemeanor assaults. It is rare that anyone with more than a one-year sentence stays in jail. Women who are arrested are more likely to spend time in jail awaiting trial because they are

*Approximately 5 percent of all those convicted of crime in America are women.

less able to make bail or pay bond fees, and are rarely released on their own recognizance. (A study conducted by former Colorado Supreme Court Justice Jean Dubofsky documented the comparatively *longer* time women spent in jail when charged with the same crimes as men. She suggests that gender-biased decisions about bail, which exist throughout the criminal justice system, are responsible.)

Analysis of the first one hundred cases in which I have completely evaluated a battered woman before her trial shows that 25 percent have been totally acquitted. Another 40 percent have been found guilty of a lesser charge than murder but placed on probation. Thus, two-thirds of these women have served no time in prison even though almost all were originally charged with first-degree murder.

Almost 10 percent were sentenced to less than two years; 14 percent were sentenced to between three and fifteen years; and 6 percent were sentenced to between twenty years and life.* Almost all of those evaluated (96%) were charged with first-degree murder; only four (4 percent) were so convicted. Three out of those four women were too poor to pay for their own defense, and one of those three was Black.

Surprisingly, for women in prison who have been convicted of murdering their batterers, the prison circumstance actually may prove beneficial to them in certain ways. For many, this is the first time in their lives that they have been able to spend significant amounts of time alone, thinking about their lives; it is

---

*In numbers, five women were in this last category; and in two of those cases (Helen Martin and Edith Burhle) expert witness testimony was not admitted. Interestingly, both of these cases went on to be widely cited in other legal opinions, used by prosecutors to keep other expert witness testimony from being admitted. They remain as two of the four cases nationwide in which the appellate court has refused to permit the jury to hear Battered Woman Syndrome testimony. It is my belief that, if retried today, the expert testimony would be admitted but the final outcomes would probably be the same. Juries still have trouble believing that battered women who do not behave according to the stereotypes have the right to act violently in self-defense.

their first time in a community of women, and, thus, their first experience of mutual support. Many say that, no matter how terrible prison life may be, it is nevertheless better than living with the batterer.

As there are no uniform standards nationwide, the conditions for women in jail vary widely. Overcrowding and lack of staff, problems in jails across the country, are even more serious in jail space reserved for women. In a recent visit to a southern California jail, I had to conduct an interview in a room right next to "the hole," where six screaming women were held. They were being punished by being ignored when their basic human needs were not met, including food, water, toilet paper, and tampons; they were denied basic human respect and attention. In another jail, I had to wait my turn to use the barely private Contact Room, or face the prospect of conducting a confidential interview in an open row of seats, where others sit so close that they cannot help but overhear their neighbors' discussions. It is not unusual to hear stories from the women about sadistic and cruel wardens, and sexual exploitation by male guards and prisoners—and even other women. Since security and order are prized, inmates can be moved only at certain times, causing them to wait for long periods before and after interviews. In the San Bernardino, California, jail, for example, where there are hundreds of women awaiting trial, it is not unusual to wait for as long as an hour while the guards locate an inmate. Once they even "lost" a client of mine for a few days. (It is difficult to remember that these women are presumed innocent while awaiting trial.) However, recent lawsuits against certain state prisons have upgraded some conditions in local jails, too.

State prisons, or penitentiaries, are where those convicted of felonies (serious crimes against the state) are usually kept after sentencing. They, too, vary in their conditions; few have ever provided adequate services for women. Most states have only one state facility for women prisoners; in many states, it is simply a separate building on the men's prison grounds. Usually, it is located a great distance from the major urban or metropolitan centers, creating a hardship for the women's families and severely limiting rehabilitation or work-release opportunities. Most prison training opportunities reflect the sexist standards of society, usually training women in financially limited pink collar skills.

Virtually no psychological counseling services are available, except to those whose craziness violates the rights of others by causing grave disturbances. Even then, it is more likely the woman will be labeled a troublemaker and sent "down in the hole" (into solitary confinement). Rarely do women prisoners have personal access to redress of justice; they get to use the law libraries, which are easily available to men, only after midnight, if at all. Like the rest of the criminal justice system, prison has been a male domain. But the system is changing.

U.S. Bureau of Justice statistics indicate that, since 1974, the female prison population in the United States increased 206%, to 22,646 as of June 1985. (These data pertain only to prisoners in state and federal prison, not local jails.) The rate of growth in 1985 was twice as high for female as for male prisoners: 13.3 percent for women and 7.7 percent for men. (Still, fewer than 5 percent of all prisoners are women. According to Angela Browne, in a recent analysis of national homicide statistics,* the number of women who have killed men, the largest category for women who kill, had its first significant decrease ever in 1979, remaining at this lower rate since then. Browne points out that in 1979 battered women's shelters also became more widely available to women. She suggests that, when given alternatives to killing in self-defense, battered women are likely to seek out those alternatives.)

How can we understand such a large increase in such a relatively small population? The Bureau of Justice suggests that women are more likely to be held responsible for their criminal acts in this era of women demanding equality. Some psychologists have raised the possibility that women who might otherwise have been sent off to mental health institutions are now finding their

*To be published in *Law and Society Review* in 1989.

way into prisons because of the serious cutbacks in mental health treatment funds. The deinstitutionalization programs of the 1970s have created many problems, including a larger population of homeless women and of women who commit violent acts. It is difficult to say what percentage of this newly identified group are battered women, and even harder to predict how many of them may find themselves in a position where they have to use deadly force to stay alive.

There are also those who suggest that the women's liberation movement brought with it an increase in violence among women as they integrated with men in a violent society. Frieda Adler, who has written about women who commit violent crimes, is one of those proponents. Much of her work is speculative, based on psychoanalytic theory rather than empirical data. Those who hold to this viewpoint believe that women cannot help but emulate men's violent behavior as they compete with them in the aggressive world outside of their homes. But, if this were really so, the rate of violent crimes would be rising at an even faster pace to match the large numbers of women now working in the marketplace.

Sociologist Murray Straus's latest data show that battered women are striking back more frequently now. He suggests that norms have changed sufficiently for many women to understand that they do not have to be beaten. Using force to get a man to stop his abuse, Straus says, may be viewed as acceptable protective behavior by the women who use it.*

Women who kill are considered high-status offenders within the informal prison hierarchy; and women who kill their "old men" for beating them are greatly respected by other women, most of whom have known about abuse firsthand. If they choose, these formerly isolated battered women can develop new social groups in prison—groups, to be sure, that do not follow

*See *Physical Abuse in American Families: Risk Factors and Adaptations to Violence in 8,145 Families*, by Murray Straus and Richard Gelles (Transaction Books, 1989).

"outside" rules but that nevertheless provide her with the opportunity to connect with women again. (Battered women often learn to devalue other women because of their inability to protect themselves. Their isolation from other women and their dependence upon men fosters that disconnection.) Those women who are fortunate enough to be housed in a facility where there are women's groups to help them explore their interpersonal relationships have a head start when they are on the outside again. If they can learn to celebrate other women's strengths, they can learn to love themselves. Then they are more able to resist pressure from male partners to commit crimes. They are also less likely to live in an abusive relationship.

Yet few women have exposed the fear, shame, and degradation that takes place in prison. Jean Harris, who was sentenced to serve fifteen years to life in New York's Bedford Hills Correctional Facility for killing her lover, "Scarsdale Diet" doctor Herman Tarnower, has written about the disgraceful conditions there.* The New York State Legislature, as the Colorado Supreme Court and similar groups in other states have done, appointed an investigatory commission to look into the potential impact of gender bias on women in various parts of the judicial system. Their recently published report supports Jean Harris's complaints and registers many more. They found that bias against women permeates every level of the judicial system. This report exposed the shameful conditions in prisons and jails, courtrooms, judges' chambers, and attorneys' offices. The chairperson of the commission says reform is on the way, but it will not happen quickly.

It has been widely recognized that women prisoners' children are not likely to be taken care of in their own homes; they usually must be placed in foster care or with relatives, since fathers are rarely willing or able to keep the home together themselves. The children of battered women who have killed their partners may lose both a father and a mother.

*In *Stranger in Two Worlds* (Macmillan, 1986) and *They Always Call Us Ladies: Stories from Prison* (Scribners, 1988).

The special needs of women prisoners and their children have begun to be addressed by several model programs, one of which I visited at Rentz Correctional Institution in Jefferson City, Missouri. Typical of many state penitentiaries, Rentz is an old prison, housing both men and women; it is located in the middle of the state several hours by car from St. Louis and Kansas City. When I visited in September 1984, the women's facility had more than three hundred prisoners. I was invited by a group of women inmates to give a presentation on the psychological impact of having been abused. Although I spent less than two hours there that afternoon, it made a tremendous impact on me.

Rentz houses women convicted of the most serious crimes, including crimes of violence.* Security is tight. I arrived at about 2:00 P.M. for my scheduled talk. Aimlessness and despair seemed to hang over much of the area as we passed by. Finally, we got to a low, single-story building that turned out to be the gymnasium.

The noise was deafening as we entered. All of the women inmates were waiting. Even the women "in the hole" were brought in for this big event. No one was given the choice of opting out; whether they wanted to hear what I had to say or not, the women were forced to be there.

As I took my seat on the stage, panic set in. "What could I possibly have to say to these women?" I wondered.

As I waited for the introductions, I noticed all of the security around the large room. Male and female guards were patrolling up and down every aisle and on the catwalks above us.

"How can I talk to them about uniting together with other women to overcome mutual oppression," I thought. "If I help these women unite together, those guards will freak out. They

*Shortly after my visit the women's prison was moved from Rentz to Chillicothe State Prison, two hours farther away from the populated areas in Missouri, making it even more difficult to staff programs.

won't be able to do their job, which is to control the women's behavior. The women could get so riled that they might become unmanageable. What good will I have done then?"

If ever there was a time when I contemplated fleeing the platform to avoid giving a speech, that was it! I heard myself being introduced. Then it was my turn. The sea of applause was a familiar enough sound; I stood and approached the microphone. Within an instant, I knew what I had to say. I discarded my prepared talk and began speaking from my heart.

I talked of their oppression before coming to prison and reviewed the statistics. "We estimate that about 80 percent of all women prison inmates have experienced some form of abuse. Would those of you who've experienced or even just witnessed abuse in your families, raise your hands?" Slowly at first, then with more deliberateness, women all over the room raised their hands. "Look around you," I said, "almost no one has her hand down! This is a woman's problem, whether you're behind bars or free to walk the streets. And I want to talk with you today, woman to woman."

The tension in the room broke. I could feel these women's pain as I talked. The room was so still that we could hear the creaking shoes of patrolling guards. In conclusion, I said that most of the women in that room would be out of prison one day, and that they could then choose not to be oppressed by the abuse of men. At this, the women broke into spontaneous cheers and applause.

I agreed to respond to questions. The issues these women raised indicated they understood violence on an intimate level. Some of their comments were the sharpest and most analytical and thought-provoking I'd ever heard. Some nearly broke my heart.

"What can I do to protect my five-year-old daughter who's living with my parents while I'm in here? My father sexually abused me at that age, and I think he's abusing her, too."

"My batterer is in the men's section on this prison grounds. He hasn't physically hurt me here, but he has all his friends watch me, so I'm still under his control."

"I talked about my old man beating me in the self-help group, and it got back to him. Now he's pissed at me, and I'm afraid to go back into the group."

"I think I was psychologically abused by my boyfriend, but I wanted his love so badly that I did whatever he asked. That's why I'm here. How can I protect myself so that when I get out I won't do it again, just for his love?"

And on they went. These women weren't afraid to deal directly with the issue of violence. They demonstrated that they understood how to apply theoretical concepts of interpersonal violence to their own lives; they didn't need my examples or stories to provide clarity. They had dozens of their own horror stories, and each could identify with the others. Being stigmatized together and branded as criminals made the label of battered woman easier to accept, even if just for that short hour. I had no doubt that each of them would go back to her regular "tough woman" act later on, for such behavior is necessary for survival in the prison system. But, for a brief period of time, these women had removed their masks and, silently or openly, wept.

III

THE LAW

12

SEXISM AND THE LAW

WHY AREN'T WOMEN—all women—better protected? Why can't our criminal justice system recognize and begin to remedy the tragic circumstances that turn these victims into defendants? We may ask ourselves, too, why the painful lives of so many women are so largely misunderstood by a society that seems determined to erect barriers against even listening to them, much less changing for their benefit.

In many ways, America's social, legal, and religious institutions perpetuate the myth that a woman is to blame for being battered. We must look to the guardians of the halls of power in these institutions to uncover the source of this myth, and we need not look far. Power in America is directly related to gender, class, race, age, able-bodiedness, education, and socioeconomic status. In most of these respects, there is no question that men have a distinct advantage over women.

Men are usually physically stronger than women. They are used to making decisions regarding property and relationships. Men generally are used to having power over others, especially over women, as a matter of course; their power is not considered a privilege but a birthright. (This fact was brought home to me in a personal way during my first marriage, when my husband applied for and received court permission to change his last name, my last name, and our infant son's last name, without my knowledge or consent.) In many states, a husband has the legal right to decide where the family will live, regardless of his wife's wishes. And, in many states, a husband cannot be found guilty of raping his wife.

A man's belief that, in an intimate relationship with a woman, his rights invariably supersede hers, is supported by religion and social customs, as well as the law. This belief has a long history that goes back to the beginnings of the American system of codified justice; witch-hunting was neither its origin nor its sole manifestation. Our system of jurisprudence inherited laws from the English system that upheld a man's right to beat his wife. The law stated, however, that he was within his rights only so long as he used a "stick no thicker than his thumb" to beat her with.* This statute remained on the books, in some states, until recently. Later rulings in American courts of law have implied or suggested a policy of benign neglect where marital violence is concerned. Police action (or lack of action, as it turns out) has certainly upheld this. It is also common, although never admitted as official policy, for an attorney to measure the probable amount of "prosecutable" injury a battered woman has sustained by counting the number of stitches required to close her wounds. And if battered women who kill can demonstrate serious bodily injuries (and a crime scene that backs up their story of imminent danger according to a male standard), they are most likely to be believed by the authorities; if the injuries are bad enough or permanent

*Del Martin provides a fascinating account of the origin of this and similar customs in *Battered Wives* (Volcano Press, 1976), as does Ann Jones in *Women Who Kill* (Holt, Rinehart & Winston, 1980). For a more complete discussion of the interaction between sexism, racism, and battering, see Ann Jones's *Everyday Death;* the subject of that book is Bernadette Powell, a Black woman in Ithaca, New York, who was convicted of second-degree murder in a case that might have been considered a battered woman self-defense case, had she not been Black.

enough, they may be "lucky" and escape being charged with a crime.

In light of all this, it is no mystery that batterers believe they have the right to "discipline" a woman. Furthermore, they believe that others, including legal authorities, have no right to interfere. And many battered women have been socialized to believe not only that their men have the right to beat them but that, if they are beaten, they must somehow deserve to be beaten. Even though many women understand that battering is the man's problem, they feel guilty nevertheless; despite what they know, they feel that somehow, some way, they could have done something "better" to help him stop himself.

We are left with the inescapable conclusion that most women in American society are viewed as properly occupying a marginal position—on the outskirts of power, of prestige, of adulthood itself. This marginal position is one reason why women, like minorities and other oppressed groups in any society, are judged harshly when they strike back at a powerful oppressor. And if average, everyday, "normal" women are judged harshly, women considered to fall outside the norms of acceptable female behavior (whether emotionally, occupationally, or otherwise) are likely to be judged even more unfairly. This phenomenon can be seen with special clarity in small towns, where the extent of her conformity to community standards may dictate exactly how a battered woman is judged or misjudged. The story about Dorothy, in Chapter 9, is a clear example. In fact, helping clients look as much as possible like the people who will judge them is an important part of trial preparation. Some lawyers keep suits and dresses for defendants to wear in court; the more similarity in physical appearance that exists between defendant and jurors, the greater the chance that the jurors will identify with the defendant and be inclined to judge her less harshly. Social psychologists call this "reducing social distance." Creating just the right image—for all members of the defense team—is an important part of any good defense lawyer's strategy.

Our society's discrimination against women pervades all of its institutions. Regrettably, this includes the very institutions that are themselves set up to aid women. Legal aid services, for example, ought to provide adequate services to those women escaping battering situations whose total family income seems high on paper, but who, in reality, have no income of their own. This situation is another sort of "catch 22" for the battered woman from a middle-class or upper-income home; she herself may have no economic resources, but she is often unable to avail herself of legal aid services because her husband's income is taken into account.

In some cases, these women may be pushed, out of fear for their lives, into killing the batterer. In these cases, the law's inherent sexism tends not to recognize economic desperation as a reasonable motive for returning to the batterer in the first place.

The following story is typical.

EDITH'S STORY

Edith Burhle had left her husband, Ken, after an especially brutal battering incident. She was terrified of him, with good reason. But she needed money desperately. Her hospital job in Casper, Wyoming, didn't provide enough of a salary to support a house and pay off all the debts she and Ken had accumulated during their marriage of over twenty-five years. So one day when Ken told her to come see him later at the motel where he was staying temporarily, she agreed. He promised her money that he'd owed her for quite a while.

Frightened but desperate, Edith took a shotgun with her when she went to the motel room. Maybe the gun would dissuade him from even thinking about attacking her again. And she needed that money.

Ken was there, but she was afraid of what would happen if she went inside. So she stayed outside the room, with his door opened only a crack. They talked and argued about the money for about an hour and a half. All the while, Edith kept her eye on the chain stretched across the inside crack of the door. If he made a move to remove that chain, she told herself, she'd turn and run. She didn't need a single reminder of how violent he could be. This time, with money as a source of tension, she knew that if he went out of control he might kill her.

The time wore on, though, and she realized she was no closer to getting the money than before. Ken had probably played her for a sucker again. She decided to leave.

He took the chain off the door and backed away. The door swung open.

Edith could see him bending down, as if to grab something from underneath the bed. She thought she saw a glint of silver. One of the many guns he carried, she thought.

She brought the shotgun to her shoulder and fired.

In a state of shock, Edith dumped the gun in a nearby trash barrel.

A dietitian at the local hospital, she always carried an extra pair of rubber gloves in her pocket. One fell out now near the trash bin. Later a state's attorney would insist that the presence of rubber gloves was *prima facie* evidence that she had premeditated Ken's death.

Edith's defense lawyer asked me to testify as expert witness at her trial in 1980, one year after the same Casper court allowed me to testify in Judy Austin's trial for killing her husband. Judy's jury acquitted her, agreeing she had acted in self-defense.

The retired judge who'd been called in to hear Edith's case because of the regular judge's crowded court calendar came to Casper only rarely now, having retired to Rock Springs, a peaceful community on the other side of the state. He didn't want to hear anything about these "newfangled defenses," he told me. He made sure to let me know that he "liked" what I was doing; it reminded him, he said, of the work he'd done with abused children when he was a more active judge. But, from the beginning, he also made sure to let me know that he didn't consider any self-defense plea in this case valid. Edith had gone after Ken, he reasoned; she'd never have gone to see him in the first place, he thought, if she'd really been afraid of him.

I could have told the judge and jury about the psychological defense mechanisms of minimization and denial; about battered women's survival techniques, including modes of behavior that help them adapt to and endure great abuse; about how women will act when they are desperate, for the necessities of life or for money. But this judge was obviously in no mood to listen.

He likewise refused to allow any testimony at the trial concerning the deceased's bad character. So the jury never had a chance to learn what Edith knew about Ken's violent behavior; because of this, they could not possibly have been expected to understand her state of mind at the time of the homicide. On the other hand, this judge did allow a bank teller to testify that, several years earlier, Edith had forged Ken's name on a loan application for several thousand dollars, using their joint account as collateral. She'd done this to give the money to their son without Ken knowing about it; she was afraid that, if he knew, he'd beat her. In any case, she had made good the loan a long time ago. But, when the defense challenged the relevance of this testimony, the judge said that it *was* admissible, and that it demonstrated her "devious" character.

Of course, he disallowed my expert witness testimony, in which I surely would have maintained that it is fear, not deviousness, that governs the seemingly manipulative nature of a battered woman's actions.

Under these circumstances, there was no way Edith could win an acquittal, or even defend herself at all. Too little of her story was allowed into the courtroom as evidence; the parts that were introduced were poorly explained and thus little understood by the jury. As expected, the judge refused to give the jury a self-defense instruction at the trial's conclusion. Edith was found guilty of second-degree murder; not surprisingly, the judge sentenced her to twenty-five years in prison.

All of her appeals were eventually exhausted, with the Wyoming Supreme Court upholding the original verdict. Edith was seen as a premeditative, conniving, greedy woman, willing to lie or kill for her husband's money. Discounted completely were her physical fear and economic desperation. The blindness of the legal system reinforced the socially ingrained sexism that our society uses to keep women demoralized and abused.

Fortunately for Edith, the prison system proved more equitable for her than the criminal justice system that had put her there. She was incarcerated at Wyoming's Women's Prison, one of the first state penitentiaries to be headed by a woman warden trained to understand the special needs of women in rehabilitation. After serving five years as a model prisoner (which many battered women are), she was recommended for sentence reconsideration. Parole was granted. Despite the long sentence initially imposed on her, Edith did not serve much more time in prison than women convicted of lesser offenses.

Bureaucratic Bias

Judges in most states are reluctant to restrain a man's access to his property, even when it is property jointly owned with his wife. It is a fact that *batterers often suffer no legal consequences whatsoever for their behavior.* Unfortunately, prosecution of the batterer, if and when charges are finally brought, is rarely immediate, enabling the batterer to perpetrate more violence against the battered woman. This failure of the legal system to respond to the problems of battered women in a timely way, along with the unwillingness of police to intervene at all (or, when they do intervene, to do so belatedly), are extremely serious consequences of the sexism that pervades the system.

There are antidotes to these problems, of course. An extremely helpful one is the use of trained advocates, to help battered women get around the maze of bureaucratic red tape that confronts them when they attempt to bring charges against a batterer.*

Bias in Family Law

Family law has been found to be riddled with both overt and subtle gender bias by commissioned state task forces studying the problem.†

Battered women with young children face the most discrimination. In court, appropriate expert witness testimony can clarify a battered woman's story, even in cases in which her history includes so much violence that it is difficult for a jury to believe it. Our legal system can and should facilitate speedy divorces in cases of battery; battered women who leave their husbands should be exempted from charges or countercharges of desertion. Economic restitution could be an effective deterrent to some batterers. To restore the power imbalance created by the man's use of violence, battered women often need to have sole custody of their children. Our society will benefit in these cases by placing the mother in charge as a matter of course, even if it is necessary to provide supportive training and social service assistance. The courts must support reempowerment of women and children during divorce.

---

*All involved professionals should note that it is important to keep careful records and other documentation in order to facilitate speedy, effective prosecution of the batterer.

†New York State has produced a comprehensive task-force report outlining the many areas of discrimination against women.

In Honolulu, Laura Crites has created an effective curriculum to teach judges how to overcome gender bias with battered women. In New York City, similar work has been done by Lynne Schaffran, director of the National Judicial Education Program to Promote Equality for Women and Men in Courts.

Nancy Loving, director of Family Violence Programs at the Police Executive Research Forum in Washington, D.C., works with law enforcement to better protect women and children.

After divorce, child visitation should be strenuously regulated. Any children involved should have their rights represented in a court of law, especially those children who have been sexually abused by the batterer. *Visitation rights should never be granted automatically.* This point cannot be stressed enough; too much depends on it. As we have seen in an earlier chapter, in those custody cases where a batterer is granted such rights, it is not only women but children who suffer.

SUE'S STORY

I first heard about Sue from Nancy Solomon, former director of the Denver Safehouse (one of the few existing long-term shelters for battered women). Nancy called from the judge's chambers in the courthouse of a small mountain town in Colorado.

Sue had taken her two-year-old son, Sam, and fled to the Denver Safehouse when this same judge had refused to grant her a divorce several months earlier. In a most unusual hearing, the judge had listened to Sue's husband, Ronnie, plead that the marriage was not irreconcilable. (Irreconcilability is Colorado's statutory requirement for granting dissolution of a marriage.) In an out-and-out lie, Ronnie had told the judge that he and Sue had slept together the previous night.

What really *had* happened, Sue explained to me later, was that she'd allowed Ronnie to sleep over because she hadn't been able to come up with a scheme that would get him out of the house safely. But they had not slept in the same bed; Sue was too frightened to sleep with Ronnie anymore, especially after the acute battering incident that had caused her to leave him.

That incident had ended with his firing a gun, which he'd pointed first at her, then at himself. The shot missed, hitting neither of them but leaving a gaping hole in the ceiling above their bed. This incident happened after several hours of terrifying threats and physical abuse, in which he'd beaten her terribly, breaking several bones and causing internal bleeding, all the while threatening to kill her first, then himself. Later, hospital records would document her broken bones, as well as his drunken and violent behavior in the emergency room. Police records, too, would attest to his long history of violence and wife beating.

Despite this, the judge involved in their divorce case, William Jones, refused to grant Sue a divorce, or even a restraining order. He wanted to give them time to attempt a reconciliation, he said; he also wanted to request more information concerning their marital history from the local authorities.

Nancy Solomon contacted me when Judge Jones ordered psychological evaluations of Sue and Ronnie. I was asked to perform the evaluation of Sue, while another psychologist agreed to evaluate Ronnie. Since the partners were disputing the child's placement, county social services were to perform a child custody evaluation.

It didn't take long for me to determine that Sue was a classic battered woman. A successful, bright businesswoman who had quit law school when she fell in love with and married her "mountain man," Ronnie, four years earlier, she had understood intellectually how dangerous Ronnie was but wanted desperately to believe that she could handle the situation, protecting both herself and her child. Yet, as soon as Ronnie began to abuse them, she knew she should send her two older children from a previous marriage to live with their father. Emotionally, if not intellectually, it became obvious to Sue that she'd already paid an extremely heavy price for this relatively short-lived love affair. Now, though, she refused to give up the home they'd shared. Other than her job, the house was her only remaining financial resource. She couldn't bear to face her parents, who had put up the money to help her purchase the house and who wanted to maintain with their friends and family their social pretenses about Sue's allegedly successful life.

Although he never came out and labeled Ronnie a batterer, the psychologist evaluating him did note his aggressive and abusive tendencies. In addition, Ronnie had terrorized a child welfare worker assigned to the custody evaluation, then accused her of being biased against him. Frightened as she was, the child welfare worker still had the courage to do the right thing and recommend that Sue retain custody of the child.

At the next hearing, several months later, Judge Jones agreed with professional recommendations to dissolve the marriage and place Sam in Sue's custody. But he gave Ronnie liberal, unsupervised visitation rights. This ruling is almost always the court's recommendation, in Colorado as well as in many other states, regardless of the danger it might pose to a mother and her children.

As might have been expected, Ronnie immediately abused his visitation rights. He flaunted his power and control by not bringing Sam back to Sue on time, sometimes disappearing for days on end with the boy. The child often returned to Sue telling horror stories of violence, guns, and drugs.

Eventually, the court agreed to have them meet to exchange the boy at a nearby convenience store, so that Sue wouldn't have to deal with Ronnie's intimidating presence, alone in her isolated mountain home. Because his verbal abuse and threats to her became worse as time went on, she hired a bodyguard to go with her to the store for the weekly exchanges. The bodyguard soon quit, saying that it was "too dangerous" for him. Yet the child—at two, three, four, and five years of age—was expected to visit his dangerous father with equanimity. Like most children, who have no choice in the matter, Sam accommodated and did the best he could.

One day, though, while he was at Ronnie's home, two thugs broke in and beat Ronnie up. They tied up Sam and left him in a closet. When the police finally brought him back to Sue, the child was in a state of terror.

During the prosecution that followed, it came to light that the assault had occurred around a drug deal gone sour. Obviously, Ronnie had thought little of placing his child in unnecessary danger because of his criminal life-style. But even then, Judge Jones did not try to stop Ronnie's visitation rights.

Sue's house was up for sale; she knew it was only a matter of time before she left the state. She intended to ask Judge Jones for permission to take Sam and join her older children in another state. (Asking the court for permission to move is now a required part of many divorce decrees, one more way to keep women under control.) Surely, Sue reasoned, the judge wouldn't keep both sets of children apart from their mother.

But when the time came, Sue lost her courage. She was afraid of returning to the court that had been so unfair to her. She was also terrified that Ronnie would kidnap Sam, as he was threatening to do. So she fled the state of Colorado first, taking Sam with her and then sending Judge Jones a letter explaining the reasons for her actions, including a forwarding address. She had recently gotten in touch with Ronnie's ex-wife, Kim; and what Kim had told her about Ronnie's treatment of her and of their child had frightened Sue even more.*

Kim's description of her abuse at Ronnie's hands was a replay of the torment Sue was experiencing. Ronnie still made harassing telephone calls to Kim frequently. No matter where she went or how often she changed her unlisted number, he would eventually track her down, threatening more violence to her and her family. Sometimes, Kim said, he would just show up, demanding his visitation rights without notice. Their son had been well-adjusted during the four years she'd managed to hide out and keep Ronnie from visiting; but as soon as Ronnie found them, the boy's behavior began to deteriorate markedly. Still acting out his need to coerce and control, Ronnie refused to return the boy at the scheduled end of a visit, alternately terrorizing him and attempting to win his favor with expensive gifts. Kim felt she could not afford another legal battle when she could barely put enough food on the table for herself and her child.

*Sue was not exaggerating her fears (as the court would later counter), and neither was Kim. Ronnie had kidnapped his oldest son after Kim divorced him; he'd done this immediately upon finding out that, in order to escape his incessant harassment and abuse, she was planning to leave the state. Later, I asked Sue if she thought she would have gone ahead and married Ronnie had she known about Kim's experiences with him. Like so many other battered women, Sue's answer indicated that she probably would have anyway.

It is truly frightening that Kim dropped out of sight shortly after her affidavit was submitted to the court on Sue's behalf. She may have been too terrified to stay aboveground. Worse still, there is always the possibility that Ronnie did something to harm her. We just don't know. We may never know.

Despite his knowledge of the violence in this case, Judge Jones was infuriated that Sue had left town. For some reason, he seemed to take her flight as a personal affront. He knew that Ronnie was terribly violent. But, while he himself had personally sentenced the two thugs who'd broken into Ronnie's home, beat him up, and tied Sam in the closet, he still maintained that Sue's fears were blown out of proportion. In one court proceeding, this judge actually stated that Ronnie threatened too much (as mountain men are apt to do, was the implication) and Sue overreacted.

Apparently, it was easier for Judge Jones to deny that a real potential existed for someone to die than to courageously do what was necessary to protect Sue and her child. In an astonishing display of insensitivity—and, I believe, of deeply ingrained sexism—he granted Ronnie's *ex parte* legal motions: first, to find Sue in contempt of court; second, to transfer legal custody of Sam to Ronnie. Without really sufficient legal grounds for doing so (and without a proper hearing!),* in my opinion Judge Jones allowed his personal temperament to stand in the way of justice.

*An *ex parte* court action is one that is held without both parties being present. Most of the new domestic violence protection laws permit a battered woman to be granted a temporary order of protection, occupation of the family home, custody of the children, and maintenance on an *ex parte* basis, with the presence of the batterer. This is done to protect women and children from further danger, as well as from those batterers who flee and hide after a battering incident, leaving the woman with no legal recourse until she can find and serve him with the necessary legal documents. However, each state requires a more formal hearing within a specified period of time, to change the temporary orders into permanent ones. Permanently granted custody cannot be changed in this way. And in the state of Colorado, an additional ruling about change of custody indicates that it cannot even be *requested* more than once every two years, and then only under highly unusual circumstances impacting in a major way on the child's best interests.

But it was to be the child who suffered now—a frightened young boy, ordered into the custody of a known violent offender and criminal.

One more man had gotten angry with a woman for not obeying his orders. One more man had tried to control a woman with punishment, using her innocent child to force her to obey him. And he had the state's judicial power behind him.

Judge Jones's orders set a number of things irrevocably in motion.

Forced to go into hiding, Sue became a fugitive. Receiving inadequate legal advice in the state to which she had fled with Sam, she was told she had to wait until she met residency requirements before filing for a change in jurisdiction. (She should have tried to file for an emergency hearing; but, again, no one with the power to do that wanted to believe that it was an emergency.)

Although Judge Jones had led me and others to believe that he would grant jurisdiction to the other state, so that another judge could make the final decision, he refused to give up his jurisdiction when Sue finally did get a lawyer to apply for the transfer, even when the new judge personally called him with the request.

The temporary custody change gave Ronnie the right to apply to the local missing-child agency, which puts pictures of missing children on milk cartons, posters, and the nightly TV news. Because Ronnie was now legal custodian, the agency was obliged to agree to advertise in order to locate the boy. My own telephone calls to them and the calls of Sue's lawyer, attesting to the danger in which this would place Sam, did not help; although agency officials promised over the telephone not to run the ads, they later admitted to being so terrorized by Ronnie's aggressive behavior that, in an attempt to placate him, they made sure that the child's picture appeared everywhere.

Sue fled to a battered women's shelter in another part of the country. This time, no one knew where she'd gone. But her life had become miserable; no matter where she went, it seemed, she could not escape Ronnie or the terrible effect he had on her life. He'd even shown up at her parents' home, threatening to hurt them if they refused to help him get his child back.

After one full year of Sue's being in hiding, reachable only through a post office box, Judge Jones set a date to hear the contempt citation against her. Sue told her lawyer she'd be present. She was tired of being on the run, she said.

It was agreed that she would not have to produce her son at that time. The judge further agreed to search everyone who entered the courtroom, in order to make sure that Ronnie could not bring in a gun with him, as he had done before.

Sue arrived in Denver under a pseudonym and was met by a protective police escort, which took her directly to a battered women's shelter. This protective deception was a real risk; if the police had learned her real identity and checked their computer, she could have been arrested on the spot for felony kidnapping since she'd taken her child out of the state without legal permission. She also might have been killed by Ronnie, who was constantly threatening to do so. She had decided that Ronnie was a greater threat to her life than Judge Jones.

Arrangements had been made for her to be driven safely, caravan style, up to the courthouse in the little mountain town of Eagle, Colorado. Her lawyer,* myself, a friend, and Sue were met

---

*Sue's lawyer was Jeanne Elliott, the attorney described in Chapter 4 who was shot and paralyzed in court three months later. Another example of gender bias is in the disparate attitudes of the attorneys in this case. Maurice Franks, the highly paid darling of fathers' rights groups nationwide, author of a best-selling book on the subject, is rumored to work only for those who pay their fees up front. Jeanne, on the other hand, was always underpaid by women who could barely afford to pay their own rent. (At the time of her shooting, she was handling more than 170 cases in order to make a modest living.) Yet, many of her clients' battering partners were willing to spend large amounts of money on their own attorneys, in order to ensure that their wives and children ended up with nothing. Leonore Weitzman documents this and other social biases against divorcing women in her book *The Divorce Revolution.* Phyllis Chesler

at the door of the courthouse by the judge and three sheriff deputies; one was a woman, prepared to search us further if the metal
detector and pat-down indicated anything suspicious. We were
shown to a private room adjacent to the judge's chambers. So
were Ronnie and his new young wife, but care was taken to keep
the two parties apart. There was no typical waiting around in the
hallways for this hearing; it seemed that, finally, Judge Jones had
taken our concerns seriously.

Ronnie had by now fired his previous attorney and hired a
well-known fathers' rights lawyer. This lawyer had arranged for
Ronnie to be examined by an unlicensed psychologist, who was
prepared to testify that Ronnie was a nice, sweet guy who just
could not possibly have been guilty of the violent behavior of
which he was accused. (Even the judge, by now familiar with
Ronnie's history of violence, looked incredulous when this "psychologist" testified.) Armed with his new "expert" witness testimony, Ronnie's lawyer demanded an immediate transfer of custody rights. Because, unknown to Sue, *her previous attorney
had agreed to allow this unlicensed psychotherapist's firm to
conduct a new custody evaluation,* the judge's order allowed
them, rather than an unbiased evaluator, to complete a home
study.

Sue, meanwhile, became convinced that she was sitting in
another kangaroo court. She turned to me and whispered that she
was "getting out of here."

"No," I replied, a little panic-stricken, "there are six deputies in here with their hands on their guns, just waiting for a wrong
move. Don't let it be yours!"

"Okay," she agreed. Later, she would say that it had been
my obvious distress that had persuaded her to stay. Thank good-
ness for the strength of the positive relationship between therapist
and client!

---

describes its negative impact on women's ability to parent their children in
Mothers on Trial.

It was difficult for all of us who had been involved in this difficult and dangerous case to listen quietly to the untrained mental health "professional" testify. He claimed to be a psychologist (a criminal act, in Colorado, for those who do not hold a license to practice psychology) and no one knew differently at the time. Nevertheless, the "psychologist" arrogantly offered opinions about Ronnie's personality, based on a single day's testing, ignoring previously established legal, psychological, and medical data to the contrary. This was simply a custody case, he claimed, with an angry, vicious ex-wife denying her decent, innocent, nonviolent-unless-provoked husband access to his own son. (Newer versions of this theme currently parade before family courts as Parental Alienation Syndrome. Whatever it is called, gender bias against mothers continues to mask maltreatment of children, who are often forced to spend time with dangerously abusive fathers. A new underground movement, called Sanctuary,* has been formed to give support to mothers, like Sue, who feel that they must flee from those courts where they cannot get justice. Although I believe that it is an extremely serious move to change identities and locales and to hide, some women see it as the only possible way to protect their children.)

Jeanne Elliott argued a motion requesting that Judge Jones reconsider his initial change of custody order. She cited case law highlighting the lack of due process in this case, which violated current state custody procedure.

At this, the judge became incensed. He proceeded to lecture from the bench for close to fifteen minutes, taking pot shots

---

*In February 1989 *People* magazine printed a story about the volunteers who provide sanctuary and of several fleeing parents who used their limited resources. As of this writing, it is my understanding that all of these people have been found by the FBI and arrested. In some cases the children have been sent back to their alleged abusers, unprotected. Dr. Elizabeth Morgan has been in jail on a Washington, D.C., judge's contempt order for almost two years now; she has refused to reveal the whereabouts of her daughter to protect her from the sexual abuse that Dr. Morgan and her experts (but not the judge) believe she was subjected to by the father.

at everyone, but mostly at Sue, Jeanne Elliott, and me. He admitted that Jeanne might have legal authority on her side; but he had no intention of turning the child over to Ronnie, he said, unless the home study ordered showed that it was safe. He also refused to review a report from the child's current psychotherapist, because "psychologists can put things in children's minds," he opined as he stared directly at me.

As abruptly as he had begun the tirade, he stopped. He refused to hear any more, advising Jeanne that she "knew what she could do" if she didn't like his opinion.

Then he stormed out of the courtroom.

As dramatically as it had begun, the hearing was over. Sue was ordered to turn her son over to Ronnie in thirty days in order to ameliorate her contempt of court conviction.

How Jeanne Elliott managed to stand perfectly still during Judge Jones's outrageous tirade is something that still amazes and mystifies me. Personally, I wanted to scream at him—something like: *Can't you see what you're doing? You're fueling this man's harassment and abusive behavior by letting him think that he has the ability and the right to parent his child. You are sending a message to the entire community, trivializing his violence against two women. You are refusing to acknowledge that he has put his own child at risk of physical harm because of his violent criminal life-style. He does not listen to your orders requiring timely visitation exchanges and flaunts his inability to follow the required parenting skills in the state's Children's Code. Batterers rarely have the ability to parent children without some use of violent coercion. And you are fattening the pocketbook of a misogynistic attorney. Surely, you must know that, by feeding your own ego, you are putting a child's life in danger. His therapist reports that he already has recurring nightmares. All because a woman defied your unjust orders—terrified for her life because you failed to use your power to help her. Where is your sense of reason? Where is your sense of justice?*

Of course, I kept my mouth shut. But he isn't the only judge in the nation who is taking children away from good mothers.*

Those of us on Sue's defense team barely contained ourselves as we were escorted by sheriff's deputies to the small airport, about twenty miles away, in Eagle-Vail. Sue was scheduled to fly into Denver on a small commuter plane, so she could safely connect to other transportation at the larger airport there. Emotionally wracked, though, she realized that she was unable to leave just yet. All of us, in fact, were terribly upset at this unexpected outcome. And we feared even more violence before it was over.

"Let him send me to jail for disobeying his orders," Sue bravely said, trying to relax over dinner in nearby Vail. "Why is he making my child suffer because of what I've done trying to protect him?"

None of us could answer that. But we were all silently obsessed, I think, with trying to come up with an answer—some answer, any answer. As we talked and ate, I realized that my stomach was squeezing itself into knots; I'd felt that way since the early afternoon, when it had become clear that a fair hearing would not be held. As I tried to keep Sue from falling apart, I found

---

*National judges associations have been trying to deal with the problem; state court judges usually attend one or more meetings per year where they discuss these kinds of issues. Richard Price, an acting superior court judge in New York City and a vice-president of the American Judges Association, has used his considerable influence by lecturing and writing about gender bias in general and violence against women specifically.

Unfortunately, most judges' knowledge of battered women is limited to personal experience or short exposure at professional meetings. Rarely do they get out into the community to see, at first hand, the impact of the escalation of violence against women and children as it is occurring. Ask anyone who is out there in the community dealing with these problems, though, and they will cite numerous stories similar to Sue's. Phyllis Chesler has given many examples in her book *Mothers on Trial* and provides a theoretical analysis to help understand this serious social problem.

it difficult to deal with my own physical pain. So I ignored it, and it got worse.

At last, armed somewhat with knowledge of what Jeanne's next legal steps would be (including the unusual move of going to the Colorado Supreme Court on an original writ),* we finished dinner and drove the two hours into Denver.

During the next month, Jeanne researched, prepared, and submitted the motion to the Colorado Supreme Court. With only four days left before the deadline when Sue was ordered to turn Sam over to Ronnie's custody, the Supreme Court justices ordered a stay in the proceedings. This meant everything was on hold, as if the clock stopped until the Supreme Court decided what to do. Judge Jones was ordered to "show cause" why the high court should not reverse his orders because they did not conform to the law. The days for his time period ticked off slowly for Sue, who was still wondering what she would do if Sam couldn't stay with her. But Judge Jones let it go without response, and his orders were vacated by the higher court judges. We could hardly celebrate the victory at that time. Jeanne had been struck down by another violent husband's bullets in another courtroom. She lay fighting for her life as Sue and Sam regained some control of theirs.

Sue was now back to the original change of custody proceedings filed by Ronnie. Sandra Pfaff, another well-known Denver battered woman's rights attorney, took over the case. Judge Jones was now scrupulously following the law; he permitted Michael Lindsay, a psychotherapist well respected for his work with violent men, to conduct the new custody evaluation. Mike didn't have any difficulty recognizing Ronnie's pattern of violent behavior and the danger it posed to Sam. After several conference calls with Sam's therapist, Michael Lindsay recommended that custody remain with Sue and proposed a schedule of supervised visitation that slowly increased Ronnie's time with his son based on Sam's tolerance and emotional reactions. By the time of the hearing that fall, Maurice Franks no longer represented Ronnie, who said he

*Which she eventually won.

was out of money. Judge Jones did not change Sam's custodial parent and did order visitation according to Michael Lindsay's recommendations. It is almost four years since the last court hearing, and Ronnie has not complied with the visitation schedule. Sue says Sam is growing up sturdy and secure in her home, with her other children nearby to be his companions.

Jeanne and I were alone in my car as I drove home later. I shared my physical distress with her, and vowed to pay attention to the distinct messages my body was trying to give me. The conversation led me to the inevitable conclusion that I would have to stop accepting any battered woman custody cases at all for a while. They were making me physically ill.

At the very next staff meeting in my offices, I shared this decision with my associates. Some of them were eager to continue the custody evaluations themselves; so Lon Kopit, our only male associate, assumed administrative responsibility immediately. I agreed to continue as a supervisor and consultant.

In a way, I had been temporarily as defeated by the sexism of a single male judge—representing the sexism of an entire legal system—as Sue had been.

Saying What Needs to Be Said

As we have seen, trial judges have a great deal of discretion in determining the conduct and outcome of courtroom legal procedure. Yet how many judges in our male-identified, male-dominated courts are sensitized to women's issues? Very few, indeed, have ever taken the time to think about the prevailing male norms and their own adaptations to them. It is extremely difficult for any judge, whose job is to uphold a particular social order, to rule against the prevailing norms of the system. And the prevailing norms of our criminal justice system work against women, especially those who kill. In our culture, women are not supposed to use violence, even to defend themselves against a potentially fatal attack.

Battered women especially are in a double bind. Leaving the batterer is, in many cases, more dangerous than remaining; as we have demonstrated, separation is the time of greatest volatility and peril in battering relationships. But staying with the batterer brings with it inevitable physical abuse, an ever-lingering threat of death. Whatever the battered woman does, she simply is not safe.

How does one convince men of this truth, though, men who have never experienced such a paradox in their own lives?

Saying what needs to be said in our courts of law, again and again if necessary, is a step in the right direction. But battered women often cannot speak for themselves. And women's ways of describing the world are frequently at variance with the descriptive process required in the courtroom.

Women tend to see events as occurring in patterns rather than in discrete individual increments or incidents. What a court calls factual information is well understood by most women only when it is supported by context and background. Women tend to see a man's facial features and the clothes he is wearing, as well as hear his words. Their interpretation of the emotions expressed by his nonverbal body language provide as much important information as does his verbal message. Women also use their prior knowledge or history of a situation in order to assign meaning to an event. Things that happen within a known context take on a different meaning than those occurring in a random pattern. Women try to figure out why certain events occurred, in order to understand them. "What happened" in a particular situation often blends, in a woman's mind, with her own analysis of the process.

In this sense, separating the facts from what people think about them or how they are interpreted (that is, within their context) is simply an artificial device; it's certainly not the way women know the world best. Given women's need to be involved in relationships with others, opinions count as much as facts to them. Such distinction does seem to be typical of male thinking, however. In the male model, events are seen as factual entities, taken separately from the context in which they occurred; intellectual understanding is separate, too, from process analysis. Patterns may be perceived, but usually they are not interwoven in the male mind with discrete individual incidents. Men, therefore, can more easily tell their stories using the rules of the legal system.

To fit into this male world, many women do learn to think in this overly rational way. But it is not their natural voice.

Rules of evidence require that only factual accounts of discrete individual incidents be given. Process analysis is considered to be "opinion," which is viewed as providing less reliable information than "the facts," and is thus generally disallowed as testimony, unless offered by an expert witness. In a courtroom, the contextual background of events is considered extraneous; the rules of evidence do not permit lawyers to discuss it, except in their opening and closing arguments. Legal truth is proven by each side presenting its very best "factual" position, then letting judge or jury decide which position seems most plausible.

But this system is a perfect setup for denying women justice. While most men function well in such a system, most women do not.* Women often prefer to explain incidents by telling stories; they give a reliable narrative account of events, and of how they and others feel about them. But narrative stories are not admitted as evidence, even when the narrator is on trial for

---

*The noted scholar Elise Boulding writes, in *The Underside of History: A View of Women Through Time,* of the "critical mass" necessary to change men's ways to those accommodating women. She suggests that a "tipping balance" occurs when 30 percent of a group is female. But will we have to wait until the percentage of women accused of crimes increases to such a high level before the Rules of Evidence begin to take women's ways of knowing and of expressing into account? I hope not. Certainly, the stories we have told here make a compelling case for instituting such changes and accommodations now.

her life. When judges (or lawyers) direct women to stick to the facts, women often have trouble, because women, in general, have trouble separating discrete factual events from the general patterns of their lives. The stark courtroom atmosphere (often compared to an exclusive men's club) further intimidates women. Women tend to interpret courtroom neutrality as hostility, reinforced by too few smiles and lots of impatience. Judicial intemperance and angry commands also inhibit women from telling their own truth.

For battered women, these conditions may especially magnify their perceived sense of danger. They are rarely able to act as effective witnesses on their own behalf, at least not without a great deal of assistance.

An expert witness, however, is allowed latitude to use context in the opinions expressed, telling the battered woman's story from her perspective in a more male-approved way.

Important Legal Precedents

Several legal decisions rendered over the last decade have helped pave the way for battered women's self-defense cases. They cast a ray of hope along the heretofore lonely, dark road women have traveled in our criminal justice system.

In the mid-1970s, Joan Little stabbed a jail warden with an ice pick as he forced her to perform sexual acts on demand (she'd been imprisoned for an unrelated crime). In defending herself against his abuse, she committed a violent act. But the act itself was found to fall under a "lesser of two evils" doctrine, a tenet of law whereby it is recognized that sometimes an individual may commit a lesser criminal act that prevents a more serious criminal act from occurring. In a sense, all acts of self-defense fall under that doctrine, as the intent of both persons is to use violence. A person can be found to be justified in using actions that under other circumstances would be considered criminal or evil. Joan Little asserted a self-defense plea, and was acquitted, even though she was an impoverished, angry, southern Black woman doing time for another crime and had stabbed a white warden to death.

Women's rights groups hailed this decision as a victory for all women who resist rape by killing their attackers. But the celebration was short-lived. It soon became clear that, in many jurisdictions, *the woman had to be blameless in bringing on the attack* before her violence could be deemed defensive and not retaliatory. (We all know the lies surrounding rape victims, who are often accused of having "asked for it" because they were seductive or didn't take better precautions to protect themselves.)

In her landmark book, *Women Who Kill*, (Holt, Rinehart & Winston, 1980), Ann Jones describes the historical shifts in cultural understanding of why most women kill and explores their subsequent treatment at the hands of the court. She demonstrates how women in the eighteenth and nineteenth centuries who poisoned the men who abused them—women who previously had led virtuous and "ladylike" lives—were often excused for their behavior and escaped punishment completely, whereas those who defied the sex-role standards of their time were usually put to death. During periods when women were more vociferously demanding their rights, those who killed men were punished more severely than they might have been during relatively "tamer" times. Obviously, the emergence of a North American women's movement in modern times places us in a historical context of strife between men and women concerning women's rights.

Jones also introduces statistics indicating that throughout history a fairly stable number of women kill, accounting for about 10 to 15 percent of all homicides. Thus, the percentage of homicides does not rise; rather, *the number of women punished by our justice system fluctuates, according to the social norms and perceived vociferousness of women's rights groups at the time.* In fact, Angela Browne's analysis of the homicide statistics kept by the Centers for Disease Control (CDC) indicates that, for the first time since the CDC began to keep this data, in the period 1979–1981 there was a decrease in the number of women killing men, but an increase in the number of men killing women; yet the numbers of women being sentenced to prison keeps rising. These findings support Ann Jones's data.

Historians of the American West like Richard Maxwell Brown have traced changes in the original American legal standard calling for a *duty to retreat* from any attack; that is, for a violent act of self-defense to be deemed legally justified in a court of law, the intended victim was legally required to show "good faith" attempts to escape from the attacker before acting violently in self-defense.* Brown demonstrates that, as the West became settled, the duty to retreat became, instead, the *duty to stand one's ground.* That is, it became an individual's legal duty to defend what was his against any other individual's attack.

I have used the masculine pronoun deliberately in discussing Brown's theories. In written or oral histories of the American West, this attitude, implying a duty to defend oneself or one's property from attack, seems not to extend to women. Women in our culture have long been expected to rely on a father, a son, or a husband to defend them.

Despite the legal statutes existent in most states allowing any individual to stand his or her own ground on his or her own property (rented or owned), women are still expected to use means other than violence to escape from physical attack. Although not legally required in fact, it is true in practice that the burden of proof falls on any battered woman who kills to demonstrate why she did not turn and run instead. The real question should be, of course: why did the batterer not let her go?

Unless a jury has been given a specific jury instruction that defines the woman's legal right not to leave her own home, an acquittal on grounds of self-defense is unlikely.†

*Brown's commentary was offered at a conference on Violence in the West, held in 1979 at Eastern Oregon State College, LaGrande, Oregon.

†Massachusetts probably has the most restrictive self-defense statute, requiring evidence of a "cooling off" period, as well as evidence of an attempt to retreat. However, after a two-day admissibility hearing on December 28–29,

In addition, studies show that most women tend to exaggerate and overreport their own acts of violence, whereas men tend to underreport theirs.* These tendencies also work against a woman taking the witness stand in her own defense when she is on trial for her life.

Obviously, battered women (like women in general) are not as well trained in physical combat as are men. Men learn to use parts of their bodies as weapons. To fight equally with a man, a woman usually needs a weapon.

This reality has been acknowledged by an important new, ground-breaking standard established by the Washington State Supreme Court in their 1977 *State vs. Wanrow* decision.†

Yvonne Wanrow, a small, petite Native American woman, shot and killed a man when he entered the house where she was staying. The man was someone she believed had previously molested a neighbor's child. When he approached her, drunk, it was late at night; tension was high. As Yvonne would later testify, she'd been so terrified that he'd harm her and the children in her care that she had armed herself with a loaded rifle and sat vigilantly, awaiting his threatened arrival. She had recently broken her leg, which was in a cast; she was therefore unable to move out of the way quickly or leave the premises when he stormed in on her. At that point she picked up the rifle, then fired the shot that killed him.

1988, a Springfield judge ruled Battered Woman Syndrome testimony admissible in the case of a woman named Lisa Becker Grimshaw, who was on trial for conspiracy to commit murder.

*See, for example, the work of psychologist Dr. Gayla Margolin at the University of California, Los Angeles, and social worker Dr. Daniel Saunders at the University of Wisconsin Medical School in Madison.

†*State vs. Wanrow*, supra 559 p. 2d 548 (1977) 558.59. The state Supreme Court's forward-looking decision, based on the arguments presented, was to grant Yvonne Wanrow a new trial. In fact, she never had her new trial. A plea to manslaughter, with no additional jail time, was offered her; she decided to take it, ending her legal battles and putting the past behind her.

At her first trial, the presiding judge refused to give the jury instructions for a self-defense verdict. He himself stated that he simply did not understand why Yvonne had "just sat there" holding a gun, waiting for what seemed to her to be the inevitable. Wanrow was convicted of murder; but the decision was over-turned on appeal because of the judge's error in not giving the jury accurate instructions.

In its decision, the Washington State Supreme Court jus-tices put forth an argument that would prove an essential part of the beginning steps toward making American courtrooms more equitable places for women. Their decision supported recent scientific research on the negative, unequalizing effects of sex-role stereotyping and behavior. First, the Court recognized that using male standards, including the masculine pronoun, in a self-de-fense jury instruction could create a cognitive set in jurors' minds that might prove prejudicial to a woman defendant; therefore, this would in and of itself deny the woman equal protection under the law. Also, since the legal standard is an individual's reasonable perception of danger, the Court ruled that *a woman's reasonable perception of danger may differ from a man's.*

Furthermore, the Court went so far as to establish what is now known as the Wanrow jury instruction, a ruling now ac-cepted in most states. This is what the Wanrow court said:

> The instruction (as given by the trial court) leaves the jury with the impression the objective standard to be applied is that applied to an altercation between two men. The impression created— that a 5′4″ woman with a cast on her leg and using a crutch must, under the law, somehow repel an assault by a 6′2″ intoxicated man without employing weapons in her defense, unless the jury finds her determination of the degree of danger to be objectively reasonable—constitutes a separate and distinct misstatement of the law and, in the context of this case, violates the respondent's right to equal protection under the law. The respondent was entitled to have the jury consider her actions in the light of her own perceptions of the situation, including those perceptions

which were the product of our nation's long and unfortunate history of sex discrimination. . . . Until such time as the effects of that history are eradicated, care must be taken to assure that our self-defense instructions afford women the right to have their conduct judged in light of the individual physical handicaps which are the product of sex discrimination. To fail to do so is to deny the right of the individual woman involved to trial by the same rules which are applicable to male defendants.*

This decision was hailed as the beginning of a new standard of justice in our nation, one that may acknowledge the necessity for ruling differently in cases involving women. This just and long-overdue ruling recognizes the supportive scientific data demonstrating different behavioral standards for men and women. It was a breakthrough and a real beginning.

We who advocate for battered women can only hope for more breakthroughs of a similar nature. For if justice is to truly be justice, it must be so for all people: justice untainted by sexism or oppression; by the needs of cruel individuals to tame and control; by the needs of men in our society to keep economic, social, and legal power all to themselves, and to keep others, especially women, on the outer fringes of their inner circle.

---

*State vs. Wanrow, supra 559 p. 2d 548 (1977) 558.59.

13

LEGAL ISSUES

O UR LAW IS BASED on the intent of an act, as well as its consequence. Homicides have different degrees of legal culpability, and not all are considered criminal acts. It is the state's burden to prove that a defendant actually committed the act, and to demonstrate beyond a reasonable doubt the defendant's state of mind at the time of the homicide.

If a person holds a reasonable belief that she or he needs to defend her or himself from imminent death or bodily injury, then the homicide can be found to be justified. That is called self-defense.

If a police officer kills in the line of duty, that homicide is often said to be legally justifiable. If a convicted criminal receives the death penalty and the state carries it out, that too is legally justifiable homicide. Each death may be morally wrong, but in neither case is it murder, nor is it punishable under the law.

If a person plans to kill someone and carefully executes the plan, it is called premeditated, deliberate, or *first-degree murder.* If the homicide wasn't planned, but the act was such that a death would obviously result, it is *second-degree murder.* (First-degree murder is said to be committed knowingly, while second-degree murder does not have that element.) But both acts are considered intentional, and so are labeled murder. Some states add an additional category that takes special circumstances into account, raising murder to a *capital offense,* one in which a conviction automatically calls for either the death penalty or life in prison with no possible parole. Such a homicide needs to be particularly brutal, with aggravating circumstances. This category is usually reserved for mass murderers, serial killers, those who kill in a particularly heinous way, those who lure or lie in wait for their victim, and those who hire a killer. Most of the noted killers who fall into this category are men who have been abuse victims at some time in their lives. But some battered women who have hired others to kill their abusive mates have also faced the death penalty.

Other legal categories by which a homicide can be judged are "nonintent" crimes, usually called *manslaughter.* In this category, something happens to cause an impulsive act, perhaps an interaction between the perpetrator and the victim that "provokes" the act. *Voluntary manslaughter* is said to occur when an individual is aware that a death can result from her or his behavior but is nevertheless in such an emotional state that he or she does it anyhow. (In this case, the emotional state is said to interfere with the ability to form intent.) *Involuntary manslaughter* is when a person engages in reckless behavior that accidentally results in someone's death. In some states, involuntary manslaughter can be charged as a misdemeanor rather than a felony. (A felony is a more serious crime than a misdemeanor and has a worse punishment. Misdemeanors are often punished by fines and less than one year in jail.)

If an individual is suffering from mental illness that impairs her or his ability to know, or diminishes or alters the intent to act, then the level of responsibility can be affected; in many states, it is lowered one category. In others, a special *guilty but mentally ill* category has been legislated. Because this last category is so new, there are as yet very few practitioners who understand all of its implications.

In all of these categories, the result is the same: someone

is dead. But the defendant's *state of mind,* the *legal intent,* and therefore the *level of responsibility* is different in each. The punishment is different, too. Intent crimes are assigned longer sentences than those deemed accidental. If there are aggravating circumstances, a trial court judge can double the sentence. If there are mitigating circumstances, a lesser sentence can be imposed.

Women account for approximately 10 percent of all the homicide perpetrators in this country. Since the establishment of a system of battered women's shelters, that rate is going down.*

Admissibility Issues

A successful battered woman's self-defense case almost always revolves around her ability to prove *reasonable perception of imminent bodily danger* at the time of the homicide.

What is allowed as evidence or as relevant testimony in a trial, and who is allowed to testify, have a particularly crucial bearing on the outcome of any homicide case in which the defendant is a battered woman. In my experience as an expert witness, admissibility issues have been a constant source of concern. In the early days (until the mid-1980s), when asked to act as expert witness on the behalf of any battered woman who had killed, I never knew whether my testimony would be admitted in court by the presiding judge. Although less common today, admissibility issues still dominate the evaluations and preparations for the trial. Since these issues are of such concern for anyone involved in litigating or in providing other professional support for battered women, they bear some exploration here.

In most states, self-defense definitions require demonstration that the woman has used the least sufficient amount of force necessary to prevent bodily harm. Such a definition is often trans-

*According to Angela Browne, in a presentation at the American Psychological Association Annual Convention, Atlanta, Georgia, August 1988.

lated to mean proof of why the battered woman did not leave her relationship. (As we have seen time and again, leaving the relationship does not mean that the battering, abuse, and harassment will stop.)

In nearly every case in which a battered woman kills her abuser, there exists that psychological bond between her and the batterer (a result of the woman's learned helplessness), which renders her incapable of acting effectively to escape or to save her own life, without killing him. Not one of the women in the cases in which I've testified said that she intended to kill her husband or boyfriend; each woman did say that she had simply intended to stop the batterer from hurting her any more than he already had or from killing her, and that she believed no other way of stopping him would have worked at the time. Some women, as we have seen, intended to kill themselves as a way of stopping the unendurable suffering of their lives, but something happened— perhaps a resurgence of their own autonomous survival instinct— and they killed the abuser instead. The informed expert witness is the only person, in these cases, qualified to point out that *the psychological reality of these women justifies their actions.* * Their state of mind meets the requirement of reasonable perception. Battered women who kill do so because it is the only remaining way they can see out of a physically life-threatening and emotionally and psychologically untenable circumstance. Their actions are motivated by terror—terror bred in them by the learned helplessness they have developed as a result of living with a repeating and worsening Cycle of Violence that they do not understand. (The fact that the violence seems, to many of them, to be entirely random and unpredictable suggests that they effectively have been brainwashed.)

*   *   *

*Psychologist and lawyer Charles Ewing, in his book *Battered Women Who Kill* (Lexington, 1987), suggests that many battered women kill the abuser when they believe they are at the point of psychological death. Although I agree with his analysis, I am talking only about actual physical death here.

My first experience with the overwhelming controversy surrounding legal issues of admissibility in these cases came the second time I worked as an expert witness, during the Beverly Ibn-Tamas trial. Beverly's attorney, Bill McDaniels (then with the prestigious Washington, D.C., law firm of Williams and Connolly) had not prepared me for the possibility that no expert witness testimony would be admitted at all. The first inkling I got of that was when I entered the courtroom for the first time and saw the largest group of spectators I had yet faced during a trial.

Judge Stewart had excused the jury and agreed to listen to McDaniels's offer of proof, or proffer, of my testimony. Even though this was only my second time testifying as an expert witness in a criminal trial, I could sense that this particular courtroom was not going to be a friendly one. I remember feeling my voice shake as I glanced up, occasionally, at the spectator section. Lined across the back wall were the dead man's Black Muslim friends, staring directly at me (in what seemed, at the time, to be a menacing and intimidating manner). For the first time, I was aware that someone might want to hurt me for doing this; for the first time (but not the last), it occurred to me that I ought to consider giving it up. After all, I mused, I could be sitting in a quiet office back in Denver practicing one-on-one psychotherapy, a far less dangerous way of putting feminism into action.*

Most of the questions asked me were ones I would later recognize as standard legal questions posed to any expert witness. But this was only my second case; I felt that I was walking through a mine field blindfolded. Not knowing what the "correct" legal procedures or responses were, I could only give answers based on my on-the-spot interpretation of the questions. Still, some of

---

*Actually, this fear was instructive for me, as it allowed me to understand firsthand how battered women themselves often feel in a courtroom. Such fear may paralyze a woman, rendering her silent or, at the very least, rendering her testimony ineffectual. The fear I felt that day almost succeeded in robbing me of my own voice, too.

these questions were in "legalese"; I was sometimes unable to figure out what words I needed to say to meet the requirements of a legal standard I really did not know anything about.

The key question, it turned out, was this:

"Dr. Walker, is the study of battered women a recognized diagnostic category in your profession? By that I mean does it appear in any of the typologies used to recognize mental health disorders?"

Although I was almost brand-new in the forensic testimony business, my instincts told me that everything rested on the way I might answer this question. And, unknowledgeable as I was about what the correct legal response would be, I had only a minute or two at most to think it through and respond. What a dilemma! If I answered affirmatively, Judge Stewart might allow my testimony; but, in that case, it would be for the purpose of labeling Beverly Ibn-Tamas mentally disturbed, not for the purpose of validating her reasonable perception of imminent bodily danger (the self-defense standard, and her defense attorneys' preferred course of action). Battered women advocates were struggling to keep such a category out of the mental health classification system* for just that reason.

"No," I responded, finally, "there are no typologies or classification systems of which I am aware that currently list battered women as a category. But the DSM revision group, which is

---

*In 1977, the major diagnostic system in use was the *Diagnostic and Statistical Manual of Mental Disorders,* 2nd ed. (DSM-II), published by the American Psychiatric Association. It is used by mental health professionals and agencies to classify patients. The DSM-II did not have a category under which battered women might properly fit. In 1980, the Post Traumatic Stress Disorder category would be added to the new edition, DSM-III, giving professionals an appropriate classification for battered women. (Later, too, in 1980, the medical typology *International Classification of Diseases,* 9th ed. [ICD-9] added a battered woman category.) But the truth was that, in 1977, few mental health professionals recognized battered women as falling into any mental health category other than the erroneous diagnosis of masochism.

authorized to develop the new DSM-III, are considering including it as a new category in the forthcoming edition."*

A few minutes later, Judge Stewart ruled that my testimony
would not be admitted in this trial.

Shocked and disappointed, I heard him state that he believed, based on my sworn testimony, that whatever I had to say
could not be considered reliable because the psychological field of
study was not yet well enough developed to support expert opinion.†

I believe that my commitment to forensic psychology—the
translation of psychological principles of understanding of human
behavior into the language and principles of the legal process—
was sealed that day. My own personal frustration, of course, was
high; a great deal of work had gone into my preparation of proffered testimony, and I wanted very much to have some positive
influence on the fate of this tortured, much-abused woman.

Yet, despite my disappointment that day, I had much to
learn about proffered testimony. Such testimony is terribly important, even when ruled inadmissible. And it was to have a great
deal of bearing on the Ibn-Tamas case as well as other battered
woman self-defense cases in years to come.

Beverly was convicted of second-degree murder. But Judge
Stewart found mitigating circumstances in her case and sen-

---

*Field trials had begun in preparation for the DSM-III, and there was
debate about listing various syndrome subcategories under the Post Traumatic
Stress Disorder diagnosis. Feminists agreed that the danger of clinicians, who
primarily use the DSM-III for treatment purposes, mislabeling battered women,
rape victims, incest survivors, and such was too high, and they agreed to omit
subcategories. The debate resurfaced in 1986 when the DSM-III-R was published, and is currently being reargued in preparation for the DSM-IV, due to
be published in 1992.

†According to attorney Peter DePaoulis, who was Judge Stewart's clerk
at the time of the Ibn-Tamas trial, the decision was a difficult one for this judge
to make. Usually, Stewart allowed the defense broad latitude in presenting
evidence to a jury. In fact, he had personally leaned toward admitting my
testimony, but could not justify it, DePaoulis felt, because of the lack of developed available data in the field of battered women's psychology at the time.

tenced her to only two years in prison. She also received credit for the five months she'd already served in jail, spent another seven months in prison after being sentenced, and was then released on probation.

Meanwhile, the legal controversy set in motion by her case began to swirl around her. As soon as the trial was concluded, her attorneys set about preparing an appeal. In the appeal process, proffered testimony can be crucial. In this case, the defense prepared an appeal to the effect that Judge Stewart's refusal to admit my expert witness testimony had been an abuse of his discretionary power (since such testimony would have been critical in educating the jury about a battered woman's state of mind at the time of the homicide).

The appeal process took six years. Even though, at the end of that time Beverly Ibn-Tamas had finished serving her sentence, this appeal case resulted in a new standard for admissibility of self-defense testimony for battered women that would have an impact nationwide.*

For me, the long, back-breaking process of appeal was an eye-opening introduction to the real world of American law. It is a process that deserves some description here.

Judge Stewart had ruled my testimony inadmissible because he said there was "insufficient knowledge" in the field upon which "reliable" expert witness testimony could be based. In her appeal, Beverly's attorneys stated that, since I could be qualified as an expert in psychology, particularly clinical psychology, and since there was information in the field of psychology that would refute many lay myths about battered women, Judge Stewart had erred in not permitting my testimony; he should have let the jurors decide how reliable such testimony was. (Legally, the jurors' deci-

---

*To their credit, the firm of Williams and Connolly underwrote the entire six-year process financially. Even though the outcome of Beverly's trial was a sort of victory (because her final sentence was so light), her attorneys had the foresight to understand the usefulness of winning an appeal, for the sake of battered women who would come to trial in the future.

sion on this reliability is referred to as "the weight of the testimony.")

In the appeal process, paperwork is paramount. Trial transcripts have to be typed; affidavits and legal motions have proscribed time periods for response. Even with bright, efficient law clerks working for them, appellate court judges are swamped with more cases than they can possibly handle. More than two years later (in late 1979), the District of Columbia appellate court handed down its first opinion on this appeal.

The court agreed with the defense's argument that the average juror needs some education concerning battered women, education that might be provided by expert witness testimony basing their judgment on what is called the "beyond the ken of the average juror" test. Thus, the judges ruled that such testimony meets the critical test of being more probative than prejudicial, and they reaffirmed that the expert witness has to be qualified. But they added two additional tests of admissibility: first, the expert must have recognized credentials in the field to be qualified to give testimony; second, in order to admit expert testimony on battered women, there would have to be a sufficiently well-developed field of study on which an expert witness could base her testimony. A psychologist with high-level qualifications and credentials might unnecessarily influence the jury, it was thought, by the strength of the impression gained from her or his credentials, rather than by the strength of any factual evidence she or he presented. Since these issues had not been clearly set out to guide the presiding trial judge in 1977, the appellate court sent the Ibn-Tamas case back to Judge Stewart with the intention that he review his original decision.

The defense immediately asked Judge Stewart to hold a hearing where they could present evidence to meet the criteria established by the appellate court (they claimed that they had not known of these criteria in 1977 either; if they had, they would have asked me additional questions on *voir dire* and would like the chance to do so now). Judge Stewart refused.

I was angry. I felt as if the prosecution's legal documents

in this appeal process were misrepresenting my qualifications, my research and clinical work, and the field as a whole. But there was nothing I could do to stop them, even though I felt, at the time, that I was being mischaracterized with blatant and intentional lies, and that my career was at stake. Attorneys on both sides of a case always write their legal documents to reflect their best possible advocacy position (and unlike in the fields of science and psychology, no one really takes their sometimes-exaggerated statements seriously until a judge rules on them).

Judge Stewart made a new ruling quickly: he would *not* hold a new hearing based only on the admissibility question; he had no intention of reopening the Ibn-Tamas case, and his original decision would stand. That was all.

But that wasn't quite all. The defense decided to file another appeal. This time, they submitted affidavits from other professionals who had been named in the prosecution's response briefs (during the first appeal) as being critical of my work. These colleagues stated in sworn affidavits that my research used perfectly acceptable methodology, even though I was a feminist, and that in many instances my results were similar to their own. I was personally delighted that my colleagues were willing to take the time to do this, even though in their own work they may have favored the use of methodology different from mine. The affidavits supported the defense's contention that, as scientists, all were agreed that there now existed a sufficient body of information in the field of battered women's psychology on which an expert opinion could be based.

This second appeal sat in the appellate court for four more years. No word came down as to what was holding up the judges' decisions.

To my way of thinking, it didn't seem as if it ought to be so terribly complicated; all they had to do, I thought, was to rule on whether or not Judge Stewart had been in error. If they affirmed the appeal, the prosecution would probably drop the charges; retrying Beverly would serve no purpose at all. She had already served all the time in prison she would have served without any appeal. But if the appeal was affirmed and a new trial won by the defense, it might clear her name, erasing any record of her felony conviction.

In the meantime, the first opinion issued by the District of Columbia appellate court was beginning to have lasting impact nationwide. This opinion clearly spelled out when an expert could give testimony concerning a battered woman's reasonable perception of danger to support a self-defense plea; it also mandated use of a three-part test of potential expert witness testimony (called the Dyas Test) and ruled that such testimony could provide information that might assist a jury in its deliberations. Because this opinion was issued by a court with the standing of a federal court, its weight was respected by various state courts. It was making a difference in the trials of battered women around the country.

Oddly enough, too, the recorded statements that I thought would ruin my reputation actually helped establish my career as an expert witness much more strongly. If an attorney wanted to know about case law concerning the admissibility of expert witness testimony, she or he could look it up in the published legal opinions. There, they would find my name as the qualified psychologist mentioned in the opinions, which I thought had so misrepresented me and my profession.

It wasn't until 1983 that the appellate court finally ruled on the second appeal, in favor of Judge Stewart. By then, enough state supreme court opinions existed to render the final decision on Ibn-Tamas less important.

The practical outcome was a very good one.

In another case, however, the outcome was quite the opposite. This story bears telling as an example of how a battered woman's life may be ruined by the whims of a trial court judge, one who, perhaps for personal reasons, was determined to rule any defense-supportive expert witness testimony inadmissible.

DONNA BECHTEL'S STORY

An Oklahoma woman, Donna Bechtel, had recently been widowed from her husband of more than twenty years when she met Ken and fell in love with him. Ken was a hard-drinking high roller who always seemed to have plenty of money and who loved the boating crowd that sailed the inland rivers and waterways of America. Donna had worked hard all her life, becoming a real estate broker in the small town she'd called home all of her life. She owned property and had money in the bank. Her children were grown and out of the house, which was a good thing, she guessed, because none of them liked Ken when they met him.

Ken was a top-level salesman for a large oil company; as it turned out, it was his company expense account that provided all the cash for his expensive life-style. He didn't have a penny in the bank. When pressed for money to pay back a substantial loan, he asked Donna if he could borrow some of hers. The request came along with a proposal of marriage. Donna agreed to both requests. It was the first in a series of loans to Ken, loans that would eventually wipe out her hard-earned life savings.

Soon after their marriage, Donna noticed that time spent with her own friends was gradually being replaced by time spent with Ken and his boating companions, or just with Ken alone—he was fiercely jealous and possessive of her, and often had temper tantrums when Donna's children called to speak with her. The first time he hit her, in fact, was when he thought she'd been spending too much time on the phone talking with her daughter. It wasn't the last time.

Ken was transferred to Oklahoma City from the small Illinois town where they had met. Donna sold her successful business and said goodbye to her children, then moved there with him, figuring that without all the pressure of her already-established life their marriage would improve.

Instead, she found herself isolated from friends and family. Ken's drinking grew worse. So did his violence. The more time she spent with him, the more depressed she became. She never knew when he'd be pleasant and loving or mean and abusive. Eventually, Donna began to feel like she was living in hell. She began dreading the very thought of waking up every morning.

She looked into alcohol treatment programs for Ken, thinking that if he would only stop drinking his behavior would improve. She even called members of his family to ask for their help in getting him treatment. They agreed to encourage him but never actually did.

Early one morning, on the way home from a fishing trip with a group of his buddies, Ken was arrested for drunk and disorderly conduct. He had about $5,000 cash on him at the time of the arrest. By the time he got home, the $5,000 was nowhere to be seen. It was four o'clock in the morning. Donna had been up all night, waiting; she'd asked Betsy, a friend of hers, to stay with her and keep her company. But Betsy was asleep in another room when Ken staggered in, poured himself a drink, and sat down to talk with her. Donna was filled with dread.

Drinking, Ken began to lament the death of his only son (who had died of meningitis ten years earlier, at the age of nine). Donna grew more terrified. Whenever he began to talk about his son, she knew, he was about to beat her badly.

She tried to protect herself by fleeing to the bedroom and locking the door. But Ken came crashing right through. The next thing she knew he was stripping off his clothes, forcing her to the bed, trying to rape her; but he was too drunk to be really aroused. Donna struggled out from under him and ran to the bathroom. He followed her, knocked her to the floor and began to punch and kick her. She tried to fight back this time, screaming for Betsy's help. Later, Betsy would say that she'd thought she heard Donna scream; but she had been fast asleep and, at the time, it had seemed like a sound from her dream.

Ken forced Donna back onto the bed. For a moment, it seemed to her that he'd passed out. She tried to wriggle out from under him. He grabbed her again, and she fell bruised and bleeding to the floor.

She reached under the bed for the gun she kept there when he was away.

Later, Donna would remember nothing of what happened next. She must have shot and killed him as he approached her.

Then, with shaking hands, trying desperately to calm herself, she smoked a cigarette.

She woke Betsy and they called the police. Donna was arrested and charged with first-degree murder. The chief judge, Joe Cannon, a friend of Ken's, found an attorney to represent her, and in an unusual move Donna was granted bail, and released from jail to await her trial. Afraid that her attorneys were incompetent, after a time Donna fired them and hired new ones who turned out to be no better, failing to interview her extensively or to inform her about how they were handling her few remaining financial assets. The attorneys all wanted Donna to plead to a lesser crime, but she wouldn't do it. She didn't believe she was guilty of anything except protecting herself. So she went to trial.

Donna was found guilty of first-degree murder and sentenced to life in prison. But that is not the end of her story.

Donna refused to go quietly. She filed an appeal that took three years for her to win, three long years in prison.

By then, she had contacted members of a battered women's shelter staff who put her in touch with Garvin Isaacs, one of the best and most honest defense lawyers in Oklahoma. A board member of the National Association of Criminal Defense Lawyers, he shared his new client's dilemma with other board members; they referred him to our offices in Denver.

Swamped with work, I at first told him that I would have to refuse to take on another case; I could not possibly meet and evaluate Donna for him, much less agree to provide expert witness testimony. But when he told me that the women in Donna's hometown were holding bean suppers as fund raisers for her defense, I was moved. Eventually, I agreed to meet with Donna herself. When I met her and listened to her story, there was no doubt in my mind that she had been horribly battered in her relationship with Ken; she had had nothing left, in the end, but her own terror. She had never planned to kill him that morning, nor had she thought about what she did at all. She had operated in a state of traumatic shock, going on blind instinct alone. Listening to her, I was certain that, if I had the chance to testify before a jury, the jury would agree.

But in April 1988, in Oklahoma City, Battered Woman Syndrome testimony was ruled inadmissible by the judge presiding over Donna's second trial. Nor was Donna herself allowed to testify to much of the abuse she had experienced. There was some question as to whether or not this judge had been pressured to give this ruling by powerful political forces in Oklahoma City. It seemed that at least one member of the Oklahoma City judiciary had been part of the boating crowd and had bailed Ken out of jail on the morning of his death. Garvin Isaacs appealed to the State Supreme Court, asking for an untainted judge to preside over the trial; his motion was denied.

The entire trial was a sham, a mockery, one of the worst travesties of justice I have ever been unfortunate enough to witness. The defense believed that evidence was ruled admissible or not according to the trial judge's whims. In the end, Donna was found guilty and returned to complete her life sentence in prison.

Hers was another woman's life ruined by men of power and privilege—men in high places, with too much to hide.

The Dyas Decision

Records of trial testimony usually are transcribed only if an appeal is filed. And usually only the defense can ask to reverse a conviction or win a new trial on appeal (usually based on some legal error made in the first trial or in procedures leading up to the first trial). Criminal cases in which the defendant is acquitted are never appealed—although occasionally a legal issue raised in such cases is sent to the appellate court for clarification in future cases— since, under the Constitution, a defendant cannot be tried twice for the same crime. (Had Beverly Ibn-Tamas's self-defense plea been successful, for instance, there would have been no record of her trial testimony available in the legal literature.)

In the past, psychologists were permitted to evaluate and comment on a defendant's state of mind, in most legal jurisdictions, as part of determining whether or not the defendant knew right from wrong at the time of the alleged crime. This commentary, called a competency evaluation, has been traditionally used when an insanity defense is contemplated. So a psychologist measuring and discussing a defendant's state of mind is not a new phenomenon in our courts.

But a self-defense statute, in most states, calls for proving a defendant's reasonable perception of imminent danger. This standard does not measure incompetency but rather uses psychology to help a jury understand how a defendant might have reasonably perceived herself to have been in danger at the time of the homicide. And trial court judges have the authority to decide whether or not to allow *any* expert witness testimony in a specific case. When experts make authoritative statements in court, they are likely to be quite persuasive. Therefore, criteria have been set to try to limit expert witness testimony, so that such testimony does not have the effect of outweighing other factual evidence.

The case law setting the standard (now used in most courtrooms) for determining the validity of expert witness testimony was set forth by the United States Supreme Court in *Dyas vs. United States.* The Court's words were:

1. The subject matter must be so distinctively related to some science, profession, business, or occupation as to be beyond the ken of the average layman;
2. The witness must have sufficient skill, knowledge, or experience in that field or calling as to make it appear that his opinion or inference will probably aid the trier in his search for truth; and
3. Expert witness testimony is inadmissible if the state of the art of scientific knowledge does not permit a reason-

able opinion to be asserted even by an expert. (Opinion at pp. 632–635)

Although the Dyas decision* does seem to give trial court judges broad discretion in determining whether to admit an expert witness's testimony, a number of convictions have been overturned by state appellate courts that ruled that not admitting such testimony was an abridgement of the defendant's rights and therefore an abuse of judicial discretion.

In a number of these decisions (*Smith vs. Georgia, Anaya vs. Maine,* and *Kelly vs. New Jersey,* most notably) the state supreme court justices also reiterated that jurors could not ordinarily be expected to be able to draw conclusions based on a defendant's behavior; they specifically suggested that a need existed for a qualified expert witness to explain a battered woman's behavior to a jury. In the case of *Smith vs. Georgia,* the state supreme court ruled for allowing an expert witness to give a professional opinion as to whether the defendant had, or had not, acted in self-defense. And in the case of *Allery vs. Washington* (1984), the Washington State Supreme Court ruled that a defendant claiming to be a battered woman was entitled to an evaluation by a psychologist to prove her claim; otherwise, the attorney would risk being declared incompetent to provide her with an adequate defense. (In 1984, in the *AKE* decision, the United States Supreme Court ruled that indigent defendants are entitled to psychological evaluation to determine their state of mind at the time of an alleged crime, at the state's expense, if necessary.)

Best of all, perhaps, the New Jersey Supreme Court ruled, in the case of *Kelly vs. New Jersey* (1984), that the fact that the

---

*Prior to Dyas, a less comprehensive test, called the Frye test, was used to determine admissibility of testimony; it basically allowed a trial court judge to decide to admit evidence or testimony if it could be deemed useful in any way to the trier of fact. The current federal Rules of Evidence have returned to the simpler Frye test of admission of expert witness testimony, as have the laws in those states where the rules of evidence conform to the federal standard.

state legislature had passed laws to protect battered women specifically indicated that they were entitled to be treated as a special group in special danger, and were thus also entitled to have an expert witness explain their reasonable perception of imminent bodily danger to a jury to bolster a self-defense case. The New Jersey Supreme Court has thus come closest to redefining the "reasonable perception" standard within the context of Battered Woman Syndrome.

Less than ten years after the trial of Beverly Ibn-Tamas, battered women could more often than not be supported by expert witness testimony admitted during trial.

Partial Admissibility

Once the courts made it clear that state-of-mind testimony for battered women would be admissible, prosecutors all over the country began arguing for a limit on what evidence would be admissible. Their fear was that juries would be prejudiced emotionally by evidence concerning the batterer's brutality toward the woman, rather than by the facts presented about her actual perpetration of the homicide.

This situation is brought to light in the following story.

JANET'S STORY

Janet's trial was held in the small northern California town where she'd killed her abusive husband, Tony.

During pretrial motions, the prosecutor attempted to exclude any testimony concerning Tony's previous conviction on a charge of felony child abuse and his subsequent sentence to the Atascadero State Hospital's special sex offender's program—testimony the defense considered crucial to its case.

The judge agreed with the prosecution that such information would be too prejudicial for the jury to hear and, in a pretrial motion decided even before I had testified, ruled that it would not be admitted. The judge was concerned that the jury might rely on such emotionally charged information to acquit Janet, overlooking other pertinent information that might prove her guilt. As would be expected, of course, the defense argued against this motion.

When it came time for me to testify, Janet's attorney filed a motion for the court to reconsider its previous ruling, based on the fact that the rules of evidence permit a psychologist to testify as to all information relied upon in supporting a professional opinion. Despite the fact that it had occurred more than twenty years ago, I found Tony's conviction on the child abuse charge relevant for two reasons: first, it confirmed his tendency to use violence within the family; second, it supported Janet's statement that he was a generally abusive man. Janet knew that he'd sexually abused a child. And this knowledge, I believed, had contributed to her fearful state of mind on the day that she shot him. After all, she had reasoned, if he could do that to a child, he could do worse to her.* So, to my and the defense team's way of thinking, the information was both pertinent and probative, in that it added credibility to the defendant's assertion of self-defense. The judge would have to weigh its probative value against its potentially prejudicial impact.

In this case, the judge modified his original opinion. I was permitted to testify that "Janet knew the deceased had been accused of an offense of a violent nature against a child, had been found guilty, and had spent some time being punished for it in a special rehabilitation program many years ago." In order to ensure

---

*Daniel Sonkin, Michael Lindsay, Edward Gondolf, David Adams, Anne Ganley, Kevin McGovern, Daniel Saunders, Joseph Giovannoni, and other professionals who have interviewed batterers participating in both voluntary and court-ordered treatment programs (and who have compiled a good deal of research data on batterers in general), tell us that these men all admit to having difficulty respecting other people's boundaries. Additionally, a very high percentage of them are sexual abusers of children.

that I didn't say anything too prejudicial, I was ordered to write down my testimony in the exact words we'd agreed on, and to read it to the jury in response to agreed-on questions by the defense attorney.

The testimony proved, in the end, to benefit Janet. The jury returned a verdict of involuntary manslaughter, rather than the first-degree murder charge requested by the prosecution. Janet was sentenced to two and a half years in the state penitentiary.

Janet's verdict never was appealed, as it would have been an expensive and time-consuming process that probably would not have been completed by the time she finished serving her sentence.

In another California case, in 1988, the Riverside County judge presiding over the trial of a woman named Brenda Aris seriously limited the expert witness testimony admitted; the result was that the jury had a chance to hear about Battered Woman Syndrome in general, but not as it applied specifically to the defendant.* The result of this judicial limitation imposed on the nature of the admitted expert witness testimony was that Brenda Aris—a woman so battered by her husband that, at the time of her arrest, she was covered from head to toe with black and blue marks—was found guilty of second-degree murder. The defense team in this case had been hoping—reasonably, I thought—that the jury would find she had acted in self-defense or would deliver a lesser verdict of voluntary manslaughter, but these hopes rode on expert witness testimony. The judge, in addition to excluding much of my testimony concerning Brenda's state of mind at the time she'd killed her husband, failed to give the jury a self-defense instruction prior to their

---

*Brenda shot and killed her husband, Rick, while he was sleeping (or passed out), fearful he'd resume beating her when he regained consciousness. A careful explanation of her specific actions by a qualified expert witness would have helped her case, I am sure.

final deliberation. Another woman, beaten and silenced, was further abused by the court system.*

When dealing with circumstances of great violence, it is quite possible (and at times probable) that concerns other than justice, or even the law, will determine what evidence or testimony a presiding trial judge will admit. Until there are standard rules governing the admissibility of expert witness testimony in every kind of case—until such time as admissibility of testimony is no longer left to the sole discretion of a single judge in each case—outcomes will vary, and some women will suffer.

Conspiracy Cases

Most battered women who kill do the actual killing themselves. Some, though, are entirely unable to defend themselves directly. Frequently, these women, often the most seriously terrorized and abused of all battered women, turn to others they perceive as having power and plead for their help. Later, these women may face charges of conspiracy to commit murder, and juries are notably less lenient in conspiracy case decisions.

Rarely, though, are these cases anything like the typical "murder for hire" cases one hears about in the media. Money rarely changes hands. More often, the actual perpetrator has heard nauseating tales of the batterer's violence and has decided to take the law into his own hands. Sometimes, too, the perpetrator does not intend to actually kill the batterer; he wants, most of all, to protect the battered woman (and, in some cases, her children) from further harm.

DONNA YAKLISH'S STORY

Donna Yaklish testified at her trial in Pueblo, Colorado, in May 1988 that she'd been so frightened of her husband, Dennis,

*Brenda's case has been appealed to the California appellate courts.

a narcotics detective and state champion body builder, that she'd asked several people to kill him. Dennis had been threatening to kill her for a long time. They'd been married for ten years, and during that time he had supplemented his body building with self-prescribed steroids (synthetic derivatives of male hormones that enhance muscular buildup but that are known in some instances to cause aggression and violent behavior as well; the emotional reaction to steroids is so common, in fact, that among certain athletes it is called 'roid rage). He'd also beaten her savagely on more than one occasion. In addition, Donna knew that his first wife, Barbara, had died under mysterious circumstances; he had been investigated in the case, but there was not enough evidence against him at the time, except the statements of Barbara's children, who hated and feared him.

Eventually, a twenty-year-old and a sixteen-year-old boy accepted Donna's request. Although earlier there had been vague talk between one boy and Donna of some life insurance money, all she had ever given them was ten dollars, here and there, for gas money. Eight months after Donna's initial request, the brothers shot and killed Dennis as he got out of his car on returning home from work at 2 A.M.

A lawyer who had been a body-building crony of Dennis's offered to protect Donna when she was charged with conspiracy to murder. Eventually, though, he seemed to become abusive and controlling toward her, too. When a conflict of interest arose, the case was turned over to an excellent criminal defense lawyer in Denver, Stanley Marks. After an evaluation, Donna spent the next six months in therapy with me, learning how to depend on her own natural strength rather than continually trust in muscle-bound but unworthy men to fulfill all her needs.

The presiding judge at her trial, Judge Jack Seavy, admitted my testimony, but he made it clear to everyone involved that he did not personally believe Battered Woman Syndrome could be responsible for Donna's state of mind when she had set Dennis's death in motion. The prosecutor had asked for special circumstances to be added to the murder charge, making this a death penalty trial.

After a very emotional and highly publicized trial, the jury found Donna not guilty of murder. However, they found her guilty of the lesser conspiracy charge. Ignoring the probation department's presentencing recommendation for probation, Judge Seavy sentenced her to forty years in prison—in my opinion, using the court and a woman's life as a way to express his own ignorance of a battered woman's plight.

There is nothing pleasant about any battered woman's self-defense trial. But conspiracy cases are often especially ugly and frightening. The following story is about one of the most frightening cases I ever worked on as an expert witness.

HELEN'S STORY

Long battered and abused by her husband, Ron, Helen Martin eventually became terrified that he would fulfill his threats to blow up the expensive home they shared, while she and her five-year-old daughter, Angela, were inside it, to get his hands on $1 million of insurance money. (These weren't empty threats on Ron's part; at a later hearing in Helen's case, I heard at least one demolition expert testify that Ron had offered him a considerable sum of money to do it.)

Allegedly, Helen hired someone to kill her husband. The word "allegedly" is used here because there is absolutely no evidence that she sought out the killer, nor was he ever paid any money. Later, Helen would admit discussing a plan with the killer, after he'd approached her in a bar as if he knew who she was, but she would also claim that she'd called it off at the last minute and that the killer had refused to listen to her. Ron Martin himself was rumored to have been a small-time crook. In fact, he'd told his wife details of several killings he claimed he'd been hired to carry out. He never went anywhere without a bodyguard. And rumors on the street confirmed that, at the time of his death, he had already hired someone to blow up their house, as he'd threatened.

Clint Almond, Helen's defense attorney, was prepared to assert self-defense, bolstered by Battered Woman Syndrome, at trial. An alternate mental health defense would have lowered the level of criminal responsibility but would not have justified or excused the alleged crime. On the other hand, a diminished capacity form of insanity defense would have forced the presiding judge to allow my expert witness testimony, as well as the testimony of Helen's psychiatrist, Wayne Stillings.

As it was, the judge seemed prepared to rule against admitting our testimony altogether; he was interpreting Missouri's statutes as disallowing a self-defense plea in the case of a preplanned conspiracy because he couldn't understand how this met the "imminency" requirement.*

I spent several days in the small town of Hillsboro, just outside of St. Louis, where the trial was being held in 1982. From the beginning, nothing seemed to go right. The motel I stayed in did not even have a lock on the door (the better motel in town was where the jury was sequestered, and I was not permitted to stay there). Eventually, I moved in with Clint and his wife, attorney Marcia Brody, at their home.

Since I was not allowed to watch the trial progress, as, day after day, one or another witness was excluded by the judge, I sat in Clint's office from morning until evening, alone except for quick consultations with the defense team during their brief recesses. I could not know what the other witnesses had said. At night, Clint, Marcia, and I went through the day's events and attempted to plan for the next day's proceedings. I could not shake my dismal, gut-level feeling that I was somehow in danger, that this trial was

---

*"Imminent" means "about to happen," as though someone is at the edge of a cliff and about to fall off. Many battered women find themselves in such a situation, only to be saved and given a temporary reprieve. Given the escalating nature of battering behavior, "imminency" refers to a reasonable perception that, as the abuse starts again, it will cause serious bodily harm or death.

not going well, that there was something other than a mere legal proceeding in the air.

Louise Bauschard, director of the Women's Self Help Center, a counseling and advocacy organization in St. Louis, agreed with me. As she was not scheduled to testify, she sat through the trial herself and later said that the entire town seemed controlled by some unidentifiable malignant force.

For one thing, it seemed that the judicial cast of characters in this town remained the same, with different people merely changing sides every few years: the same attorneys seemed to take turns at being prosecutors, defense attorneys, public defenders, and judges. It was difficult to know who was on which side. I trusted no one; neither did Louise. She and I validated each other's paranoia, in a way. After a few days' exposure to the trial and the town, neither one of us believed that Helen Martin would be able to get a fair trial or a good defense.

Rumors of organized crime involvement pervaded the atmosphere around us. It made sense, in a way, that some organized crime racketeers had wanted Ron Martin dead for their own reasons, and that they had set Helen up to let a hired killer into her home to assassinate Ron when his own bodyguard was away on an errand. I began to feel almost certain that this was the case when a local television reporter told me that the bar in which Helen had originally met the hired killer had some connections with a South St. Louis gang that had ties to organized crime in Las Vegas. I don't know whether he intended to intimidate me or to warn me when he also told me about the mysterious disappearances of several other witnesses.

But this perception was mere speculation, after all—although it was interesting (to say the least) that the local bars, where many small-time hoodlums in town hung out, supposedly were preparing to celebrate Helen's upcoming conviction.*

Personally, all I wanted was for Helen to get a fair trial.

---

*On the afternoon the jury delivered a guilty verdict, the reporter told me that many of these bars offered customers a free round of drinks.

Helen had been raised in Yugoslavia, fleeing to America with her family when the Communists had taken over. I believe that she was young and naive when she'd first met Ron and that, although she found out he was a professional killer before she married him, she had been intrigued with his high-rolling life-style and the large sums of money he threw around. After years of abuse and battery, the marriage wore her down, and her fear of Ron was accompanied by a fear of the mob. Once her daughter was born, though, she was forced once and for all to face the truth of what her husband was. No matter what her connections had been with other criminals, I had no doubt that she *had* been a battered woman and that, like other battered women I'd evaluated, it had been reasonable for her to fear for her life.

But circumstances were to make it impossible to get these, or other facts, before the jury.

I don't know exactly when it was that I realized Clint Almond would not be allowed to call any other witnesses, except Helen Martin. He *had* prepared several witnesses to testify as to Ron's violent criminal character, but the judge ruled their testimony inadmissible. He also prepared to call psychiatrist Wayne Stillings and me as expert witnesses, but we were allowed to testify only in front of the judge (to ensure a proper record), never in front of a jury. The judge disallowed our testimony, too. Even those who could have testified about Ron's violence toward Helen or about his search for someone to blow up his own house were unable to testify.* Their testimony was ruled inadmissible in some cases; many of these witnesses had criminal records themselves (which hardly would have added much credibility to Helen's case).

Worst of all, Clint seemed unwilling to explore any links to organized crime. I couldn't tell if he felt they were unsubstantiated or simply not relevant to a good defense, or if he himself was

---

*One of the most important reasons to assert a self-defense plea is that it allows full testimony about the decedent's history of violence witnessed by others, supporting the defendant's claims of reasonable perception.

afraid of exploring such links because—and perhaps this was the unspoken truth underlying the strange, frightening atmosphere of this entire trial—it might put his own life or career in jeopardy.

After my testimony was disallowed, I asked Louise Bauschard to drive me to St. Louis immediately. I was anxious to get on the last available flight to Denver. Both Louise and I were pretty spooked by then. Fearing the ignition was bomb-wired, we even asked someone else to start her car for us. (It was difficult to remain internally calm after listening to those demolition experts, who had coldly described just how simple it was to kill someone.) In any event, I arrived at the airport in St. Louis unscathed. It felt better than it had ever felt before to settle into an airplane seat and know that I was on my way home.

Helen was sentenced to spend the next fifty years in Renz Correctional Facility in Jefferson City, Missouri.

She handled her conviction much better than I did. Louise Bauschard began visiting her in prison on a regular basis and eventually helped her start a self-help group there for battered women. From prison, Helen fired her attorney and hired another one to work on her appeal.

The appeal was denied, with the Missouri Supreme Court upholding the trial court judge's decisions to disallow both a self-defense plea and expert witness testimony. But the appellate court did suggest a special hearing to determine whether or not Helen had received a proper defense. (The court based this recommendation on the fact that Clint Almond had never even asked for a diminished capacity or impaired mental condition defense.) About three years later, in January 1985, a hearing was held in the same courtroom where the original trial had taken place, in front of the same judge.

Louise Bauschard picked me up at the airport in St. Louis. We spent the night at her house, preparing for the trip to the courtroom in Jefferson County the next day. Both of us were dreading it. As soon as we arrived, the same old feelings of omnipresent evil overwhelmed me; I literally felt that I had to force my feet to move, one in front of the other. I found myself wondering why on earth I had let Louise and Helen's new attorney talk me into coming back. But I told myself that, like it or not, I was there, and I had to do my very best—for Helen and for all the other battered women I'd ever known. Then, I told myself, what I really had to do was to get out of there as quickly as possible. The dull, continual sense of fear really was crippling, just like battered women say it is.

Helen looked like a completely different woman. Gone was her former gaunt pallor; gone was the familiar expression of fear. She radiated self-confidence, looked healthy and pretty. I could only imagine how terrible her marriage to Ron had been all those years, for her to have blossomed in prison, doing a fifty-year sentence, with no chance of parole.

That day, I testified that I had provided Helen's attorney with all the necessary information culled from my clinical interviews and evaluations. In my reports, I mentioned that I had found evidence of severe depression that, along with the Battered Woman Syndrome from which Helen had suffered at the time, could have supported a limited-responsibility mental health defense. But I insisted that I had not known Missouri law and that, therefore, I could not be expected to have used their legal language at the time of Helen's original trial. Such a defense, which would have had to be requested and was not assumed feasible from trial testimony, would have automatically dropped the level of charges from conspiracy to commit murder down to manslaughter, because the requisite mental condition to premeditate would not have been present.

For his part, Clint Almond blamed Helen for his failure to use such a defense. His associate, Edward Williams, testified she'd been aware that, if convicted of manslaughter, she would not have been able to inherit any of Ron's life insurance money* (under the

---

*Ron Martin had kept a life insurance policy on himself, as well as on Helen, of almost $1 million. After his death, Helen signed over her share to their young daughter and her lawyer. She allowed Ron's family to have the rest, so

law in most states, an individual cannot profit from a criminal act). It was Helen, he claimed, who had not wanted to take that chance; she'd wanted to gamble at getting all of the insurance money. But, although Clint had had her sign other directives she'd requested from him, against his legal advice, he never had her sign anything on this one.

Helen, in turn, denied the truth of Clint's statements. He had been the one, she stated, who wanted her to go for "all or nothing" where the insurance money was concerned. She stated that it was he who controlled the entire conduct of the defense case, he who told her exactly what to do. Her testimony in this instance is entirely consistent with what I know about the behavior of battered women. Most battered women are still so malleable at the time of trial that they are likely to defer completely to their attorney's judgment. Helen stated that her only strong requests, at the time, had been that her daughter be well cared for and that the baby-sitter, a friend who had cared for her from birth, not be dragged into the proceedings.

I know that Clint Almond and Marcia Brody had been excited about the possibility of using a novel approach in this case. They'd been intrigued by the concept of Battered Woman Syndrome. And it had seemed to me at the time that they believed, as I did, that Helen Martin had been a severely battered and abused woman. But the fact remains that they could have (and, as defense attorneys, probably should have) held on to the option of using a mental health defense, especially once they realized that a self-defense plea simply would not work. Instead of serving fifty years without parole, Helen might already have completed her time in prison if a mental health defense had been successful.

I believe, too, that the judge might have permitted a late notice of mental health defense; he implied, at the special hearing, that he would have done so. In that case, expert witness testimony would have been deemed admissible before the jury.

---

that she would control enough, on her own, to pay for her own defense. Only her attorneys know exactly how much of it was spent, but others estimate that it was all gone by the time her trial ended.

And, had I known that such an option existed at the time, I certainly would have tried to persuade both attorney and defendant to attempt it.

At the time of this writing, Helen Martin has served seven years at the Missouri Women's correctional facility. She has lost all of her legal motions to date. There are other steps she can take, but she is totally out of money. And no lawyer seems willing to carry her case any further now. Louise Bauschard helped get a law passed making it possible for a battered woman to introduce expert witness testimony on her behalf.

Death Penalty Testimony

It should have been expected that, after working on first-degree murder cases, I would eventually be asked to consult, evaluate, and testify on cases in which special circumstances were charged, allowing the prosecutor to ask that a battered woman be put to death.

Most of these cases are unusual. They involve behavior and violence even more gruesome than the usual violence of battering situations. And the realization that another woman's life may literally be in my hands is always a frightening and humbling one.

SARAH'S STORY

Sarah was twenty-three when she became involved with George. Already a habitual user of marijuana and an occasional user of methamphetamines, Sarah thought he was attractive and fascinating. Later, she would describe his magnetism as irresistible. He made her feel worthwhile by spending hours getting high with her and listening to her talk about herself, something no one had ever done. (This is similar to the situation Hedda Nussbaum testified to during Joe Steinberg's trial for the murder of their adopted daughter, Lisa.) Her mother had abused her when she was growing up; her father had deserted the family when she was an infant. She was vulnerable to his brand of charming seduction.

George told her secrets about himself, too. He told her he'd beaten up all his former wives, each one for justified reasons, he said. He told her about his prison record, too, and about the fact that he earned his money by killing people.

Still, Sarah wasn't scared. She loved George and the exciting way of life he offered. She knew she would be different from the other women in his life; he would never have any reason to hurt her.

It didn't take long for the first battering incident to occur; it happened during the first three weeks of their relationship. George beat Sarah badly for talking to another man, tied her up, and threatened to inject poison into her veins. Then he said he'd leave her in a deserted area to die. But he didn't.

Instead, he took her with him as they set off on a cross-country trip, beginning the first of what would end with at least three killings in which she would later admit complicity. George used her to lure a man to his death; for this, he was paid $5,000. For the second killing, they dressed up like college students and kidnapped a twenty-year-old girl who picked them up hitch-hiking. George raped and sodomized the girl, then choked her to death and buried her in the desert. Sarah was with him during everything except the murder and burial. The next week, he forced her to participate with him in kidnapping and strangling another young woman.

When they were arrested, Sarah continued to profess her love for George. She proudly showed police the tattoos he'd given her, along with a terrible stab wound he'd inflicted on her leg just before the second murder. But for a long time, Sarah would not discuss George's violence toward her. Even when she began, slowly, to recount the incidents, she did not seem to understand the brainwashing effects he'd had on her.

Sarah was charged with murder, with aggravating or special circumstances. The prosecutor asked for the death penalty. The judge in this case refused to sever her trial from George's; they were tried as codefendants.

My testimony was allowed during the regular part of the

trial, rather than just the penalty phase (where psychological testimony can be used for mitigation, to reduce a death penalty to life without parole). I testified that Sarah had been George's victim, too, even though she had been unaware of his psychological hold over her. Despite the evidence of learned helplessness and the undeniable presence of battering and the Cycle of Violence, Sarah believed that she loved George. She knew she was in danger of being killed by him, too, but she believed that if she did what he told her to do and proved that she loved him, she might manage to stay alive. For months after they were jailed, she continued to write him love letters, all of which were introduced as evidence against her at the trial.

If it was love she felt, it was a terrifying love. She had identified with her oppressor as a way of trying to cope with the extreme stress and violence of her life with him, and the perpetual high risk of her own death. She had helped him murder other women to maximize her own chances for staying alive. All this took place in less than six months of her life.

As I write this, the jury in Sarah's first case has brought back its verdicts. They have convicted her on all counts as charged and they have given her the death penalty. The trial for her second case is scheduled to begin soon. Whatever the outcome, Sarah's fate by age twenty-seven is sealed.

Admissibility of Testimony on the Federal Level

Another important interim step taken by the legal profession in its attempt to deal with troublesome admissibility issues came during the federal court trial of Mary Player, a battered woman who shot and killed her Marine husband on the military base where they lived. (The fact that the homicide occurred in base housing at Camp Pendleton is the reason for her case going into federal court in the first place.) I was involved in this case as an expert witness for the defense.

MARY'S STORY

In 1981, Mary Player shot and killed her husband, Joseph, in their home in Camp Pendleton, a U.S. Marine Corps base in San Diego.

A poor Black woman, originally from North Carolina, Mary was assigned an attorney from the Federal Defender's Office in San Diego. Luckily for her, this particular group of attorneys has a national reputation for their brilliant performance at trial, and they were not about to let Mary down. She was the third battered woman attorney Mario Conte would represent. (Later, he would confide that her case had caused him so much emotional anguish that he considered death penalty work easier.)

Mario reviewed all legal precedents, then talked with other defense attorneys who had taken similar cases to trial. He knew his first hurdle would be to persuade the presiding judge, Judge Leslie Nielsen, to admit expert witness testimony concerning Battered Woman Syndrome.

There were a number of disturbing elements in Mary's personal history that an expert witness would have to explain. The state prosecution had already lined up witnesses to testify as to Mary's "haughty" and "snobbish" nature. This charge, sometimes masked under the mental health term "narcissism," or intense preoccupation with oneself, is a charge often made against battered women by those who fail to realize that the battered woman's survival often depends on her preoccupation is with her own safety, her own life and death.

Mary's claim was that her husband would beat her whenever she showed any interest in friends, so she stayed away from other people socially. There was legal record of a child abuse investigation in which she had covered up for Joseph; he had, at the time, supposedly been watching their four young children while she worked at one of the two full-time jobs she held to help support the new car he'd bought and to help pay off his drinking and gambling debts.

Most damaging of all was the fact that there were witnesses

for the prosecution who were prepared to state that Mary had tried to kill Joseph on several previous occasions. She had, in fact, threatened him once with a gun, when he wouldn't stop beating her.

Only an expert witness could explain to a jury whether or not she had been initiating violence herself, or merely responding to her husband's brutality.

Mary herself would be a poor witness on her own behalf. She'd developed a thick outer shell to protect herself from her life of constant pain. But her protective behavior made her appear defensive and angry; it often did make her seem "haughty" or "snobbish," as the prosecution's witnesses were prepared to state.

Even after reviewing videotapes of herself, designed to help her practice changing the way she looked and sounded, Mary simply could not alter her appearance. And, for a jury to believe a defendant, the defendant must appear to be like them; similarities, not differences, must be emphasized, especially where physical appearance is concerned. But Mary Player had devised a certain psychological strategy for preserving her own mental stability: she had chosen, throughout the years of abuse and beatings, to emphasize her own uniqueness; she needed to feel that she could be "somebody," and the attempt to make her fit a more "average" mold resulted in her sinking into suicidal depression several times while she was awaiting trial. Beaten emotionally as well as physically and sexually, there wasn't enough time for even an able and compassionate professional to help her drop some of her defensive stance. In this situation, only an expert witness could explain her behavior and appearance, in a sympathetic way, to the jury.

Mario Conte had been busy contacting most of the known researchers and professionals who had previously testified in similar cases. When he decided to hire our firm, he felt he had a good chance of getting my expert witness testimony admitted at trial by supporting it with affidavits from other experts in the field. Richard

Gelles,* Suzanne Steinmetz,† and others he contacted were all willing to prepare and sign sworn statements attesting to the fact that there was a field of study on battered women that contained sufficient data upon which reliable and valid professional opinions could be based; furthermore, each consulted expert swore that they knew my work and found me qualified to testify as to Mary Player's state of mind.

In a special motion hearing, Judge Leslie Nielsen accepted Mario's argument and ruled that my expert witness testimony would be admitted. All of us on the defense team were absolutely jubilant. In 1982, five years after it had first been admitted in state courts, Battered Woman Syndrome self-defense testimony was about to be admitted in a federal court.

Several other lawyers in the Federal Defender's Office worked with me on preparing my testimony. Attorney Gene Iredale spent hours helping me prepare for cross-examination.

At trial, the direct testimony went off as well as it had when Mario and I prepared it. Then came the cross-examination. Despite prosecutor Pam McNaughten's apparent need to prove herself "tougher" than most, it seemed to be going well, that is, until a severe blow occurred that might have had my entire testimony stricken from the record.

McNaughten asked me to produce my raw data: a copy of the Battered Woman Syndrome Questionnaire and the MMPI answers obtained directly from Mary Player during a clinical evaluation procedure. As was my normal practice then, I had brought neither to court. I did have the scored MMPI profile and report written for me by Dr. Lynne Rosewater, who did all of our analysis at that time, but, as was customary, she had not returned the computerized answer sheet that the prosecution was now request-

---

*Sociologist Richard Gelles, Academic Dean at the University of Rhode Island, is a researcher and author of many studies on domestic violence.

†Sociologist Suzanne Steinmetz, a professor at the University of Delaware, has authored several domestic violence studies. She has provided important data in other areas of family violence, notably sibling and elderly abuse.

ing. (Mary's answers to the Battered Woman Syndrome Questionnaire had been summarized in the Draft Summary of Notes and
used to write a report, which I did have.) The original forms had
been given to a research associate for data entry on our computer.

I explained all this to Judge Nielsen. I also explained the
psychologist's code of ethics, which does not normally permit
psychologists to turn over raw data (including notes and raw test
data) to those untrained in its use.

"Other psychologists do it all the time," said the judge.

"They should not be doing so, your honor. The American
Psychological Association (APA) Standards for Providers of Psychological Services and the APA Code of Ethics do not permit
such a practice. Anyone who does so is in violation of state
administrative law and is jeopardizing his or her license to practice
psychology."

"I don't care, Dr. Walker. You will have those materials in
this courtroom by nine o'clock tomorrow morning, or I will strike
all of your testimony. Do you understand?"

Oh, no, I thought.

"Yes, sir," I answered.

After all of Mario's creative work in getting expert witness
testimony admitted in this trial, would everything be lost now?

It was already 2:30 P.M. in San Diego; that meant that it was
3:30 P.M. in Denver and 4:30 P.M. in Cleveland, Ohio (where
Lynne Rosewater's psychology office was located).

Luckily for me (and for the defense) my long-time assistant, Roberta Thyfault, was there at the trial. As prosecutor
McNaughten continued with her cross-examination, I could see
Roberta lean over to confer with Mario and with Tim Levya,
Mario's investigator; I knew that, if anybody could locate the
necessary data and get it to us on time, Roberta could. Her brilliant
administrative skills had kept our Denver offices functioning on
several occasions when everyone else had been ready to throw
in the towel. I continued, meanwhile, to be cross-examined, helpless to do anything myself.

By 5:00 P.M., I learned that my faith in Roberta and the rest of the staff was more than justified. She had contacted all those involved. Angela Browne, working on the research analysis in Denver, managed to locate the necessary Battered Woman Syndrome Questionnaire form and, despite one of the worst winter snowstorms in the history of Colorado, she delivered it to Stapleton Airport in time for it to be sent air express. In Cleveland, Lynne Rosewater located the answer sheets requested; she, too, drove through a terrible snowstorm to get the material out on the last plane to San Diego that night. Rarely have I been prouder of the professionalism and commitment of the people I am fortunate enough to work with.

Like many investigators and attorneys, who put in long hours during trial, Tim Levya waited at the San Diego airport for both flights to arrive in the dim hours of the night. He made copies of all necessary documents; and by 9:00 A.M. we were in court with the raw test data on hand. Judge Nielsen accepted the documents matter of factly, obviously without any knowledge of or, at least, any intention of acknowledging the panicked efforts we'd expended getting them there according to his orders. (This taught me a lesson that should be noted by other budding expert witnesses: always try to have all your raw data with you, especially when going out of town to testify.)

In the end, though, it was well worth it: my testimony was admitted in federal court. Battered Woman Syndrome testimony by an expert witness has been allowed in other federal court cases since, based on the precedent set in the Mary Player case.

And, in the end, Mario Conte's brilliant legal footwork paid off. Although Mary Player was found guilty of second-degree murder, Judge Nielsen sentenced her in the mitigated range of two years and then later reduced the sentence to less than one year. So Mary retained her voting and other rights as an American citizen. (Citizens who are convicted of a felony and spend a year or more in state or federal prisons lose some of their civil rights, such as the right to vote. In some states, though, a petition for pardon to the governor can restore those rights.) She returned home to continue raising her four daughters, hoping that each one of them would grow up one day to be "somebody special."

The legal issues in battered women's self-defense cases are many and varied. And they can be difficult to resolve. Our legal system has made great strides over the last decade in beginning to cope with the complex issues in cases involving battered women who kill. But many more advances must still be made before justice can be done as a matter of course. It is my profound hope that I and other expert witnesses will continue to be part of helping this process go forward.

14

THE MAKING OF
AN EXPERT WITNESS

OR ME, the path toward becoming an expert witness first came into focus while speaking at the Violence Against Women conference in May 1977, at the University of Washington in Seattle. While I had done some public speaking before on the issue of battered women, I was still somewhat naive about the publicity that can be generated when a speaker addresses large, informed audiences in an activist community. I had finished my talk, and opened up the remaining time to a question-and-answer period.

All of a sudden, a challenging question came from the audience:

"What do you suggest as a short-term approach to keep battered women from getting killed?"

"We need highway billboards," I quipped, "with a large picture of John Wayne looking displeased, shaking his finger and saying that you're a sissy if you beat your wife."

This line got a big laugh, which encouraged me to continue.

"And if *that* fails, a woman should be allowed to defend herself to the point of killing the abuser, rather than dying herself. I'll help provide her with a defense, should she have to stand trial."

Once those words were out of my mouth, I was sorry I'd said them. My only previous experience with this country's legal system had been in traffic court and in divorce court. I felt that it was really presumptuous of me to even think I might be able to help defend a battered woman in criminal court; I didn't know what I was talking about.

Little did I suspect, however, that those few regretted sentences would form the essence of many wire news service reports that night.

The next morning, headlines in newspapers across the country read:

NOTED PSYCHOLOGIST TO DEFEND
BATTERED WOMEN WHO KILL!

In Billings, Montana, the noted criminal defense attorney Charles ("Timer") Moses read this story with more than usual interest. Five months earlier (in January 1977), Miriam Griegg had shot and killed her husband, Bob. When arrested and charged with deliberate homicide, Montana's equivalent of first-degree murder, she had asked Timer to represent her. Reading a newspaper article about the Violence Against Women conference in Seattle, Timer thought that perhaps the facts of his new case pointed to something novel: a new self-defense strategy, based on the psychological state of mind of a battered woman, even though such a defense was unprecedented at that time.

Within a few days of returning to my Denver offices, Jack Lindsay, Timer's investigator, had called to inquire about my availability. Timer, he said, was interested in using me as an expert witness in Miriam's upcoming trial.

I panicked.

"I don't know anything about testifying in court," I stammered, feeling trapped.

"Mr. Moses can teach you that," Jack reassured me. "Are you willing to come up here and interview our client?"

"I don't know. From your description of the facts, she does

sound like a battered woman, and it does sound as if she believed that her life was in danger when she shot and killed her husband. But I've never done anything like this before."

Timer came to the phone then, and he too tried to reassure me that my remarks in Seattle hadn't been totally out of line.

"If you can teach me about the psychology of battered women, Dr. Walker," he bargained, "I'll teach you how to explain it to a jury."

The next week I was on my way to meet with Timer and his staff and to interview Miriam.

When he met me at the airport in Billings, Jack Lindsay fit my urban expectations of a real-live western man: tall and physically powerful, he wore tough reptile-skin boots but had a warm, caring personality. It was instantly clear to me that he loved and respected his boss.

Timer Moses was unlike anyone else I've ever known. He, too, was a big man: about 6'4" tall, in his mid-fifties, with a thick shock of white hair. He spoke slowly, deliberately, fiddling with his pipe as if to measure out each word before speaking aloud.

Jack was the pilot of Timer's single-engine Cherokee plane. The two of them were a familiar sight throughout the Northwest.

I soon learned that Timer was like a superior chess player in his approach to the law, thinking out his overall strategy in large chunks, in advance. He always began with a thorough review of legal theory, then developed creative approaches to the practical applications of theory in each case. Whenever he arrived at an intellectual point that pleased him, his eyes twinkled and he broke out in an enormous, engaging smile. Timer was a lawyer's lawyer, studiously cognizant of the larger picture into which each case might fit. Lawyers in that area of the country frequently consulted him for his advice on particular theoretical points or asked him to advise them on legal strategy or even to act as cocounsel on especially difficult, complicated cases. His reputation was impeccable. And I would later attribute a great part of my eventual success as an expert forensic witness to Timer's expertise and patience, and to his consummate willingness and capability in teaching me what to do in court.

He told me little about the case initially, explaining that he wanted me to interview Miriam and form my own opinion first before bothering me with legal details. So I spent the better part of two days interviewing and evaluating Miriam in a small room in a local motel.

Miriam looked frightened. The anticipation of having to discuss this traumatic homicide with some psychologist who was still a stranger to her must have been extremely stressful. Still, nothing in my background or training could really have prepared me for what Miriam said. She began describing her ten years with Bob as many other battered women had before. The abuse had begun slowly, she said, with slaps, shoves, pushes, punches. It had then escalated in a regular pattern. Bob became progressively crueler; his physical and sexual abuse of her worsened. She'd felt that she could not protect his children (from his prior marriage) from his physical abuse when they visited; as a result, she became increasingly reluctant to let them stay for very long. Also, she said, he had been so intensely jealous that he rarely let her out of his sight. She remembered learning to look down at her shoes when walking around so that he could not accuse her of flirting with other men. To avoid a scene or a beating, she would let him accompany her to the door of the washroom in a restaurant, wait outside for her, then accompany her back to their table. When Bob loudly complained that she was "fooling around" with her sixty-year-old boss, she quit her job.

She described several acute battering incidents. After one beating, she'd gone to work with her face so swollen that she was unable to open her mouth wide enough to eat. (Later, at trial, some of her former co-workers testified that they remembered bringing her soup for lunch.) She described how, another time, she was awakened in the middle of the night to see Bob standing by the bed with a hatchet, first-aid cream, and bandages. He'd forced her to listen to him describe how he would smash her kneecaps so she couldn't ever leave him; then, he'd explained calmly, he would nurture and take care of her, guarding her smashed kneecaps against infection with the first-aid cream and bandages. By that time, Miriam had been beaten enough to know that he meant a lot of what he said. At the same time, she thought of him as if he were a little child, constantly needing her attention; she couldn't acknowledge to herself that he was, in fact, a pathologically intrusive and dangerous man.

Yet there seemed no way for her to escape him. One night, shortly before the final battering incident that had driven her to kill him, he'd hurt and frightened her so badly that she ran from their house, planning to walk the seven miles to her mother's place. A police car picked her up while she was walking along the road, still wearing her nightgown, and drove her there. Once at her mother's, Miriam was too frightened to tell her family what had happened. She suspected Bob of planting electronic surveillance devices in her family's home, as he'd threatened he would do. Eventually Bob himself drove up that night, acting as cheerful and charming as could be. So gentle and kind had he been toward her, in fact, that he was able to persuade her, terrified as she'd been, to return home with him. When he acted like such a gentleman, she said, no one in her family would believe that he habitually abused her.

After that incident, she told me, Bob was on his "good" behavior for a longer time than usual. Even when they spent several weeks visiting his family back East during Christmastime—an event that would usually set him off—he seemed able to maintain his "good" behavior without a single battering incident. But during a New Year's Eve party back at their own home, under the influence of too much alcohol, he cornered Miriam in the kitchen and accused her not only of flirting but of actually engaging in sex with one of their party guests. The accusations and hateful threats had begun again. Miriam knew that, when he got started like that, a beating would soon follow. Nevertheless, she tried to continue to be a gracious hostess.

Several hours later, when the party was over, she found she

had fired five shots from the handgun Bob had thrown at her, demanding that she use it on him before he shot her to death. Within a few minutes it was Bob who lay dead, sprawled bleeding across the floor in their bedroom.*

After I completed the interview, Timer and I talked. I told him what I knew about the psychology of battered women in general and about Miriam in particular. He told me a few things about courtroom law.

First, he said, would come all the legal motions. Lawyers could try to have certain evidence disallowed, bring other evidence in, and otherwise get the presiding judge to define exactly what conforming to the Rules of Evidence would mean in the case in question. Often, the attorneys would write out their arguments, usually citing other case decisions supporting their positions. Many motions would be resolved without oral argument, summarizing the written points; others would receive a hearing before the presiding judge. The resultant rulings could often be critical to the outcome of a case. And certain of these motions would be directly related to expert witness testimony.

Timer and I discussed jury selection to some extent, but at that time I was too much of a forensic novice to offer any advice. Instead, I listened in fascination as he described how he went about questioning potential jurors. It became obvious to me that good trial lawyers inevitably learn how to sense jurors who might be favorable to their client's position. Each side has a certain number of challenges at their disposal, allowing them to dismiss a potential juror without cause. If a juror admits bias, or reveals other reasons that might prevent him or her from considering the presented evidence objectively, the judge has the right to dis-

*Much of Bob's violent behavior toward Miriam was so horrendous that it was not all introduced as evidence at her trial. But by the time the trial was over, it was clear to everyone in the courtroom just how mentally disturbed as well as abusive he had been. It took the jury only a few hours to agree that Miriam had definitely been defending herself, with good reason, when she shot and killed him; they found her not guilty.

qualify him or her for cause, that is, without either attorney
having to use up a challenge; this can become quite important,
as each side gets closer to using up all their challenges. Our legal
system calls for a defendant to be judged by a jury of his or her
peers; sometimes, that standard is quite difficult, if not impossible,
to achieve.*

Choosing the right jury, then, is a critical phase in every
trial. I remember Timer talking about his plans to ask several
questions on *voir dire* that would get all the potential jurors
thinking about defensive actions they themselves might have
taken to save their own lives during a frightening incident. He and
I had to discuss possible *voir dire* questions in advance; witnesses
are generally excluded from the trial at all times except for those
when they are actually testifying (this rule of witness exclusion is
an attempt to prevent collusion or bias in testimony; it is sometimes not applied to expert witnesses, who may need to observe
the proceedings in order to form an opinion). It was clear to me
that he wanted to use the *voir dire* jury selection period to set the
mood of this trial from the beginning. Timer wanted every potential juror to start thinking about what it would mean to feel in fear
of dying, to feel the need to aggressively defend oneself, even to
use physical force in self-defense. He believed that this would
encourage the eventually selected jurors to identify with his client.

Toward the end of the selection process in Miriam's case,

---

*In most jurisdictions, twelve jurors and two alternates are chosen. All
sit through the entire trial and, in some instances, even deliberate together, in
case one of the regular jurors cannot continue duty for some reason; but only
twelve vote, and they must unanimously find that the state has proved its case
beyond a reasonable doubt, in order to deliver a verdict of guilty (except in
Louisiana, where it takes only a majority vote). In first-degree murder or capital
murder cases, in which the death penalty is being requested, a "death qualified"
jury is chosen; this means that any potential juror who states that he or she is
morally opposed to the death penalty or states that under no circumstance could
he or she sentence someone to death is automatically excluded from serving on
the jury. In fact, social psychologists have found that "death qualified" juries in
general are more likely than other juries to convict a defendant. But the United
States Supreme Court has not ruled such juries unconstitutional.

Timer had eleven women and one man seated in the jury box, with one challenge remaining. There were two women still in the panel, both potential jurors, should he exercise his challenge. Back in 1977, the popular belief was that women judged women victims more harshly than did men during rape trials (the psychological explanation for this was that, by blaming the victim for what had happened to her, the women jurors would feel safer, more assured that it couldn't happen to them; it made them somehow feel reprieved). Would this hold true for battered women defendants, too? Or would women identify with another woman in this case? Even if they had never been physically abused themselves, would the psychological oppression of all women become an implicit unifying force in the courtroom? Timer decided to find out. He exercised his last challenge and excused the man, taking his chances with an all-woman jury.*

Once a jury is chosen, each attorney gets the opportunity to address it, presenting his or her view of the case in what is called an opening argument.

The prosecution goes first, since it must present the elements of the alleged crime and prove its case. The defense may present its argument directly afterward or wait until all the state's evidence has been presented. Since the elements are clear in most self-defense cases involving battered women, many defense attorneys choose to make their opening statement before the prosecution's evidence is presented, so jurors can view any presented evidence while keeping both sides' versions of events in mind.

Some attorneys believe that cases can be won or lost during opening arguments. Prosecutors must be careful not to promise more than they can actually deliver through the evidence; and defense attorneys must decide whether to challenge the state's evidence or simply put forward a case of their own. I've often wondered, in this regard, what jury members think when the

---

*In all the cases in which I've testified, I've seen only one other all-woman jury—in Opal's case (described in Chapter 6), and she too was acquitted.

defense promises them that they will hear from an expert witness concerning Battered Woman Syndrome and then, because of admissibility issues that go unresolved, they are never presented with the promised testimony. Do they feel cheated? Are they resentful of the prosecutor for objecting to expert witness testimony? Do they resent the defense attorney for not keeping his or her promise?

Presentation of evidence comes after the opening statements. First, the prosecution presents all its available facts; then the defense does the same.

The evidentiary part of the trial marks a presentation of facts within a ritualized context. In the direct examination, the attorney calling a particular witness asks questions (usually of a general nature, so that the witness appears to recite facts naturally, without having been coached by the lawyer). These questions must follow proper legal form, and the answers must be directly responsive and factual. If either question or response do not conform to the rules, the opposing attorney can object. The presiding judge must then decide whether the objection will be sustained or overruled. Sometimes, the judge will simply ask the questioning attorney to restate a question differently. Opposing attorneys often use objections, however, to break a witness's train of thought or stop the flow of an especially damaging piece of testimony. (If there are too many frivolous interruptions, though, the jury may begin to suspect the disruptive attorney of having a weak case.)

During bench conferrals over objections and rulings, I always attempt to make eye contact with various jurors. This is an important and useful technique for any expert witness. Subtle eye-rolling, or slight knowing smiles, convey a powerful message: *We are all here in this alien land, where a great fuss is being made over incomprehensible rules, when all we want is for them to let us get on with the story.* Like all nonverbal behavior in a courtroom, this must be done in good taste, but it can be most effective in enhancing one's perceived credibility as an expert witness.

When direct examination is concluded, the opposing attorney may conduct a cross-examination, the purpose of which is to find and challenge all potential weak spots in the testimony. Discrediting a witness by demonstrating previously proven unreliability, exposing discrepancies in testimony, and exposing a bold-faced lie via impeachment are typical strategies. If all else fails and a witness seems otherwise faultless, the cross-examining attorney may raise doubts in the minds of jurors by using shifting verbal emphasis and innuendos. All possible techniques are used. Cross-examination has its own proscribed question-and-answer format; the questions are generally longer (often trying to mislead the witness by giving inaccurate information, by assuming facts not in evidence, or by restating an earlier statement, giving it a different meaning through changed emphasis). The witness, on the other hand, is expected to give short answers, preferably yes or no. Again, the tempo and rhythm of a cross-examination often determines whether or not it holds jurors' interest; objections or a witness's requests for water or for a restroom break can ruin the established pace.

Timer taught me that a good cross-examination is planned in advance and mapped out in chunks of questions, sequences that may be upset by a witness asking the attorney to repeat a question, taking extra time to think, searching through a file, or asking for clarification. (These strategies should be used carefully and sparingly, since feigning too much ignorance or appearing to be too disruptive can result in a jury's disregarding one's testimony.) The key to getting through a tough cross-examination with flying colors is to stay calm and listen to each question carefully, then give just the right amount of information necessary for a reasonable response. If an opposing attorney is asking questions in an angry or hostile manner, I try to get him or her to do something courteous for me, like filling my water glass. I also try to engage him or her by smiling, laughing, or talking during recess, so the jury can see that I am not intimidated. The witness who can stay cool and unruffled during a tough cross-examination adds immeasurably to his or her credibility.

Expert witnesses are not treated like other witnesses, and

an additional *voir dire* proceeding carried out initially to qualify them as experts allows them to give their opinions as well as recite factual information. In essence, an expert witness teaches the jury how to interpret the evidence as would an expert in this field. Using the witness's up-to-date résumé (listing education, training, work experience, research, relevant honors, professional member- ships, published articles or books, professional presentations, and expert testimony admitted elsewhere) and other pertinent infor- mation, the attorney questions the expert witness in a way that establishes that he or she has requisite qualifications. To impress a jury, attorneys sometimes spend a half hour or more conducting this *voir dire*. This procedure is especially important when the other side is planning to call their own expert, who disagrees with the opinion of the defense's witness.

The opposing attorney also has the right to question any expert witness. This cross-examination is only supposed to con- cern an examination of qualifications to determine if the witness may be admitted as an expert; however, many opposing attorneys try to use it to chip away at a witness's credibility so as to mini- mize the importance of her/his opinion in the jury's mind.*

A common strategy of prosecutors is to ignore an expert witness's impressive credentials and to focus instead on what he or she is *not*. This approach is important for any mental health professional acting as a forensic witness to know about, and I

*A favorite tactic used against me early on was to pick at my doctorate degree—which was granted from an American Psychological Association-ap- proved program in psychology at Rutgers's University School of Education, but which was an Ed.D. degree in psychology, not a Ph.D. An Ed.D. has less prestige than a Ph.D., although requirements are often the same as in my program, and appearances count in a trial. To offset this status differential, I took a rigorous examination and in 1979 was awarded the Diplomate in Clinical Psychology from the American Board of Professional Psychology, recognizing my excellence in performance of clinical psychology. That coveted status, which is so highly regarded and recognized that it substitutes for licensing examinations in most states, helps overcome the unwarranted bias against my hard-earned Ed.D. But even today, opposing attorneys still use this technique on me, but with little or no success.

examine the pitfalls and danger points here in order to inform other psychologists who may find themselves in similar positions, and to help potential jurors recognize such ineffectual techniques.

"You are not a *medical* doctor, are you?" a prosecutor may ask derisively.

"No," the expert witness psychologist will respond, honestly.

"Tell us the difference between a psychiatrist and a psychologist, Doctor," the prosecutor may then sneer.

At this point, the expert witness will have a chance to pontificate about his or her field of psychology. Psychology, the expert should point out, is the study of all human behavior, not just of the disordered behavior that psychiatrists study. Psychology, the expert witness should proudly say, provides the behavioral science foundation underlying any medical doctor's specialization in the disease process. In fact, psychologists such as myself have taught behavioral science courses in the nation's medical schools

Quickly, the image of "lowly psychologist" will fall apart. The prosecutor, though, may switch from his or her attempt to discredit the profession to a demeaning of the title.

"But it isn't really correct to call you Doctor, is it—un—uh, is it Miss, or Mrs., or Ms. . . . ?" (Ms. will be pronounced "Mizzzz," with teeth showing through the prosecutor's extrawide smile.)

This is the time for the expert witness to respond calmly, as though the question asked were perfectly legitimate.

"As a scholar in the field of psychology, who has earned a legitimate doctorate, it is customary and proper to use the title 'Doctor' when addressing me," the witness responds, adding, "This is true for women as well as for men." The witness can then turn to the women and men on the jury, make eye contact, and smile sweetly as though sharing a secret with them.

As an alternative, but only when the expert witness is fairly sure that the prosecutor appears particularly pompous and obnoxious to the jury, she might give a slightly bemused smile, or else put hand gently to mouth, as if to stifle a giggle. At times, one may even, safely, laugh out loud. If the presiding judge is tolerant and good-humored, it may also be appropriate to crack a mild but appropriate one-liner joke; this will make the expert witness seem like a real person to the members of the jury, not some angry radical feminist or academic elitist, but a human being with a wide range of emotions, like them.

All of these ploys, while harmless, enable the expert witness to exercise some control within the strict limits of a highly ritualized and often mystifying process. In addition, they help preserve one's dignity and self-esteem.

The jury instructions, given by the judge to the jury at the conclusion of the trial's other phases, are the judge's explanation to the jury about how to interpret what they have heard within the framework of the law, based on the evidence presented. All the pieces must be put together to create a reasonable theory concerning the case. It is not just what the facts show that counts; ultimately, it is how these facts fit into a legal structure, itself composed of laws created by the legislature and shaped by judicial precedent, that will determine the valid outcome. Yet it is still the impression created in the minds of jurors by testimony, sometimes expert witness testimony, that may supply the unstated but underlying emotional fabric supporting a final verdict.

"Your job is to teach the jurors what you've taught me about the psychology of battered women," Timer Moses told me, all those years ago. "That means that you have to get their attention and hold it. Courtroom drama is one way to capture it. But you can't always be dramatic, or else they'll begin to distrust you. You need to find a really comfortable style, and you need to tune in to how they're reacting to you at any given moment."

I understood immediately what he meant. After all, I'd already been a teacher for fifteen years, and a good teacher must learn techniques for grabbing students' attention and keeping it. Working with Timer and preparing for that first trial felt like learning the rules of a new game of logic. In the end, it wasn't such alien territory, after all.

"When I ask you a question," he said, "look at me first, as though you're listening, then thinking. Then turn slightly, like a quarter-turn, toward the jury, and look at them while you answer. Even though I ask the question, be sure that you respond to them. Try to be natural, not too stiff. And above all, don't use psychological jargon. But don't simplify everything so much so that the jurors think you're being condescending toward them."

"That sounds like the balance you have to strike when you're teaching a basic undergraduate psychology course," I replied.

It became clear to me that, to teach a jury about battered women, I would need to talk about some old social myths about women, explaining why these myths did not really hold true, and then I'd have to describe the new research proving that other old ideas about women are outdated. Once some general principles had been explained, I could apply them to the defendant, discussing how she did or did not fit the pattern.

Timer also taught me to pay close attention to the total impression I created in a courtroom.

Given that legal deliberation is an unfamiliar activity for most jurors, they will look for any available clues to help guide them in their judgment. (As it is truly difficult to discern how juries make up their minds, attorneys try at least to be consistent in their presentation of a case.) Lawyers all over the country attend seminars to learn how different colors and styles of clothing affect people's moods, how modulation of voice, stance and position, humor, toughness, and use of expert witnesses in a courtroom may influence a jury's collective consciousness. In turn, lawyers instruct defendants in such aspects of behavior as how to dress in court, how to sit, and proper demeanor.

Timer did the same for me. He wouldn't rehearse my testimony; he decided that he wanted me to appear personable and spontaneous.

"You're too attractive. You don't look like a psychologist or a scholar," he said. "Go out and buy a pair of eyeglasses, and charge it to us. Wear a simple dark dress or suit. And use very little makeup. Don't dress like too much of a sophisticate. Don't dress shabbily, either, just because this is a small town in Montana. People here are proud, but they're not fancy. We want them, most of all, to be able to identify with you."

He even took me out to eat out at different restaurants around town, and suggested I observe how people dressed and sat. What I learned with Timer still holds true for any case I am involved in today: jurors expect a psychologist to appear professional, so I wear something in accordance with that expectation, but make sure that it's comfortable. This way, they're free to listen to me rather than to struggle with any contradictions between how I look and what I say. The only exception to this rule is when I anticipate a nasty prosecutorial attack on my feminist beliefs; I then will try to appear a little "extra" feminine.

I remember how strange it felt, donning a pair of noncorrective eyeglasses. They did make me look a bit like a bookworm, but I never felt that they did me much good; in the end, Timer agreed. "When the trial's over, you can throw those glasses away, Dr. Walker. You really don't need them to appear scholarly."

I never wore them again.

Timer taught me well. And he conducted a brilliant defense for Miriam. Six months after she'd killed her battering husband, Miriam was acquitted—able to begin a new, violence-free life, in contrast to Joyce Hawthorne, who killed her husband, Aubrey, during that same month of January in 1977, but whose case took nine years before it was done.

And, although I really did not know it at the time, I was embarked upon a new career.

Good defense attorneys choose expert witnesses carefully, quickly dropping those whose competence, presentation, ethics, or integrity cannot stand the scrutiny of the public eye.

"Everything you do can and will be exposed in a hotly contested trial," I was told from the first.

"Each side wants to win, and we'll do whatever is necessary to achieve that goal. If you can remember not to take all the attempts to make you look like a fool personally, you can survive the process."

I learned that this was so; trial law was competition at its finely tuned best. I realized quickly that, on the witness stand, I had better be able to back up my professional opinions with data. Otherwise I'd look mighty foolish up there.

Lack of familiarity with the system can intimidate a novice expert witness. Psychologists frequently forget that, on the witness stand, we are not to speak unless asked a question or ordered to do so by the judge. (In normal teaching and clinical practice, talking is the psychologist's trademark.) If we are unfamiliar with the adversarial process, we may expect that our objective approach to scientific data will be respected as neutral. But once an expert witness agrees to testify for one side or another, as opposed to being just the court's witness, there is no more neutrality in the legal arena.

It was painful at first for me to learn that everything I'd ever written professionally could and did come into a trial, usually presented by an eager prosecutor who was attempting to decrease the impact of my testimony by encouraging the jury to view it as "biased." Favorite quotes from my book *The Battered Woman* began to show up in trial after trial. (I often wondered how all these prosecutors knew to underline the exact same sections.) Opposing attorneys were especially fond of using my feminist political views against me.

"If Dr. Walker is a feminist," they reason, "then she's in favor of women killing men."

In court, I am not about to deny my feminist perspective. Even if I wanted to, which I most assuredly do not, it happens to be the case that every book, paper, and speech I've produced in my career presents my belief that, in this society, men and women are not equal, that mental health is affected adversely by that inequality, and that feminist psychologists have a responsibility to use their knowledge to help women achieve equality by speaking out against, and hopefully eradicating, all forms of discrimination. Nowhere in any of my work do I advocate that women kill men! Yet, sections of my published work are frequently quoted completely out of context—sometimes even to the point of using unrelated sentence fragments—to falsely demonstrate that I am a preacher of dangerous ideas. And prosecutors, generally employees of a state legal system with far-reaching tentacles, tend to network with other prosecutors.

It was during a trial in Fort Wayne, Indiana, that I first realized the full extent of prosecutorial networking to other attorneys and related colleagues. As I was waiting in a separate room for witnesses (who are excluded from the courtroom unless testifying), the defense attorney rushed in urgently.

"Dr. Walker, are you a widow? How did your husband die?"

"Why is that your business?" I asked, stung by the personal nature of the question, intruding as it did into a painful part of my life.

I soon learned the answer.

Apparently, while both attorneys were discussing trial strategies in the judge's chambers, the prosecutor had revealed that he had contacts in Denver who told him my husband had suddenly died. Without any supporting information whatsoever, the prosecutor suggested that I too might have been a battered woman who got away with murdering a man, and that I therefore had no right to testify.

I assured the defense attorney that I had not been battered by my late husband, and that I had nothing to do with his death, as proven by the cause of death, which appeared on his death certificate. The unfounded rumor was thus quickly dispelled, but I was furious. It shouldn't ever have come up in the first place.

When it came my turn to testify, I entered the courtroom and took the witness stand. The prosecutor, trying to appear both congenial and intimidating, approached me, proudly waving a psychological report I had written several months earlier concerning a case in Denver. Knowing that psychological reports are supposed to be kept confidential, I asked him where he'd obtained it. A friend of his, he told me, a lawyer in the Denver D.A.'s office.

To be sure, this seemed to be one of the most unethical prosecutors I had dealt with to date. I was appalled at the lengths to which he seemed willing to go for a conviction. Clenching my teeth but keeping a smile on my face so that the jurors (reentering the courtroom after a recess) would not discern my real feelings, I whispered to him:

"You can ask me anything you want to about this case or about my research on cross-examination. But try getting out of line with just one personal question and I'll haul you right back in here with a civil lawsuit."

Still smiling and feigning self-confidence, I continued with my testimony that day. Sure enough, the prosecutor's cross-examination was much milder than his earlier bluster had threatened. I am sure that my own refusal to be intimidated by his bullying tactics and his questionable ethics changed his behavior toward me. It may also have helped the defense win that case; the battered woman defendant was totally acquitted.

Not all of my contacts with opposing counsel, though, have been hostile. In a number of cases, we've established good relationships based on mutual respect for both psychology and the law. In other cases, we'd already established good relationships through other community work involving the promotion of more effective prosecution of batterers and follow-up of domestic violence/assault cases.

Norm Early, Denver's current D.A., and his predecessor, Dale Tooley, are good examples.

Norm's interest in victims' rights and domestic violence began way before my arrival in Denver in 1975. He headed the district attorney association's efforts to prosecute abusers while protecting victims, as well as having served on the board of directors of Park East Mental Health Center, a tough, community-based job, and helping persuade Dale, then his boss, to begin one of the first domestic violence prosecution units in the country. Dale didn't need much persuading; he already worked well with a number of women's rights groups in town.

Once, during a particularly tense period when the Colorado
Coalition for Justice for Abused Women (fondly known as JAWS
by its supporters) was negotiating with the Denver police department and the city attorney's office to avert a possible lawsuit, Dale
and Norm attended a meeting in which they were clearly aligned
with JAWS' demands. Their postion infuriated Captain Montoya, who had been authorized to speak for the police department. Mostly women lawyers sat all around the table. I was the
only psychologist present. After some remark I made (which no
one can remember now), Captain Montoya became even more
enraged. One of the JAWS attorneys, the only man present
representing us, Robert Hill, sitting next to me, tried to no avail
to calm him down by explaining what I'd just said. Without
warning, Montoya exploded.

"If you women think you can sue the police department,
then you have another think coming! You'd all just better hold
on to your jock straps!"

At first, none of us believed that we'd heard him correctly.
Finally, Dale Tooley broke the silence, using his diplomatic skills
to wrest a promise from the city's attorney to keep these talks
progressing; shortly thereafter, he ended the meeting. When the
city and police representatives had left, the rest of us burst out
laughing. There was something hysterical in the laughter; we'd all
been holding it in for so long.

Afterward, whenever a controversial topic came up, we'd
whisper to each other something like, "You'd just better hold on
to your jock strap!" And immediately each of us would break into
uncontrollable laughter.

Eventually the new mayor, Federico Pena, appointed a new
police captain and manager of public safety, who worked more
cooperatively with this community group, which eventually became the core of Denver's highly acclaimed Project Safeguard, an
advocacy program on behalf of battered women.*

---

*Project Safeguard received part of its funding from the Department of
Justice. It became one of several model programs nationwide focusing on sup-

The opposing attorneys I have liked the best are those willing to learn as much as possible about the consequences of domestic violence, those who are willing to revise their future legal strategies in the name of justice.

After he lost one of the early battered woman self-defenses in Colorado, Jim Franklin, an assistant D.A. in Colorado Springs, suggested that his boss (D.A. Bob Russell) invite me to come and train their staff, the staff of the sheriff's department, the police, and other concerned people in the community. Bob Russell had previously formed one of the first child abuse prosecution teams in the nation and was quite receptive to such a suggestion. We had been on a panel presentation together at a National District Attorneys Association meeting. Jim Franklin is now a judge; I have faith that he and some of his colleagues will be instrumental in furthering the efforts of their community to reduce the high level of intrafamily homicide and violence that exists there.

The behavior of judges in the courtroom can directly affect the outcome of a trial. Those who are impatient and discourteous and who demonstrate intemperance in the court can place a favorable outcome for the woman in jeopardy, as such intemperance has a chilling effect on all who come into the courtroom. People want to disbelieve the terrible tales of brutality told by the battered woman and other witnesses, including the expert. It is the judge's responsibility to go beyond simply admitting such testimony; she or he must create a proper atmosphere for it to be given equal weight with all of the other evidence. The judge's perceived attitude can help jurors pay attention to or invalidate battered woman syndrome testimony.

State judicial disciplinary committees are charged with hearing grievances against judges who blatantly exceed their judicial discretion. However, more subtle behavior that has a high

---

porting battered women and children while encouraging the legal system to arrest and prosecute abusers.

probability of creating a chilling effect on justice must be directly
dealt with at state and national judicial forums.

The prosecutors who have given me the hardest times are,
unfortunately, other women, even those who are self-avowed
feminists. It sometimes seems to me that they have to convince
themselves to hate me in order to do their job.

Expert Witness Techniques

Early on, I decided that for ethical reasons I could first work on
a case only as a consultant or a clinical evaluator. Then, if my
results supported the defense's strategy, I would agree to be available to testify during a trial. (If my results did not support the
defense's side of things, I made up my mind that I could not and
would not discuss them with anyone but the defendant and her
attorney.) Today, many state laws protect the psychologist's privilege and consider the expert as part of the defense team. Some,
however, do not.

I also decided early on that I would consider both the
defendant and her attorney to be my clients, and that I would
then claim the privilege of confidentiality for both of them. This
privilege allows psychologists to function in an atmosphere of
client trust, thus maximizing the beneficial potential of therapeutic work. Thus, unless I am called to testify in court and am given
permission to do so by the client(s), I consider myself bound by
these rules of confidentiality. (The only exceptions occur in cases
in which I suspect child abuse or child neglect, or if I have
evidence that someone involved is in danger of seriously hurting
herself or others.)

Confidentiality rules are critical in legal cases for several
reasons. First, the standard of American justice is such that an
individual must be considered innocent until proven guilty
beyond a reasonable doubt, and it is the trier of fact, not the
psychologist, whose role it is to make such a pronouncement.
Second, defendants have the right to remain silent, all the way

through to the end of an entire trial, if they so choose. Third, the evaluator may learn information that could prove incriminating to the defendant without being proved true. (Although in my own practice, I do try to corroborate a defendant's story with other sources, psychologists are not primarily factual investigators; we can investigate only for psychological consistencies.) Fourth, the unwritten ethical code pledge taken by licensed psychologists is similar to the Hippocratic Oath taken by doctors: we pledge to do no harm to a client intentionally; and to disclose confidential, sometimes embarrassingly personal information in a public forum without permission is undoubtedly harmful.

A request for my help as an expert witness may come from a lawyer or an investigator; less often, it comes from a woman defendant herself, from another mental health professional, or from a battered women's shelter. I've evolved a sort of formulaic response for handling an initial inquiry like this. It may prove helpful to other professionals to describe it here.

I first spend a lot of time, if possible, on the telephone, getting the facts of the case, seeing if the case meets with my criteria, "feeling out" what the lawyers are like, what the defendant's motivation for committing homicide or violence may have been, finding out if the people involved with the defendant's case are able to afford my services.* I also like to get a feel, in advance, for what the trial community will be like.

In any case, I send each inquirer a packet of information from our Denver offices. I tell them that, whether or not we agree

---

*If not, I usually direct them to local people who might help find an expert who will testify in my place. Sometimes, if the defense attorney is court-appointed through the public defender's office, the state pays my fees. Vince Aprile, an attorney in the state Office of Public Advocacy in Kentucky and former President of the National Association of Criminal Defense Lawyers, has helped lawyers find the necessary money to pay my fees from public funds if the client is indigent. The National Clearinghouse on Defense of Battered Women in Philadelphia also provides such assistance. Still, most defendants are limited by lack of funds.

to work together, they must become as thoroughly educated as possible about battered women. If I am called back (usually within two to four weeks) and agree to do so, I sometimes act on a consulting basis, reading three or four hours' worth of material concerning the individual before deciding whether or not to take on the case.

If I decide to take the case, I and my staff conduct a thorough two-day evaluation with the defendant. Whenever possible, the defendant comes to our Denver offices. Sometimes, though, I must travel to wherever she is, preferably with an associate but often alone. It is still an eerie feeling to land in the airport of some strange city, not knowing much about who or what awaits me.

In preparing for a case, I familiarize myself as much as possible with "discovery material" (police reports, indictments, past history, police-recorded statements). When accompanied by an associate, I let her perform the longest part of the interview, using the Battered Woman Syndrome Questionnaire, which is conducted using a standard form developed in one of our research projects. I myself do the clinical interview, which lasts several hours, using the MMPI, which is mostly self-administered, and sometimes other tests. Once in a while, we ask local qualified professionals to become involved as consultants. They, too, may do some diagnostic testing. The entire process is painstaking and very thorough indeed. I then spend several weeks evaluating the materials we've collected and interpreting the defendant's tests, after which I put together a summary of my notes, including the defendant's abuse history and, if the attorney has requested it, a psychological report.

I discuss these results with the attorney and the defendant and sometimes send a copy of my understanding of factual information to them for corrections. It is very important that these materials not fall into the hands of a prosecutor prematurely, before all the facts are in. One typo or mistake on my part could cast doubt on my client's story.

In that connection, it is also terribly important for any expert witness to be entirely aware of such factors as the defendant's legal rights or waivers of confidentiality. An expert witness puts her reputation, her career, and sometimes her life on the line, to say nothing of the fate of the defendant.

Most murder trials last one to two weeks (except in California, where six weeks is usual and six months is not unheard of). If the testimony of the expert witness is admitted, she must remember that the job to be done is to educate the jury and the court, not just to state her own beliefs concerning the client's guilt or innocence. As a mental health expert, she observes and notes symptoms, tries to understand what they mean in relation to this specific case, and testifies in the area of her own personal expertise.

As I learned from the outset, working with Timer Moses, an expert witness needs to *appear* a certain way to the court and to the jury, because she will be continually scrutinized while on the witness stand. Depending on the setting—some are more formal than others—and the region of the country, the expert witness must be careful to dress appropriately. Most importantly, she must be a good and effective teacher, using language that is neither jargonistic nor patronizing. Testimony may run three hours in the morning and three hours again in the afternoon, with only two short breaks. The task of being an expert witness requires one to think and evaluate quickly and consistently on the witness stand. Obviously, it is demanding and exhausting.

The expert witness should find out in advance whether or not the community in which the trial is to be held has a lot of social prejudice concerning "feminists"; depending on what the community norms and perceptions are, she may try to "soften" her image (to appear as stereotypically "feminine" as possible) or else try to appear entirely "plain" ("average" and "scholarly" at the same time). I always ask an attorney to advise me concerning

such matters as community "dress codes" and terms or mannerisms that might prove offensive to a jury.*

The most important thing in any trial is rapport with a jury.
The expert witness wants a jury's attention to be fixed on her
whenever she speaks; only then does she know for a fact that she
may be succeeding in making them believe. Any jury, I think, is
capable of understanding what a college class understands regarding scientific method and research. The expert witness can also
explain how any decision was arrived at, which often provides the
extra bonus of preempting or undercutting the prosecution's
cross-examination a little.

Initially, the use of a psychologist or other non-M.D. mental health professional as expert witness was really an expansion
of accepted trial practice. Everyone was kind of "winging it" at
first. Now our courts are starting to see better-prepared expert
witnesses: serious, thoroughly qualified professionals who know
exactly what they are doing. And in 1981 the American Psychological Association, acknowledging all the forensic activity of psychologists, some of whom also testify as expert witnesses, permitted the formation of the Psychology and Law Division. In
addition to all the qualified local professionals around the nation
who may testify as expert witnesses for battered women who kill,
I have personally trained about ten psychologists specifically to
work as expert witnesses in these cases.

What makes a good expert witness?

*One of the other facts of life in our legal system is that lawyers need
to coexist with presiding judges, with prosecutors, and with all the other legal
professionals on their circuit or in their locale. Defense attorneys have their
careers and futures to consider, too, futures that stretch beyond the outcome
of any one trial. Some of them may live in small towns; they need to maintain
and preserve a certain reputation. All of these factors may create complex
situations during a trial—situations that unfortunately may not be resolved in
the best interests of the defendant. Until our legal system is much reformed,
though, there is often no way around this problem. The expert witness should
be prepared to find herself in the midst of such situations more often than she
might like.

A sense of drama.

A willingness to take risks.

An ability to think quickly under stress, to be highly verbal, to be a bit of an exhibitionist when required.

An expert witness must have a high level of self-confidence and self-esteem. She must also be obsessive-compulsive when it comes to detail; such an attitude ensures a healthy respect for the process.

The expert witness must, above all, be well prepared.

And she must be a good teacher who can use relevant examples and keep an audience's interest.

I am proud of the fact that more than 25 percent of the defendants for whom I've testified have been fully acquitted and two-thirds have never served a minute of time in jail.

15

JOYCE HAWTHORNE
TODAY

JOYCE HAWTHORNE'S LEGAL DESTINY took nine years to play itself out, nine long years after the death of her battering husband, Aubrey.

This woman endured three murder trials. In each instance, attorney Leo Thomas, faithful to his client and her cause throughout the long, bitter, heart-breaking process, arranged for her to be out of prison on bail and filed an appeal. The third appeal he filed was again based on prosecutorial misconduct (the prosecutor had insisted on using Joyce's forced "confession" to the police as evidence in the third trial, too, thereby impeaching her) as well as on judicial refusal to allow my expert witness testimony.

The Florida court of appeals finally handed down a decision in favor of the defense in 1986, four years after the final appeal had been filed. Included in the court's opinion was a strong condemnation of the blatant misconduct of the prosecutor in this case. The opinion also strongly intimated the presence of judicial misconduct (from two out of the three judges on the panel) and agreed that a fourth trial was warranted to amend these damaging procedural errors. The appellate court also made it clear that, in its opinion, expert witness testimony could be admitted in the new trial it ordered.

Before the fourth trial could begin, however, Leo Thomas submitted a motion to the new presiding judge, Joseph Tarbuck. This motion stated that it would constitute cruel and unusual punishment to force Joyce Hawthorne to endure a fourth trial, for the same crime, after all she had been through. Leo moved that her case be dismissed. And Judge Tarbuck agreed.

After nine years, Joyce Hawthorne was free.

I would have celebrated with Leo, I think, when I heard the news from him via telephone, but in a way we were both a bit too exhausted from the nine years of legal process to openly express our jubilation at the final outcome. And if we were exhausted, one can only imagine how Joyce herself felt—tired, relieved, pleased, maybe a combination of many emotions, and, of course, validated. Finally, through painstaking legal documentation, Joyce got to tell her story, and the appellate court judges believed her.

Joyce also decided to take her story directly to the American public. She appeared on popular television talk shows, on "Good Morning America," "The Oprah Winfrey Show," "Phil Donahue," "People Are Talking," and "Merv Griffin," among others. The enormous support she has received from those who listened to her tale of horror has been healing. It has helped her live through the long days and nights when she didn't know whether or not she'd wind up returning to prison. It helped her want to live and to continue raising her children.

Most of Joyce Hawthorne's five children are doing well these days. During the past twelve years, they've grown to adulthood.

Joyce herself is looking for work.

She has not had a single date with a man in all this time, but is thinking about it more favorably these days.

She has changed her name, and is considering moving away from Pensacola now—to start her life again, she says. And she is also considering going back to school to earn a counseling degree. She would like some day to be able to help other battered women on a professional basis.

Joyce is still in the process of shedding her "victim" status, of picking up the pieces and moving on. Involvement with the legal system keeps women on the fringes of society, and she, like many formerly battered women, is moving inward—closer to the core, closer to life, light, and status as a healthy, whole, nonvictimized human being.

ACKNOWLEDGMENTS

IN WRITING THIS BOOK I have been able to share the stories of some of the bravest women I have known. The battered women who have killed their abusers in self-defense also became widows at their own hands. They have grieved for the men they once loved as well as for the death of their own hopes and dreams, while at the same time they are relieved that they no longer have to put up with their abusers' behavior. Destined to die by their violent partners, these women cheated their destinies by fighting back and killing the batterer instead. Rarely do they understand the feminist political ramifications of what they have done, which I have tried to analyze and write of here. In fact, rarely do they understand right away that they have actually killed their violent partners. They never really wanted anyone to die; they only wanted their partners to stop hurting them.

My work with these women who have killed in self-defense has spanned the past twelve years of my life. I have seen many changes in the legal system as well as in the field of psychology, where professionals are now willing to take on the difficult job of acting as expert witnesses on behalf of these women. I could not have continued my own work without the support of some of these psychologists and experts, many of whom have become my

331

good friends. Psychologists Lynne Bravo Rosewater in Cleveland; Daniel Sonkin in San Francisco; Mary Ann Dutton-Douglas in Fort Lauderdale; Toby Myers in Houston; Laura Brown in Seattle; Julie Blackman at Barnard College in New York City; Charles Ewing in Buffalo; Leonard Haber in Miami; Geraldine Stahley in San Bernardino; Margaret Nichols in Atlanta; Dan Saunders in Madison, Wisconsin; Lois Veronen in South Carolina; Toni Appel in Fort Lauderdale; Hannah Evans, Marjorie Leidig, and Kathy Jens in Denver; Vicki Boyd and social worker Karil Klingbeil in Seattle—all have provided peer support for me and for one another at various times when the cases got rough and the women's stories would not leave my mind. Louise Bauschard, founder of the successful St. Louis Women's Self-Help Center and forerunner of the model programs for battered women in the nation's prisons that I write about here, has also remained a good friend and colleague; perhaps our friendship was sealed as we drove away safely from Jefferson County and the trials in Hillsboro, Missouri, described in this book.

I couldn't have completed this book without the help of my staff at the Battered Women Research Center, the Domestic Violence Institute, and Walker & Associates in Denver. Angela Browne and Roberta Thyfault, who stayed on at the Domestic Violence Institute long after the Battered Women Research Center closed in 1981, were the interviewers for many of the women in the book. Together we shared so many heartbreaking as well as funny stories. Both have left the Denver area to go on to professional careers of their own; Angela as a researcher in Massachusetts and Roberta as an appellate attorney in San Diego. They gave me courage, support, companionship, and love during those early years when we were trailblazing in uncharted areas. Nina Sokol, my dear friend of twenty years now; Diana Huston, a former student at Colorado Women's College and one of the original interviewers for *The Battered Woman,* even before the Battered Woman Research Center was established, and now head of our New England office; and Lon Kopit, who insisted I had to train men as well as women to work in this field—all have remained associates and interviewers throughout the years. Other interviewers included Terry Bernard, Mary Ann Bolkovatz, Janice Bondi Burns, Glenace Ecklund Edwall, Emili Rambus, Miriam LaTorre, Jan Ferguson, Tom Rhodus, and Joan Leska. Sandra Corierre, our office and special-projects administrator and my special confidante, always found a way for me to clear time to work on the book. Joyce Schiebout typed earlier versions of the manuscript. I cannot thank them enough for their friendship and for providing consistency in an ever-changing field.

I could not have accomplished my task as a psychology expert witness without the friendship and support of many attorneys as well, who gave so much of themselves to make sure their clients as well as other battered women had a chance at justice. Many of us have become good friends, including Timer Moses in Billings, Montana; Leo Thomas in Pensacola, Florida; Mario Conte in San Diego, California; John Edmunds in Honolulu, Hawaii; Vince Aprile in Frankfort, Kentucky; Barbara Hart in Pennsylvania; Bruce Lyons in Fort Lauderdale, Florida; Elizabeth Schneider in New York City; Garvin Isaacs in Oklahoma City and now in Santa Fe, New Mexico; Nancy Gertner in Boston; Marjory Fields in New York City; Bob Ryan in Billings, Montana; Geraldine Russell and Judy Sanders in San Diego; Robert Sanders in Covington, Kentucky; Fritz Aspey in Flagstaff, Arizona; Betty Rocker in Sacramento; Ellen Yaroshefsky of the Center for Constitutional Rights in New York City; Paul Mones in Santa Monica; Janet Hoffman, Larry Matasar, David Falls, and Phil Margolin in Portland, Oregon; Otha Standifer, John Barnett, and Richard Aronson in Orange County, California; Steve Nardi in Kalispell, Montana; Don and Barbara Jordan and Allan Spears in San Bernardino, California; Don Bersoff and Kit Kinsport, the APA attorneys in Washington, D.C., who wrote the *Amicus Curiae* briefs in Hawthorne and Kelly; as well as many others too numerous to mention here.

Denver attorneys Jeanne Elliott, Kathy Bonham, Wendy Davis, Shelly Don, Cathlin Donnell, Norm Early, Lainie Edinburg, David Eisner, Joe Epstein, Loyce Forest, Robert Hill, Richard Hoesteler, Eileen Lerman, Stanley Marks, Bob Miller, Caroll Multz, Sandy Pfaff, Richard and Robert Podoll, Larry Posner, Jackie St. Joan, and Marshall Quiat have become good friends as we have struggled to resolve our own lives as well as those of our clients.

In 1987, the National Clearinghouse for the Defense of Battered Women was formed and located in Philadelphia, Pennsylvania. Director Sue Ostoff and her staff provide technical assistance to lawyers and experts who are involved in legal proceedings concerning battered women and their children. Thanks to them, I no longer have to do the job of educating attorneys and battered-women advocates alone. They have developed a superb library of legal briefs, trial transcripts, psychological papers, and other materials. Acting Judge Richard Price, in the Supreme Court in the Bronx, New York, is among many judges who have carried on the fight to remove gender bias from the nation's courtrooms through his role in the American Judges' Association. Judge Sandra Rothenberg in Denver and Judge Frances Wong in Honolulu have taught me much about the judge's perspective on domestic violence.

Thanks also go to my feminist writer friends, including Ann Jones, Phyllis Chesler, Sharon Silvas, Barbara Seaman, Marlene Sanders, Pauline Bart, Diana Russell, and Susan Brownmiller, who lent me their own muses when mine seemed to disappear for a while. Photographer Donna Ferrato has captured the look of battering couples with her camera. Her work helped me see the reality of the consequences of violence even more clearly.

And the list goes on. I have met so many wonderful people each time I have spoken or testified in another case. I wish I could thank them each one individually. Every year new advocates join the battle to protect battered women and their children, while most of the old ones stay on, sometimes in new roles after returning to school to get advanced degrees.

Finally, I want to thank those people who have been closest to me and have had to put up with my flying all over the country while completing this book. My children, Michael and Karen, have grown up and finished college while I have been defending battered women everywhere and writing this book! My mother, Pearl Auerbach; her special friend, Sam Hoffman; my brother, Joel, and sister-in-law, Anne, and their children, David, Jocelyn, and Rebecca; and all my aunts, uncles, and cousins have all provided a cheering section each time we won another case.

Jan Mickish, Barbara Shaw, the staff and volunteers at Project Safeguard, Dave Patron, Frank Farley, Mary McCurry Kelley, Christina Kelley, Barbara Claster, Frank Henry, Bonnie Strickland, Mel and Esther Cohen, Diane Hill, Joseph Giovonnoni, Miriam Vogel, Christina Antonopoulou, Susan Edwards, Emilio Viano, the River Raft group, and my friends from the Women's Forum, APA, and the Feminist Therapy Institute are just a few of the many who have been there for me during various phases of this project. My feminist therapy support group has provided peer support and friendship as it has at our monthly meetings for the past six years. Sincere thanks to Suzanne Keating, Maureen Hendricks, Donna Marrold, Marty Lees, Cynthia Dougherty, and Jan Thurn. I know they share in the excitement of seeing this book become a reality.

To Mary Yost, my agent, who has watched the development of my career as an expert witness and has learned to expect telephone calls from a different state each time she thinks she has my schedule memorized, I owe a great debt of gratitude for having been a constant source of inspiration, especially during the rough times. Jerry Gross offered his helpful editorial comments at a time when this was critical. Jennifer Levin was a superb editor who understood the message I wanted to convey through this book and carefully crafted the words to make it happen. And Janet Goldstein, my editor at Harper & Row, has also been wonderful support, believing that feminist books such as mine provide an essential message to promote the growth of positive mental health in the reader. Janet and the team at Harper & Row, including attorney Maggie Mulvihill and copyeditor Pat Fogarty, worked so hard to get the book into production.

Last, but perhaps most important, go my thanks to the

women whom you read about in the pages of the book. Most of the 175 battered women who have killed or seriously injured their abusers and sought out my help do not appear here and remain anonymous, the unsung heroines who cheated their destinies to stay alive. Many still keep in touch with me and as you might have expected, very few have ever been in trouble for a violent act again. To them I give a special thank you for teaching me so much as they have filled my life.

Lenore Elizabeth Auerbach Walker

Denver, Colorado
June 1989

INDEX

Abusers: abandonment of, 27, 65–66, 94, 95, 137; burning of, 25, 210–14; characteristics of, 39, 43, 71, 77, 107, 136, 218, 219–22, 237; children who become, 146, 168; conviction rate for, 53; dual personalities of, 71; legal consequences for, 241; omnipotence/omniscience of, 64, 73–75, 107, 179; profile of, 71–72, 104; seeking of help by, 44; without battered women, 46. *See also* Alcohol abuse; *name of specific case study*

Acute-battering incident, 42, 43–44, 52, 72, 76, 102, 106, 175. *See also name of specific case study*

Adams, David, 282*n*
Adler, Frieda, 228
Admissibility issues, 266–78, 281–84, 295–301, 309–10
Aggravating circumstances, 265, 266
Agnes [case study], 181–87, 190
Alcohol abuse, 44–45, 52, 71, 101, 103, 105, 114–23, 204. *See also name of specific case study*

Allery v. *Washington*, 280
Almond, Clint, 287, 289–90, 291–92
American Board of Professional Psychology, 312*n*
American Family Therapy Association, 219–20
American Psychiatric Association, 48*n*–49*n*, 269*n*
American Psychological Association [APA], 299, 312*n*, 326
Anava v. *Maine*, 280

Anderson, William, 31–41
Anger: of the abuser, 221; addressing, 203–6; as an emotion following homicide, 219; case studies about, 203–6, 208–17; creative, 221, 222; denial of, 203; and feminism, 218–19, 220; and insanity, 180; and juries, 203–6, 217; kinds of, 221; of men, 220; men's fear of women's, 218; and power, 218, 219–22; and racism, 206–18; as a reason for killing, 201; and recovery, 201; and self-defense, 219; and self-esteem, 221; and survivors, 220; and therapy, 221; and victims, 220, 221
Appeal process, 272–74
Aprile, Vince, 323*n*
Aris, Brenda [case study], 283–84
Auerbach, Anne, 185–86, 187
Austin, Judy, 239

The Battered Woman Syndrome [Walker], 9*n*
The Battered Woman [Walker], 4, 8, 317
Battered woman: definition of, 35–36, 102
Battered Woman Syndrome: and admissibility issues, 281, 283–84; and contract killings, 104*n*; formulation of, 7; and insanity, 10, 178–79; and the MMPI, 105*n*; and the perception of imminency, 26–27; and Post Traumatic Stress Disorder, 48–49; and self-defense, 10–11, 25; and state of mind, 26–27. *See also* Expert witness testimony; *name of specific case study*

Battered women: characteristics of, 39, 101–13; as hostages to child abuse, 137–38; infantilization of, 3, 137; murder of, 65; profile of, 101–13; research about, 8–9; as a universal phenomenon, 106; without the abusers, 46; as witness in their own defense, 12, 258, 261. *See also name of specific topic or case study*
Battered Women Issues of Public Policy [Commission on Civil Rights], 61*n*
Batterers. *See* Abusers
Bauschard, Louise, 288, 290–91
Bechtel, Donna [case study], 275–78
Belle, Jessie [case study], 210–14
Berk, Richard, 61*n*
Bernardez, Teresa, 221
Beverly Ibn-Tamas [case study], 33, 73–75, 176, 268–74, 279
Blame, 70–71, 158*n*, 163, 235, 259, 309
Boulding, Elise, 257
Brainwashing, 180–81, 267
Brenda Aris [case study], 283–84
Brody, Marcia, 287, 292
Brown, Richard Maxwell, 260
Browne, Angela, 62, 65*n*, 103, 227, 259–60, 300
Brownmiller, Susan, 151*n*
Burble, Edith [case study], 225*n*, 238–41
Burden of proof, 260, 264
Bureaucracy, 241–42
Burning the abusers, 25, 210–14
The Burning Bed [TV movie], 25
Burns, Patricia [case study], 66–69

337